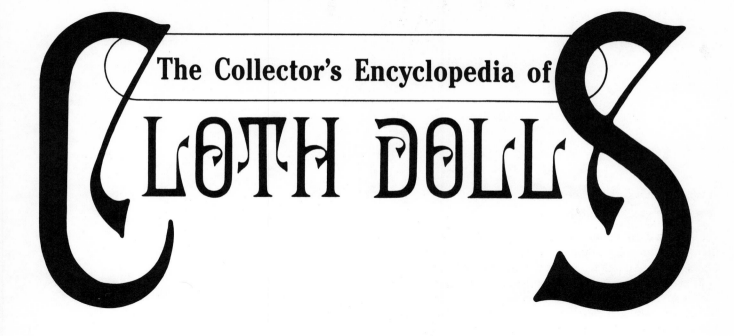

The Collector's Encyclopedia of CLOTH DOLLS

From Rag Baby to Art Object

Johana Gast Anderton

Cover Design: Heather Miller
Cover Photograph: Lightfoot Photography

The information contained herein does not constitute a
statement of any legal rights or proprietary interests in or to
any of the mentioned items. It is the intent of the author only
to furnish descriptive information to collectors and dealers.
Such information should not be construed as affecting or
evidencing any actual copyright or patent rights or the
absence thereof. The author has made every effort to be
factual and accurate and any discrepencies are totally
unintentional.

All photographs, unless otherwise credited, are by the author.
If a doll is not attributed to a specific collection, the collector has
asked to remain anonymous.

Published by

Wallace-Homestead
authoritative books on antiques & collectibles

To my husband, Harold, for better or for worse.

About the Author

Johana Anderton began writing and drawing at an early age. As a first-grader, she sent poems and drawings to the children's page of the Kansas City *Journal Post,* a local newspaper. Her mother still treasures those first published works as well as those of Johana's two sisters who now are also published authors.

Anderton began writing for collectors with a small pioneer work on what is commonly known today as "Depression Glass." Before going out of print, *The Glass Rainbow: The Story of Depression Glass,* went through eight printings and is now considered a collector's item in itself.

Turning to her first love, dolls, she began to chronicle their history and to identify the dolls of this century when she discovered there were no books on the subject in the libraries. Her *Twentieth Century Series* now includes four volumes, plus a price guide edited by her sister, Carol Gast Glassmire. Two more are planned for release in the next two years, including a second volume of *Sewing for Twentieth Century Dolls,* which is now on the drawing board. She is also working on a series of paper dolls in full color and has published numerous black-and-white sets

designed for collectors. Also for collectors will be a series of dolls' heads that she hopes to have produced by a mold company.

Collectors will recognize Johana Anderton as the author of many articles for collector publications, including *Western Collector Magazine, Collectors News, Mid-America Reporter, Doll Castle News, The Dollmaker,* and *The Bottle Gazette,* among others. Selected columns and articles from these publications have been compiled in a soft cover book, *Johana's Dolls: A Reprint of Her Articles and Columns.*

In addition to collecting and writing, her activities have included teaching oil painting, instructing YWCA craft classes, and personal appearances on television, radio, and at antiques and doll shows and conventions throughout the country. She also teaches occasional workshops and does some lecturing, an activity that is necessarily limited by her full schedule.

In 1972, she founded her own publishing company, Athena Publishing Company. She reports she has worn every hat in the publishing industry except those of copy camera operator and press operator, adding with a twinkle that she could do those, too, given a little instruction and some time to learn.

During this period, she designed and produced books on a variety of subjects in the collectibles field written by several well-known authors. Of particular interest to doll collectors are *The American Doll Artist,* Vol. II, by Helen Bullard; *Dressing Dolls in Nineteenth Century Fashions,* by Albina Bailey; and *Much Ado About Dolls* by R. Lane Herron. She originated the *Collectors Art Series* of paper dolls and coloring books based on authentic antique dolls and chose fashion illustrators and fine artists to create them.

After experiencing some health problems because of overwork, Anderton sold her publishing company in 1976. Her books are now published by Wallace-Homestead Book Company, a subsidiary of American Broadcasting Company.

Anderton is the mother of a son and daughter and now has four grandchildren — "even up," she says — two boys and two girls. She and her husband, Harold, have moved to Florida, but not for retirement, she hastens to explain. Together they operate a retail shop specializing in antiques, dolls, and related items. Exploring their adopted state is a favorite spare-time pursuit, along with an occasional fishing expedition.

She is a member-at-large of the United Federation of Doll Clubs (UFDC), a founding member of the Original Paper Doll Artists Guild (OPDAG), and a charter member of The Paper Doll Collectors of Florida. Anderton is listed in *Who's Who of American Women* and the *Dictionary of International Biography.*

Contents

Acknowledgments

Does anyone ever read the acknowledgments? Anyone other than those whose names are listed, that is? I sometimes wonder, and I certainly hope so. It is in the acknowledgments that most authors express their gratitude for favors granted and for help given during the completion of their books.

Thanking someone for a kindness is often a difficult task. The words *thank you* sometimes fail to convey what a person hopes to say. I have come to airing my thanks in public, so to speak. By setting down the names of those who have helped me, I hope to emphasize my gratitude and proclaim the virtues of my friends and associates so all may know of their generosity.

And that is a good thing. Kindnesses should be remembered and cherished. Generosity ought to be rewarded and encouraged. Doll collectors are a tribe of generous, kind-hearted souls who tend to open their hearts and collections to researchers and writers. Some of the collectors and artists who helped me in this venture even took dolls to professional photographers in order that you and I might enjoy photographs of them in this book. Others spread their collections on beds, chairs, even floors, so that I might photograph each member of the crew. Still others shipped dolls to my studio so that I might undress, examine, and photograph their precious treasures. Such trust! Collectors answered my seemingly endless questions and letters and remained patient and understanding through it all.

My two sisters, Shirley and Carol, prodded, poked, and pushed me toward completion of this book. Shirley, who lives nearby, listened to me read my paragraphs on the telephone for hours at a time, making editorial comments where needed and offering me encouragement. (There were times when I would have liked to chuck it all!)

Carol, who lives in Florida, opened her home to me when I needed a winter retreat in the hope that the sunshine would clear my addled brain, thus allowing me to finish this book. She, too, did her share of encouraging and pushing. In addition, her long-suffering husband, Ted, put up with the total disarrangement of his household during my sojourn there. I am sure my entire family has breathed a collective sigh of relief now that at long last this book is finished.

My secretary, Thelma, held things together while I was hiding in Florida. She braved snow and sleet all winter, keeping up with the mail and answering the telephone, leaving me free to concentrate on my research.

A very special word of gratitude (actually, three hundred words) to my husband, Harold, who somehow manages to love me in spite of it all.

There are so many people who have contributed to this book. I could tell little stories about my experiences with many of them, but if I started, there would be no end to the storytelling. Instead, here are the names of those who helped me. If I have omitted someone, I plead for forgiveness. It was not an intentional slight. Write me and we will include your name in the next printing.

Cora Adame
Jayne Allen
Jan Alovus
Harold Anderton
Rebekka Anderton
Virginia Baldwin
Thelma Barber
Virginia Battagler
Alice Ann Beecham
Mr. and Mrs. Richard Beidelschies
Rodney Beidelschies
Anita Berg
Jack Berg
Colleen Bergman
Mary Bigelow
Doris Braden
Kay Bransky
Mary Jo Brockington
Betty Brown
Shirley Buchholz
Doralee Burger
Carolyn Burson
Joeann Calia
Ruth Causey
Cheryl Charlson
Chase Bag Company
Close to Your Heart
Antique Dolls
Celeste Cooley
LaRaine Crawford
Dorothy Cronin
Deet D'Andrade
Bee Davis
Dayne's Dolls
John Dinardo
Gladys Dluzak
Elizabeth Fahr
Dorothy Nell Foster
Sharon K. Foster
Evelyn Gaylin
J. L. Gibbins
Nell Glasscock

Carol Glassmire
Ted Glassmire
Ralph Griffith
Delene Hafner
Hallmark Cards, Inc.
Anna Haag
Daisy Hartwell
Barbara Haviland
R. Lane Herron
Maxine Hiett
Mrs. Russell Holdren
Arlene Hoy
Joel Hoy
Rebecca Iverson
Mrs. J. C. Janke
Paul Johnson
Pat Jones
Ilene Joplin
Doris Kaufman
Dr. J. E. Kendrick
Nita Kinney
Betty Kirtley
Sylvia Kittman
Clarence A. Kutz
Natalie Kollimer Kutz
Carolee Alt Luppino
Shirley Lynn
Tressa E. Mabry
Kim McKim
Barbara McLaughlin
Marian Mason
Jackie Meekins
Violet Meynen
Mrs. Shelby Mongeon
Margaret O'Rourke
Verna Ortwein
Gladis Page
Claudette Patterson
Nancy Perry
Sheila Peters
Playthings Magazine .
Beverly Port

Karen Potter
Vivian Rasberry
Bernard Ravca
Frances Ravca
Genevieve Reeves
Nancy Ricklefs
Sharon Ricklefs
Bill Riggs
Xavier Roberts
Ethel Rogers
Bertha Mae Ross
Shannon Ross
Betty Rossi
Alice Rothert
Dorothy Avey Sanders
Jane E. Sheetz
Ruth Sheinwald
Susan Shell
Orpha Siehl
Donna Stanley (deceased)
Stella Mae's Doll Shop
Ann Tardie
Mrs. Terry
Eleanor H. Todd
Ellen Turner
Mira Kosicki Walilko
Roman Walilko
Judi K. Ward
Alice Wardell
Marion Weaver
Margaret Weeks
Gerry Werner
Joann E. Williams
Sandy Williams
Harry Wilson
Win Ann Winkler
Betty Wiseman
R. John Wright
Phyllis Wright
Diann Zillner

Preface

Inspiration arrives in many cases unannounced and completely unexpected. Sometimes ideas take shape as necessity forces adjustments in one's thinking or one's plans. It was probably through a combination of such forces that the idea for this book came about.

Midsummer 1974 I was deeply involved in the completion of the third title in my Twentieth Century Dolls Series, *More Twentieth Century Dolls from Bisque to Vinyl,* which was to be released later that year. Two years of intensive research following publication of the first volume had been interrupted for about ten months in order to complete another book, *Sewing for Twentieth Century Dolls.*

As it happened, my work on the sewing book also contributed to the later volume. Research trips to museums, libraries, and other cities yielded material for both books. As my work progressed, it became only too clear that there was too much material for a single book. I had prevailed upon my publisher to increase the number of pages in the new book on two separate occasions. I knew the book could not be enlarged a third time. The retail price had already been set prior to the first enlargement and we were fast approaching a cost crisis.

Writing is a difficult occupation at best. Even more difficult is the job of editing one's own work — a task that sends many writers into something akin to cardiac arrest. Now I was being asked to *cut* my book. I had to leave out some of this marvelous research material, material that I knew my readers would want included. How could I compromise my standards, deprive my readers of the wonderful information I had gleaned from old catalogs, trade journals, and musty archives? How could I choose between photographs and catalog cuts? What could possibly be deleted?

Fortunately, happy inspiration struck. I decided to pull the huge chapter on rag dolls, combine it with the material in the rag chapter from my first volume, collect some additional information, and have another book. My publisher was pleased. I was relieved. My scruples were intact. Everything seemed promising, indeed. The tentative date for release of the proposed book was set for the spring of 1976.

It is well that most of us cannot see into the future. That tentative date flew by and the book was never completed. Poor health and family traumas created a series of problems that took precedence. My life was really no different from any one of a million other lives, but certainly not designed to contribute to meeting deadlines or writing books.

Despite a couple of bad years, I continued to collect information, record details, photograph dolls, and build my foundation for future books, never giving up the dream of finally being able to complete the eight or so books that languished in file cabinets in my office. I continued also to write my monthly column for *Doll Castle News.* This helped me keep in contact with the doll world during those years.

Then a new publisher came on the scene and my too-big book became a two-volume set. My horizons expanded once again and it seemed possible that the book on rag dolls could, indeed, become a reality.

"Telephones and typewriters do not mix," I found myself telling my family and friends. To complete the work required, personal calls could not be answered during "working hours." My workday was defined, and my needs were respected. Thus I was able to gather my thoughts and energies for the great effort required in the preparation of any book. My only distractions were the beautiful spring days I glimpsed through my window and an occasional squirrel flitting by on some important mission. From that window I watched spring turn into summer, then autumn and winter.

All the materials collected through the years — the photographs taken, the notes made, the articles clipped — came into focus as I spread them across my table and began. With wonder, I felt the years drop away and I was once again in some collector's home, handling her dolls, making entries on description cards, photographing her collection. Or I sat once more in the New York Public Library, filling out all those little blank spaces on a Form 29c in order to obtain some deeply stored volume of ancient date.

Time is a convolution of reality, an unnatural ordering of our lives in an attempt to gain a kind of control never truly attained.

In the process, we have learned to think of our lives as having a past, a present, and a future in which things, events, and even people exist independently. We have forgotten, or never knew, that each of us is the center of his or her universe, that within each of us exists the whole of what we have learned and experienced.

The mind, that great storehouse, knows no time. And to escape the barriers enforced by time, one need only allow the mind its freedom, a freedom to explore what we are and have been, and even what we wish to become. I traveled the reaches of time and space one warm spring afternoon, knowing again the friends I had made across the miles and years, handling again the photographs and clippings, the notecards and catalogs stored away so long ago and yet, just yesterday.

With a renewed sense of purpose, with a clearer vision, I was ready to begin. I had defined my goals: Give as much of myself and my energies as is humanly possible, be as fair with my readers as I can be, and provide as complete and honest a picture as I know how.

Here, then, are the results of my musings and inquiries, my investigations and searchings. The story is not complete. No story ever is. Other researchers may expand, correct, or enlarge upon—but never complete—the story that begins here.

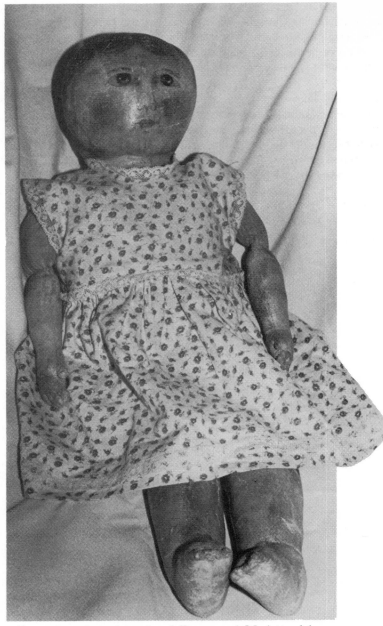

From the talented hands of Emma and Marietta Adams, sisters from Oswego, New York, comes this old rag doll with the pensive expression. The doll's head and limbs are painted a flesh color. The face was deftly applied by Miss Emma. After Emma's death in 1900, Miss Marietta continued to make similar Columbian dolls, which were usually marked with one of the sisters' names, "Oswego," and the words "Columbian Doll." (Photograph courtesy Gladys Dluzak)

1 Rag Dolls Defined

Any doll takes its designation from its head.
— Jo Elizabeth Gerken, *Doll News*

Rag dolls. How prosaic the term sounds, conjuring up pictures of floppy, worn, raggedy old dolls with embroidered features and yarn hair; misshapen, badly proportioned bodies; and tattered clothing. And yet one would have to look far to find more sophistication, more imaginative rendering, more artistry in any category of dolls. Rag dolls have been created on every level of artistic skill in nearly every imaginable form, from the most simple homemade doll fashioned of sewing basket scraps to the extremely well-executed artist dolls of the present.

Seldom do collectors consider the category of rag dolls to include anything as remarkable as a walking doll, yet such dolls have been documented by Coleman (*Fabulous Figures of Felt-Lenci,* 1977) and Gerken (*Wonderful Dolls of Papier-Mâché,* 1970). Among others, the Autoperipatetikos, patented July 15, 1862, is just such an example. The walking mechanism was operated by clockwork. The heads were not only made of bisque, china, and papier-mâché, but also made of cloth. Gerken believes the cloth heads of these dolls were made in the United States, although those made of other materials undoubtedly were manufactured in Europe.

Gerken also discusses another key-wind mechanical patented in 1868 by Hawkins and Goodwin of Washington, D.C. (There is some confusion as to whether the mechanism was contained in the doll itself or in the cart she pushes.) These heads were, to all appearances, molded from a German china head.

Another patent, issued to Carl Wiegand, May 23, 1876, was for a head made of muslin and reinforced with pasted layers of cardboard or paper, finished off with another layer of muslin inside.

Izannah Walker made some of the most sought after collector's dolls from 1850-1870, although there is some question as to the accuracy of these dates. It is known that her patent application is dated 1873, but the dolls were apparently made before and after that date. A study of a group of the Walker dolls will reveal the development of the dollmaker's skill and art over the period they were produced.

Martha Jenks Chase began making her dolls around 1880. They were of stockinette stretched over a molded, shaped mask face, all hand painted in oils. In 1893, Ida A. Gutsell patented a six-piece, intricately gusseted, boy doll printed on fabric sold by the yard.

Rag dolls historically have been used as fund-raisers, and such was the case with another doll of that year. Coleman tells of the Missionary Ragbabies created by Julia Beecher. These dolls were made of discarded silk underwear. Proceeds from the sale of these dolls went to the Missionary Fund of the Park Congregational Church of Elmira, New York.

In the last half of the nineteenth century, several other dollmakers were creating their own original dolls. Fraulein Margarete Steiff began in about 1877 to create the now-famous Button-in-the-Ear dolls. Easily identified by the seam down the center of the face, the Steiff dolls included a large number of characters as well as charming children. (Later dolls had faces of a different design.)

An unknown artist created one of the first advertising rag dolls for Northwestern Consolidated Milling Company in about 1895. The doll is a farmer boy with a cap and high boots and may have been printed on a flour sack. The trademark, Ceresota Flour, is printed on the boy's shirt front between his suspender straps. A later example of this doll wears a brimmed hat.

The period was a golden age for rag dolls. Thousands of mothers, aunts, sisters, and grandmothers fashioned dolls of materials from the ragbag, whether for lack of ready cash to purchase a store-bought doll or from a need to create.

The nineteenth century was a time of expansion and resettlement in the United States. Families were on the move and out of necessity often took with them only essential items. When a child needed a toy, materials on hand were employed to create one. A doll carved from a bent limb or sewn from scraps was often the answer. Few of these dolls have been preserved and those known examples are cherished by families both as footnotes to history and as family heirlooms. Occasionally, a particular doll has been donated to a museum or even given to a collector friend for preservation. Such early dolls are rare, and most collectors must be content with later examples.

Other sources of old cloth dolls were the companies producing flats — yardgoods printed with dolls to be cut out, sewn, and stuffed at home. Perhaps no other type of rag doll offers such variety. Many dolls in this category were used as promotional pieces, renditions of a familiar trademark such as Buster Brown Mills' famous Buster Brown and Tige. Others were chosen for their familiarity and appeal to the public, as in the case of the Santa Claus figure published by E. S. Peck of Brooklyn, New York, in 1886. Still others depicted characters from fiction or nursery rhymes.

During this period, faces were hand painted, as was the hair in many cases. A later innovation was the use of lithography, then photography, in reproducing the artwork. Horsman's Babyland Rag Dolls and American Maids with beautifully rendered faces and hair (some models quite obviously were portraits) were among the earliest of the genré. Soon every doll manufacturer was offering a similar line of dolls. Printed faces appeared in about 1907.

The rag doll trend continued into the twentieth century with these dolls a favorite of mothers and children alike. Economy of manufacture made rag dolls a highly desirable commodity on both sides of the market. They were appreciated for their softness and warmth and "dragability," something the chinas, bisques, and waxes lacked.

Around the turn of the century, J. B. Sheppard and Company featured their Philadelphia Babies, dolls with molded, painted features and hair. Similar dolls, but with beautifully printed faces, were produced by Albert Bruckner in the first two decades of the century. The distinctive Bruckner dolls had faces sewn or glued to a flat, plain head after the doll was completed.

Another handworked doll was the Mothers Congress rag doll created by Madge Lansing Mead in about 1900. These dolls featured golden curls with a blue ribbon. One of the dolls was named Baby Stuart.

Many beautiful cloth dolls were manufactured in Europe and shipped to the United States. From England came the Chad Valley dolls, the Norah Wellings dolls, and the Dean's Rag Book dolls. From Germany came the Steiffs, the Kruses, and more. And from Italy the marvelous line of Lencis arrived, along with a bevy of copies.

In the United States, the American Stuffed Novelty Company produced its own version of the Lenci child in its Trilby line. With painted features, curly mohair wig, and felt clothes, the Trilby dolls presented very strong competition to the imported Lencis.

The list could go on for many pages with every manufacturer's output through the years of this century. Rag dolls are still a very important item for many doll companies. Such modern greats as Knickerbocker, Gund, Mattel, Effanbee, Alexander, and Fisher-Price have found the rag doll market to be a lucrative one. Other, newer manufacturers have been attracted to the market as well.

There is an important point in all of this. Rag dolls are a genuine, legitimate addition to any doll collection. They are varied, usually well made, interesting, and desirable.

Still, there are those who object to the term *rag doll*. The objection is expressed especially when the term is used in reference to one-of-a-kind or limited edition dolls presently being created by some very talented artists who happen to be working in the cloth medium. Whether the objection comes from the artist or from the collector-patron, the thought is basically the same. The term lacks dignity and definition of a legitimate art form.

While it may be appropriate to seek a more fitting, definitive term for the artists' dolls, it would seem nearly impossible to delete the phrase *rag doll* from the vocabulary when referring to the dolls produced in earlier years, either by hand or in mass production. A good case for the term was made by one of my readers, Shannon Ross, who wrote to me with the following:

> Don't let anyone object to the term "rag" doll. I read in one of my magazines about a lady who makes them but hates the term as she only uses new, expensive fabric. Well, so do I (though not so expensive), but I still call them rag dolls as it has a lot friendlier sound to me, like something that was made with love and care — unlike store-bought ones. And after all, a lot of valuable quilts were made from "rags" way back when — and now, too. I use mostly the scraps from other projects, as many do, but I still think of the pieces as rags. And some of our first flags were made from rags, too! "Rags" isn't such a bad term.

Let's face it, the idea of cloth dolls originated in someone's ragbag or scrapbox. Sewing scraps or pieces cut from worn-out clothing were saved for patching or future projects. Whether we like it or not is immaterial (no pun intended). The genesis of cloth dolls is the cloth called rags, hence the term *rag dolls*.

Even a manufacturer with as distinguished a reputation as Dean's has included the word in its name. Montanari had a display of English Rag Babies in 1855 according to Constance King (*The Collector's History of Dolls,* 1978). She refers continually in her book to rag dolls and rag babies. And no less an authority than Dorothy Coleman has classified them as *rag dolls* (Collector's Encyclopedia of Dolls, pp. 513-516).

This book has been thoughtfully titled to include the word *rag*. A rag doll, for purposes of this book and in accordance with the thinking of Jo Elizabeth Gerken, Shannon Ross, and others, is a doll made of cloth. The words *rag, cloth,* and *fabric* are interchangeable as far as I am concerned and all three shall be used as such in this book.

The head of a rag doll may *not* be vinyl. It may *not* be composition or tin or bisque or any one of a number of other materials. The head of a rag doll must be made of cloth — either muslin or linen or felt or silk or even oilcloth. The body and limbs must also be of cloth, though they may be shaped or painted or stitched or jointed or stiffened.

Whether cloth is dipped in glue and molded into shape or simply cut out, sewn, and stuffed, it can be fashioned into a doll that qualifies for what I hope will become a dignified title in years to come.. a rag doll.

1S-1

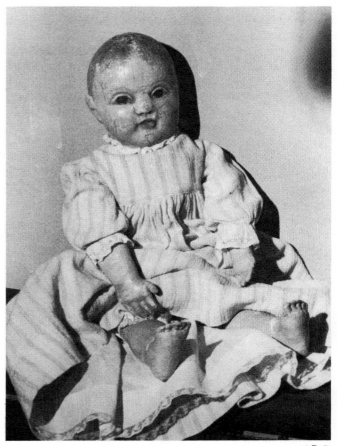

1S-2

1S-1   **The Alabama Indestructible Baby, 26½".** Made by Ella Smith from about 1904 through at least a twenty-year period. Doll is of all-cloth construction, has head and limbs covered with waterproof, flesh-colored paint. Cloth body has been slipcovered for preservation. Painted-on shoes are blue with black, hair is brown, mouth is rosy red. (Mason collection)

1S-2   **The Philadelphia Baby, 21".** Also known as the Sheppard Baby, manufactured by the J. B. Sheppard Company of Philadelphia. Company was in business for seventy-five years, closing in 1935. Dolls were made sometime during that period. This particular example belonged to a woman who was born in 1894 in Philadelphia. Head and lower arms and legs were sized, then painted with flesh-colored paint. Hair is light brown, eyes are brown, mouth is red, and doll is dressed in its original clothes. (McLaughlin collection. Photograph courtesy the collector)

13

2 A Short Course in Color Printing

One of the benefits of collecting is the opportunity for learning that appears at frequent intervals. Collectors learn of the fashions and mores, the technology and the everyday living habits of the people of the periods from which they collect. They are aware of the peoples of other times in more personal ways, perhaps, than are the historians who write the long tomes they use for reference.

On that note, I would like to take you on a little side path of learning. When I look at a work of art (which we all agree dolls certainly are), I wonder about the artist who created the piece. I think about the processes required to complete a work. I wonder, "How was this done? What was required to achieve the effect? What means were used to produce this?"

Cloth dolls have been produced using many different methods, from hand painting and hand embroidery to the most up-to-date printing processes. There are silk-screened faces and photographic faces. There are faces that were achieved with heat transfer patterns. (These are merely faces printed on paper with heat-sensitive inks that are transferable to cloth with even the light pressure and relatively low temperature of a domestic iron.) Nearly every method of the printer's art has been employed to create cloth dolls.

When many of the older dolls were printed, the color separations were done by hand. An artist painted the area of each color on a separate transparency with tiny dots (thus the term *color separation*). Printing plates were made from each transparency — one plate for black and white printing, two plates for black and another color, three plates for black and two other colors, and so on. The number is theoretically unlimited. However, the number of plates required to achieve full color is usually four. Many of the earliest dolls were silk-screened, a process that uses essentially the same basic approach, but is more like stenciling than printing.

Soon screens that relieved the artist of the monotonous task of painting dots were developed. Screens look very much like negatives of a window screen. The dot patterns are available in various sizes and shapes to suit the requirements of different jobs. Large acetate sheets of dots may be cut carefully to any shape and arranged on a layout to represent a particular color. When color proofs of these screened separations are placed on top of one another, they give a fairly accurate picture of what the final print will look like.

When a printer describes a project as a four-color job, he does not mean the finished work will show only four colors. Printing by the four-color process (red, blue, yellow, and black) results in many more shades as the process colors are printed one or more on top of the first. Thus, yellow and blue in various proportions (the proportions being determined by the size and density of the dots in the separations), become green shades from light yellow-green to dark blue-green. In some of the darker shades, small amounts of black are introduced to achieve the correct shading.

In the early days of four-color printing, the fabric (or paper, in the case of other items) was fed through the printing press four times. Each time, a different color of ink was used, depending on which plate was in the press. There was a certain order in which the colors were applied, with black usually applied last. Today, on a four-color press, all of the colors are applied at one printing.

When material is fed through a press more than once, it is essential that the plates be aligned so that each color is put down correctly. Then we say that the plates are in register. If misalignment occurs, and the job is out of register, one or more rows of tiny dots of the out-of-register color may appear as a halo around the edge of the printed form. An out-of-register piece is usually scrapped. However, they are sometimes inadvertently allowed to slip through and appear in the ranks of their more perfect comrades with fuzzy eyes and lips, or strangely patterned clothing. I have seen more than a few out-of-register paper dolls, mostly in magazines popular in the early part of our century.

The collector who has access to a high-power magnifier can appreciate the intricacy of the process described. The dot patterns show plainly under magnification, and one can see the different colors and how they were applied to achieve secondary colors and shadings.

Today the printing procedure is much the same as in early days, with the exception of the use of greatly improved, high-speed presses. (Some of the oldtimers love to argue the merits of their familiar old Heidelburg presses against the latest equipment.) The method of achieving color separations has changed tremendously, however. Today, original color art and photographs are "read" by sophisticated computers that have been programmed to detect the slightest nuance of color and shading. Printing plates are made from these computer "read-outs," but even so, the trained eye of the artist is the final test of whether or not the computer has done its job.

There are some exceptions to the use of the screen process, of course. Another method, called flooding, actually lays down a solid, unscreened color already mixed to the desired shade. This method gives a flat field of color comparable to poster art. Most of the dolls I have examined were printed by either the four-color screen process or were silk-screened, although a few were done using the flooding method.

2-1

2.2

2-1 **Lithographed Girl, 7″.** Wine-colored stockings, blue lace trim on underwear, laced boots. These dolls are usually found in played-with condition, evidence of their desirability as play objects. (Rasberry collection)

2.2 **Lithographed Girl, 15″.** Blond hair, blue stockings, brown shoes with dark pink rosettes. The soil around the mouth indicates the doll was probably "fed" by her little mother. The variety of these flat-sewn dolls is virtually endless and a collection could be established in this one area alone. (Rasberry collection)

3   The Advertising Rag

No, this chapter is not about sheet music or a dance step from the 1920s. *Ragtime* has a different meaning for doll collectors, and the advertising rag is a very specialized doll category. Advertising rag dolls stand at a crossroad between two broader classifications of dolls — advertising dolls and rag dolls. Please note, however, that this chapter will not treat the subject of cloth animals and other types of stuffed cloth advertising paraphernalia. Rather, our subject here will be dolls in human form, cut, printed or otherwise applied to cloth, then stuffed with a soft substance, and in this case, used as advertising premiums either through direct retail outlets or mail-in offers. Some were distributed flat for home sewing.

Because rag dolls are an inexpensive type of doll to manufacture (paper dolls may be a bit more economical), they are the natural choice for a company seeking a means of advertising its products through a promotion featuring some sort of premium. In addition, they have a special charm that gives them a strong sales appeal. Often the choice of premium is a doll because the manufacturer's trademark can be represented easily in doll form.

Sometimes a specific character is created especially for the promotion, given a special name, and proclaimed the representative of the product. If the image becomes popular, it may be incorporated into the general sales campaign or even become the official company trademark.

In other cases, simple economics govern the selection. A manufacturer may be persuaded to use a doll as a premium by some enterprising doll manufacturer who is holding an excess inventory of a particular item and can offer his dolls at an attractive price. In such a situation there may be no identification whatever with the product.

A few trademark dolls are merely attractive dolls wearing T-shirts, dresses, or aprons with the manufacturer's name or slogan emblazoned across the front. Often there is an attempt to identify with the targeted consumer. For example, a product that is intended for use by teenagers may be advertised by a doll representing a teenage boy or girl wearing a sweatshirt featuring the product name. Sometimes the nature of the product dictates the doll's shape and appearance. An excellent example is the humanizing of a banana to create the very recognizable Chiquita Banana trademark in doll form.

Rag dolls most often fall into the category of close product identification as is evidenced by the examples illustrated in this chapter. There are many examples of the use of long-standing trademarks-as-dolls. One thinks immediately of the Campbell Kids, Aunt Jemima, and Buster Brown, among others. Such oldtimers have been issued in many forms over the years, often undergoing somewhat startling metamorphoses in the updating process. More recent entries have also been radically changed in a few short years as advertising agencies seek to keep a fresh, yet recognizable image before the public. All of this, of course, adds interest for the collector, who often benefits (albeit through no intent of the manufacturers) from such corporate shenanigans.

As new businesses are established and others close, some of the advertising messages of former years become somewhat cryptic. It is sometimes difficult to identify a doll marked only with a one-word slogan or product name. Regionally marketed products, without benefit of national recognition, also add to the problem. Researchers and writers have done much to alleviate this situation in the past few years. Especially notable is the work of Robison and Sellers. (*Advertising Dolls*, 1980). Readers also contribute to the store of information.

An example of such sharing occurred several years ago. I had written an article on mystery dolls for *Mid-America Reporter* in February 1972. This article was subsequently reprinted in a soft-cover collection of my columns and articles (*Johana's Dolls, A Reprint of Her Columns and Articles*, 1975). One of the dolls discussed in the article was a doll I considered to be an advertising premium. Across the waistband was embroidered "Miss Supreme," obviously, I thought, referring to a product of some sort. There was, however, no indication on the doll as to its origin or to the type of product it might have represented.

In the article, I asked that readers with information on any of the dolls write to me. As a result, two collectors with identical dolls, both in the original state, wrote to tell me about them.

The doll had been printed on one-hundred-pound sugar sacks for Supreme Sugar. Printed on the front of each sack were the words "Supreme Sugar/Registered U.S. Patent Ofc." (there was no date). There was also a picture in blue of a mountain scene with white snowcaps, all in a circle with "100#" inside, under "Supreme Sugar Xtra Fine/Granulated Cane Sugar/New Orleans, La."

One of the readers, noting my reference to the embroidered features of the doll I had photographed, commented, "I can see no reason for it [the doll] to be embroidered. The instructions are just to cut out, sew and stuff."

Apparently, the person who embroidered my photographed example liked embroidery or thought the additional stitching would improve the appearance of the doll. I am indebted to Maxine Hiett and Celeste Cooley, who took the time to write about their Supreme sugar sack dolls.

The Gerber Baby

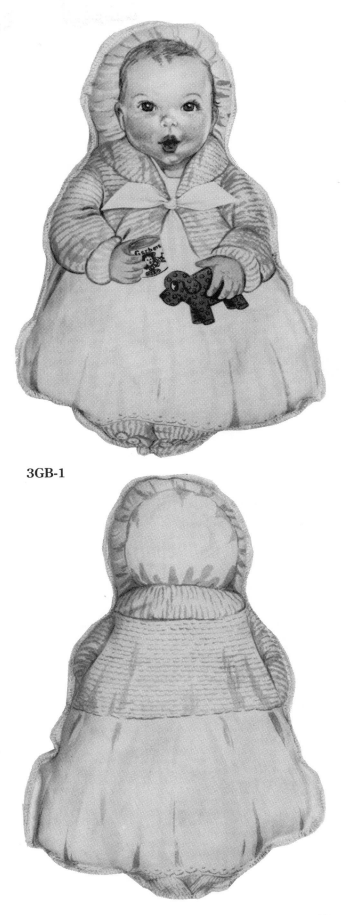

3GB-1

One of the most successful trademarks ever created, the Gerber Baby, enjoys extremely high consumer identification. Everything from feeding spoons to vinyl dolls has been used to represent the Gerber image since 1928, the year of its adoption. And yet the Gerber Baby rag doll is one of the most elusive of the advertising rags. Reasons for this are unclear. Gerber reports that nearly 14,500 dolls were distributed in 1936, the introductory year for their fabric trademark dolls, with the total number climbing to just short of the 27,000 mark by the end of 1936 when the offer was withdrawn.

In terms of today's production runs of millions and half-millions, these numbers are not high. Perhaps these relatively few cloth babies were loved and played with to the point of extinction.

The Gerber Company began work on its archives in 1977 as a part of the celebration of its golden anniversary year in 1978. An attempt was made at that time to locate one of the cloth babies through the media, since the only exhibits Gerber had were copies of contemporary magazine advertisements.

In January of 1978, Gerber received a donation that nearly completed their Gerber Baby collection. Mrs. Ida Evans of Fremont, Michigan, was able to provide not only the girl baby, but also the original mailing carton plus the advertising folder that came with the doll. The company has not given up hope of finding the boy version of the doll to complete the pair.

3GB-1   (Photographs and information courtesy the Gerber Products Company, whose registered trademark the Gerber Baby is) **The First Gerber Baby, 8″**. A soft, huggable doll designed for a baby or small child. The little girl wears a printed-on pink dress. The boy is dressed in blue. The boxes the dolls were mailed in were also color-coordinated. Note the outside seaming on the doll shown. (Photographs courtesy of The Gerber Company)

3GB-2 **The First Gerber Baby, Girl.** With her original mailing carton and the advertising folder that was included. Gerber is still hoping to find an example of the boy baby.

3GB-3 **Gerber Baby Rag Doll Advertisement.** Pictured is one of the first ads. Three baby food labels and ten cents would buy the Gerber Baby offered in the March 4, 1936, issue of the *Christian Science Monitor.*

3GB-4 **Gerber Baby Ad for Gerber's Shaker-Cooked Strained Foods.** This ad comes from the June 1937 issue of *Good Housekeeping.*

3GB-3

3GB-2

3GB-4

The Chase Bag Company

When W. E. (Bill) Riggs, manager of the Chase Bag Company's Reidsville, North Carolina, plant talks about advertising dolls, he uses big numbers. Chase is unique in the United States, and possibly in the world, in its role as producer of long runs of such dolls and as fulfiller of orders for these dolls as well. It is not uncommon for Chase to receive and process orders for hundreds of thousands of promotion dolls in a single week. But such was not always the case, for Chase did not enter this market until 1963, more than one-hundred years after its founding.

The company had its beginnings in 1847 on the docks of Boston Harbor, where West Indian gunnies, the kind of large, rough-textured bags familiarly called gunny sacks, arrived in the United States filled with coffee, cocoa beans, and raw sugar. Henry Chase began recycling these bags, which proved popular among wholesalers whose only alternative was the much heavier and more expensive wooden keg or barrel.

With the advent of the sewing machine, Henry and his brothers, Thomas and H. Lincoln Chase, were able to begin manufacturing their own bags at low cost. They acquired patents for equipment to sew bags on a continuous feed and to print brand names on the bags.

In 1866, Francis H. Ludington, forebear of the present family of owners, joined the firm and went to St. Louis, then later to Kansas City to open new plants to serve the growing needs of the Midwest after the Civil War. The company continued in the bag manufacturing business, adding new plants and expanding old ones, until they had established a solid national reputation.

It was not until they were approached in 1963 by a Chicago advertising firm about creating a stuffed doll that Chase considered stepping out of the familiar market into an entirely different type of venture. An account executive at the advertising agency tried without success to convince the company that they had the capabilities of producing dolls. Pointing out that Chase had everything required to make a doll — cloth, thread, machinery, and experienced operators — the executive finally prevailed and Chase accepted an order for 75,000 dolls. That doll was the Jolly Green Giant.

Bill Riggs laughs when he remembers how it all happened. Chase had fun trying to create an acceptable design for their client. A young artist drew the designs, which were then transferred to cloth and stitched. Then everyone involved sat around and looked at the doll, trying to decide what needed changing. Then the whole process would be repeated. After many changes, Chase finally had a doll they thought would be acceptable to their client and sent off a copy to Chicago. After three or four more changes suggested by the customer, the doll was nearly ready.

The doll was to be printed on green cloth with black detailing and a red mouth, which caused another problem. Printing red over green ordinarily results in brown. After much experimentation, the desired effect was achieved and the first Jolly Green Giant doll was ready for promotion.

That first order for 75,000 dolls was quickly dispersed, and before the promotion ended about 600,000 dolls had been sent to eager customers. But another problem emerged. Since the trucks used to ship the dolls to LeSeur, Minnesota, home of the Jolly Green Giant, held only 10,000 dolls per load, it soon became apparent that shipping costs were prohibitive and an alternative fulfillment method had to be found. The Green Giant Company asked Chase to dropship the dolls to their customers, with Green Giant furnishing the typed labels. With this operation Chase completed a partial fulfillment on a large promotion and began to think in terms of performing the entire fulfillment service for future customers.

Fulfillment is a different business than is manufacturing stuffed dolls, but Chase eventually resolved whatever problems were involved and their fulfillment program went into operation. Shortly thereafter, with the Green Giant experience to their credit, Chase began seeking orders for other promotional items. They contacted Kellogg's and obtained orders for a Woody Woodpecker doll and a Toucan Sam, both of which Chase produced and fulfilled. These two dolls brought Chase national recognition in an area other than bag production and launched them into what would become a lucrative market. (Later, Chase produced the Little Green Sprout for Green Giant. It met with little success, however, since it was never heavily promoted.)

Chase doll figures tell the story. About half a million Woody Woodpeckers have been made and mailed, while 300,000 to 400,000 Toucan Sams were produced and fulfilled by Chase. In the point-of-purchase market, where dolls are sold directly to customers at retail outlets, the numbers are even larger. During a two-year promotion of McDonald's Hamburglar and Ronald McDonald, more than a million dolls were produced. In one year, Chase shipped 700,000 of the short, fat Burger King doll while Hardee's Gilbert Giddy-Up, a first trial doll with limited exposure and length of run, totaled 150,000.

The list goes on. There were about 100,000 Florida Orange Birds, another 100,000 Tony the Tigers for Kellogg's, and 100,000 Big Boy dolls. In a Texas-only promotion, the Dairy Queen stores promoted the DQ Kid and Sweet Nell — 212,500 each. Pillsbury's Dough Boy in the first few years of promotion rang up several hundred thousand pieces before going into a doll manufacturer's line.

Mr. Peanut is Chase's all-time great in terms of length of

manufacture. This trademark doll has never been promoted except on the cellophane wrappers of vending machine product packages but it produced an average of 1,000 orders a week for many years, beginning in 1967. It is still going strong.

The Mr. Peanut doll has been made in three different sizes over the years. With production costs increasing each year, it was necessary to cut the size of the dolls. The price increases on the wrappers never quite caught up with escalating production costs.

There is no single fulfillment company in the country that would be able to handle a national promotion by McDonald's. For this reason Ronald McDonald has always been offered on a regional basis and at individual store option. Some outlets offer Ronald as a gift with certain qualifiers. Others display the dolls for direct sale. Ronald McDonald, during his heyday, accounted for from 750,000 to a million units annually and is probably one of the most popular, if not *the* most popular promotion doll ever offered.

The following is a list of promotion dolls manufactured by Chase Bag Company. Whenever possible, the company for whom the dolls were manufactured is noted in parentheses.

Alice (MD Bathroom Tissue)
Alice in Wonderland Characters (MD Bathroom Tissue)
Allergy Annie (Honeywell, Inc.)
Astronaut
Baseball Players
Bazooka Joe (Bazooka Joe Bubble Gum)
Bemco (Bemco Bedding Company)
Ben Franklin (Ben Franklin Life Insurance)
Big Boy, two-styles (Big Boy Restaurants)
Brach Scarecrow Sam (Brach Candy)
Bracho the Clown (Brach Candy)
Brunswick Dolls (Brunswick Bowling, four styles)
Burger King (Burger King Restaurants, two styles)
Casey Clown
Centsable Cuddly Characters Series
    Adventurous Ashley Astronaut
    Cowardly Culbert Caveman
    Harmonious Harvey Hippie
    Quivering Quincy Quarterback
Charlie Chocks (Chocks Vitamins)
Chaseline Clown (Chase Bag)
Cheerleader (Dairy Queen, Texas promotion)
Chiquita Banana (Chiquita)
Chore Girl (Chore Girl Pot Scrubbers)
C & H Sugar Twins (C & H Sugar)
DQ Kid (Dairy Queen, Texas promotion)
Derby Oil Man (Derby Oil)
Dolly (Big Boy Restaurants)
Dough Boy (Pillsbury)
Dough Boy with Chef Hat (Pillsbury)
Eskimo Boy (Eskimo Pie Corporation, two styles)
Farmer Brown (two styles)

Fireman (18″)
Fun Fair Clowns (Kellogg Company, three styles)
Funmaker Sprite (Wurlitzer)
George Washington and Martha (Gillette)
Gilbert Giddy-Up (Hardee's)
Gileski
Gingerman
Green Giant (Green Giant, standard size)
Green Giant (Green Giant, 28″)
Hamburglar (McDonald's, two styles)
Hot Tamale Kid (Hot Tamale Candies)
Jack Frost (Jack Frost Sugar)
J. P. Patches (Mission Macaroni Company)
Leprechaun
Lerner Newsboy (Myers Publishing)
Little Hans (Nestle's)
Little Leprechaun (Shamrock Oil)
Little Sprout (Green Giant)
Mac Miser
Mahatma (Riviana Foods)
Mattie Mae
Mets (small size, man)
Mets (standard size, lady)
Mets (standard size, man)
Mohawk Tommy (Mohawk Carpets)
Mr. Chip
Mr. Magoo (General Electric)
Mr. Peanut (Planters Peanuts, large size)
Mr. Peanut (Planters Peanuts, 18″)
Nicky (Nets)
Patient Pat (Kimberly-Clark)
Peter Pan (Peter Pan Ice Cream)
P & G Terrycloth (Procter & Gamble)
Pickwick
Pirate Girl and Boy (Long John Silver's)
Play-Doh Boy (Play-Doh)
Punchy (Hawaiian Punch)
Purple Boy
Raisin Bran Chex Doll (Ralston Purina)
Ronald McDonald (McDonald's, three styles)
Sammy Speaker
Santa Claus
Sweet Nell (Dairy Queen, Texas promotion)
Tasty Baker (Tastycake Bakeries)
Thor (Dak Meat Company)
Thumbody (Princeton Partners)
Thurd Plush
Winnie
Wizard of Oz Characters (MD Tissue)
    Dorothy, Tin Man, Scarecrow, Lion

Note: This is not a complete listing of the promotional items manufactured by Chase Bag Company. It includes only those items that fit the definition of all-cloth representations of human figures.

Sybil Ludington—A History Lesson

One of the many benefits of research is the quantity and diversity of information one finds. Always there is a learning process going on as a book is completed. Too often, much of what one discovers must remain as background material and does not become a part of the final manuscript. Here is a story I cannot resist sharing.

As previously noted, Francis H. Ludington joined Chase Bag Company in 1866, and the Ludington family subsequently took over the firm. Sybil Ludington, ancestor to Chase's Francis H. Ludington, was a feminine Paul Revere. She rode from Danbury, Connecticut, to Patterson, New Jersey, to alert her father's soldiers that the British were on their way.

Sybil was just sixteen years old when, on the night of April 25, 1777, two thousand British troops landed on Connecticut shores and marched inland toward Danbury. There they began the destruction of rebel stores, some of which included a quantity of rum. Soon, drunken Redcoats were shooting and burning throughout the community.

In the early evening, an injured messenger arrived at the Ludington home, located about twenty miles west of Danbury. He had ridden the distance with a bullet in his back to alert Colonel Ludington and his troops. Sybil volunteered to ride the forty-mile circuit to arouse her father's militia, thus freeing him to remain near Danbury to organize the regiment and lead them into battle.

That night, Sybil rode twenty-six miles farther than Paul Revere did on his famous ride almost exactly two years earlier, including some distance through a no-man's land where hostile Indians and army deserters lurked. Nevertheless, she rode successfully along her route, shouting and banging on doors to awaken her father's men. She returned to her home at dawn, exhausted but safe.

The citizens of Danbury have erected a statue commemorating Sybil's ride. It depicts a young girl seated sidesaddle on a great bay horse, clothing flying, one arm extended with a stick clutched firmly in her hand.

3A-a1

3A-a1   **American Beauty Macaroni Company, Roni Mac, 11″.** Distributed as a flat to be sewn at home. **AMERICAN BEAUTY/"RONI MAC"** printed on top of head. This mail-in offer was printed on product packages in the 1930s. (N. Ricklefs collection)

3A-1, 2   **Arbuckle Brothers Coffee (Yuban).** This company really believed in advertising premiums. They used every gimmick, including a set of four lithographed dolls to be cut, sewn, and stuffed. Here we have Jack and Jill, approximately 14″ tall. The other two were Tom, the Piper's Son, and Mary and Her Little Lamb. Jack and Jill are more stylistically alike than the Mary I have seen. The fourth doll has not come to my attention for comparison, however. More than one artist may have been involved in the creation of the set. 1931. (Author's collection)

3A-3   **Atlas Van Lines, Atlas Annie, 15½″.** Lithographed doll in two-tone blue pantsuit. Designed to be a comfort to the child moving to a new home. The Atlas Van Lines trademark is on the pocket and a tag reads: "Hi! I'm Atlas Annie. I'm here to make moving fun with my special friend. . . ." (Ad from *Family Circle,* March 8, 1977)

Moving day.
She needs you and Atlas Annie.

3A-3

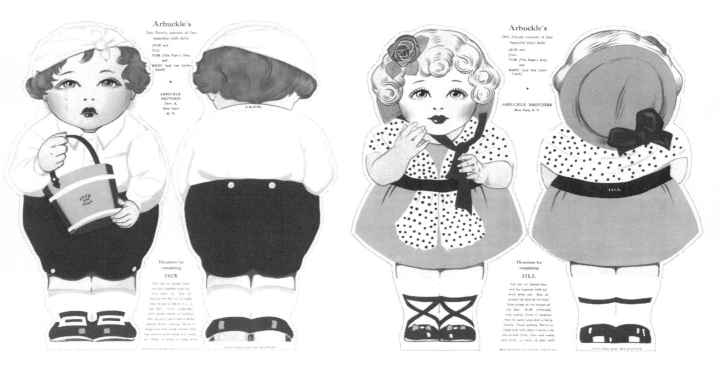

3A-1, 2

3A-4

3A-4a

3A-4a

Aunt Jemima Mills, St. Joseph, Missouri.
This company capitalized on the image of a warm, motherly Black cook to represent their products. The Aunt Jemima trademark became as familiar to most Americans as any in the history of advertising. So popular was the trademark that the idea was expanded to include an entire family — Uncle Mose, Wade, and Diana among them.

3A-4   **Aunt Jemima.** From a 1919 *Ladies' Home Journal* advertisement. Miss Nancy Green was Aunt Jemima at this time.

3A-4a   **Aunt Jemima Doll, 15″.** Lithographed on muslin, this doll wears a yellow dress with black dots and a yellow cap with red checks. Distortion in closeup is due to lumpy stuffing. Doll is marked **Aunt Jemima** on the back. This doll more closely resembles Nancy Green than most other issues known. (Author's collection)

3A-4c   **Diana, 10½″.** One of the Aunt Jemima family that also included Uncle Mose and Wade, a young boy. This Diana was a victim of careless stitching and stuffing, hence her peculiar shape. Printed on the front of her skirt is: **Aunt Jemima's/Pancake Flour/Pickaninny Doll/Diana/The Davis Milling Co./St. Joseph, Mo.** The Davis Milling Company preceded Aunt Jemima Mills. (Author's collection)

3A-4d   **Aunt Jemima, 12″.** Printed on oilcloth or plastic-coated fabric, ca 1948. The cartoon approach is used for this newer doll, also part of a set of four. Available in stores as well as through a mail-in advertising offer. (Courtesy Ralph's Antique Dolls)

3A-4e   **Uncle Mose, 13½″.** Another of the Aunt Jemima family. This doll is from the same set as 3A-4d.

3A-4c

3A-4d

3A-4e

3B-1

3B-3

3B-2

3B-1   **Bakery Girl.** An unidentified promotion doll, lithographed in bright colors, sewn flat.

3B-2   **Bazooka Bubble Gum, Bazooka Joe, 18″.** Lithographed cloth, 1973. Name on front of shirt. A Chase Bag Company production.

3B-3   **Bemco Bedding Company, Bemco, 18″.** Produced by Chase Bag Company.

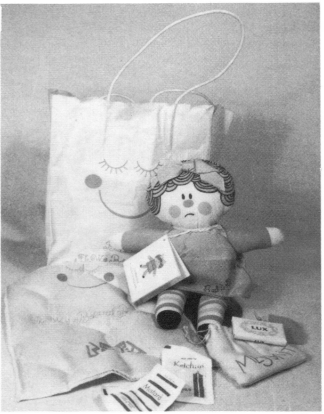

3B-4

3B-5

3B-6

3B-4	**Beta Fiberglas**™, Beta, 10½″. Came with an 8″ × 9″ bedspread, miniature shopping bag, ketchup, soap, mess kit, and sponge. On doll's dress is printed: **Bad Doll.** Original booklet reads: **I'm a Bad Doll. I'm fun to play with.** On bedspread is: **The Well Behaved Bedspread/Fiberglas/ BETA.** Lithographed cloth. (Stewart collection)
3B-5	**Bird's Eye Frozen Foods**, Minx, 11″. Dressed in blue. Part of a set of three. Merry dressed in red and Mike dressed in green complete the trio. These dolls were distributed flat as part of a frozen orange juice promotion by General Foods Corporation. Marks: **Minx** on shirt front, **1953 GENERAL FOODS CORPORATION** on back of belt.
3B-6	**Boraxo Cleaner**, Jennie, 22″. Yarn wig, imitation rhinestone eyes, embroidered mouth, lithographed body. Instructions for making the doll were included in the by-mail promotion. Advertised on boxes of Boraxo cleaner for $4.50. (Janke collection)

In the 3B-6 advertisement image:

The comp
lovable "
Jennie is
bedroom
rooms. St
with yarn
ribbon for
and Bucill
everythir
trated ex
instructio

$6.00 Value
$4.50

3B-7

3B-7   **Brach Candy Company, Bracho, the Clown, 18".** Lithographed features and clothing, plastic ruff around neck. Mail-in offer from candy wrapper. Produced by Chase Bag Company. (Rogers and Weaver collections)

3B-8   **Brach Candy Company, Scarecrow Sam, 17½".** Came with the coloring book, *Sam, the Scared-est Scarecrow,* by Robert L. May (author of *Rudolph, The Red-Nosed Reindeer*), illustrated by Ruth Bendell. Doll produced by Chase Bag Company. (Weaver collection. Courtesy Chase Bag)

3B-8

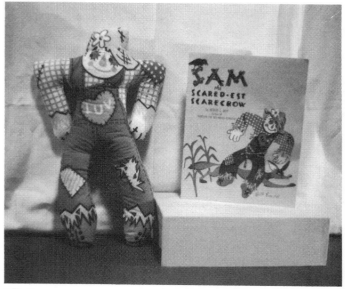

3B-8

3B-9   **Burger King Hamburger Stores, Burger King, 16½″.** A 1973 edition of this 1972 doll had a medal on the chest with **Burger King** printed on it. These dolls were offered throughout the 1970s in various forms. (Haag collection)

3B-10   **Burger King Hamburger Stores, Burger King, 13″.** Marked only **MADE IN U.S.A.** This 1977 doll resembles the actor who plays Burger King in the television commercials. Although Robison and Sellers give the size of this doll as 15″, I have measured it several times and it is, indeed, only 13″ tall. It is possible that more than one size was issued over the years. All sizes were produced by Chase Bag Company. (Author's photograph. Courtesy Chase)

3B-11   **Buster Brown Textiles, Inc., Buster Brown and Tige, 16½″ and 11″.** Offered through magazine ads as a mail-order item for $1. Marked ©**1974 Buster Brown Textiles, Inc.** On the back hip of the doll is **C1974.** This cloth doll is a new version of one from the Buster Brown Historical Collection of Memorabilia, dating to 1904. It was in that year that Buster Brown began making clothing for children. (Courtesy Buster Brown Textiles, Inc.)

3B-9

3B-10

3B-11

3C-1

Rag doll offer from C and H Brown Sug...

**Two little Hawaiians
Only $1.00 each...**

The pure brown cane sugar
from Hawaii...
with deep molasses flavor.

3C-2

3C-3

3C-1   **C and H Sugar Company, Sugar Kid, 16″.**
Silk-screened features and clothes. Sold for $1 plus
C and H oval from brown sugar box. (Hafner
collection)

3C-2   **C and H Brown Sugar Magazine Advertisement Offering the Sugar Kids.** The "kids"
were also offered on bags of white sugar during
this promotion. Produced by Chase Bag Company.
Offer expired December 31, 1973.

3C-3   **Campbell Soup Company, The Campbell
Kids, 12″.** Yellow and orange yarn hair, lithographed features, cotton bodies. Each wears a
chef's hat and outfit with a large **C** in Campbell's
logo style on hats and aprons. (1973 catalog
illustration courtesy Sears, Roebuck and
Company)

3C-4 **Campbell Soup Company, Campbell Kid Girl, 16″.** All cloth, made in Hong Kong, 1973, polyester-stuffed. The Campbell Kids are a registered trademark of the Campbell Soup Company. (Haag collection)

3C-5 **Central Flour Company, ISTROUMA, Humpty Dumpty, 11″.** Printed on 24-lb bags of bleached flour. (Robison and Sellers list their example as 13″ tall.) Printed in red, blue, and yellow on an unbleached muslin bag. (Author's collection)

3C-6 **Chicken of the Sea Tuna, Mermaid, 14″.** One of three Shoppin' Pals by Mattel, © 1974. Flesh-colored cotton and yarn hair. (Weaver collection)

3C-4

3C-5

DIRECTIONS FOR MAKING
Cut out on dotted line through both sides of sack. Lay printed side in and sew on outline, leaving an opening for stuffing. Turn right side out. Stuff arms and legs first and sew across where arrows indicate. Then stuff body.

3C-6

3C-8

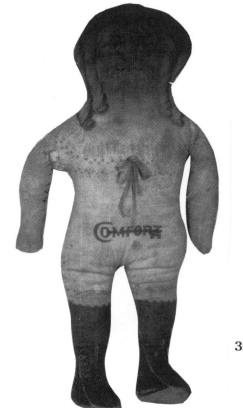

3C-7

3C-9

3C-7   **Chocks Vitamins, Charlie Chocks, 20″.** Lithographed cloth. Marks: **CHARLIE CHOCKS** on helmet, **CHOCKS** on lithographed bottles around waist. Charlie is a Chase Bag Company product. (Stewart collection)

3C-8   **Chore Girl Pot Scrubbers, Chore Girl, 16″.** Lithographed cloth, marked **CHORE GIRL** on front of apron. A Chase Bag doll. (Stewart collection)

3C-9   **Comfort Magazine, Golden Locks, 14″.** Lithographed cloth, bow on back of head. This doll was free from the magazine with a twenty-five cent subscription. Marks: **COMFORT** (with a drawing of a skeleton key through the word) and **from AUGUSTA, ME.** on the underwear. Note that the face is soiled. The doll was apparently dressed most of its years, thus preserving the body and legs.

3D-4   **Dutch Maid Noodles, Dutch Maid, 13″.** Lithographed cloth, white dress, blue vest, yellow hair, hands, and feet. This 1976 premium cost $1 with a product wrapper. (Weaver collection. Photograph courtesy the owner)

3E-1   **Eskimo Pie Ice Cream Novelties, Eskimo Pie Boy, 15″.** This lithographed cloth, flat sew-and-stuff doll was first offered in 1964 and was available until 1974 when the design was changed. The character has been the trademark of the company since the 1930s. A Chase Bag design. (Author's collection)

3E-2   **Eskimo Pie Ice Cream Novelties, Eskimo Pie Boy, 16″.** New design for the Eskimo Pie boy, 1975. Another product of Chase Bag. (Haag collection)

3D-4

3E-1

3E-2

3C-7

3C-8

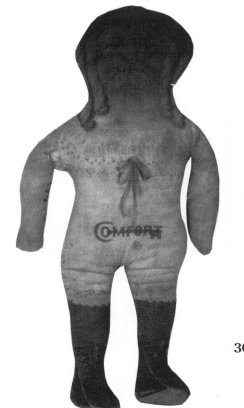

3C-9

3C-7 **Chocks Vitamins, Charlie Chocks, 20″.** Lithographed cloth. Marks: **CHARLIE CHOCKS** on helmet, **CHOCKS** on lithographed bottles around waist. Charlie is a Chase Bag Company product. (Stewart collection)

3C-8 **Chore Girl Pot Scrubbers, Chore Girl, 16″.** Lithographed cloth, marked **CHORE GIRL** on front of apron. A Chase Bag doll. (Stewart collection)

3C-9 **Comfort Magazine, Golden Locks, 14″.** Lithographed cloth, bow on back of head. This doll was free from the magazine with a twenty-five cent subscription. Marks: **COMFORT** (with a drawing of a skeleton key through the word) and **from AUGUSTA, ME.** on the underwear. Note that the face is soiled. The doll was apparently dressed most of its years, thus preserving the body and legs.

3C-10   **Cracker Jack, Sailor Jack, 15″.** Another of the Mattel Shoppin' Pals™,© 1974. Cracker Jack is a division of Borden Foods, Borden, Inc. (Weaver collection)

3C-11   **Cream of Wheat Cereal, Rastus, the Cream of Wheat Chef.** A premium for ten cents and a boxtop, this doll was offered in a 16″ size in 1922 and an 18″ size in 1930. Doll was available through various promotions until 1952. (Author's collection)

3C-12   **Cream of Wheat Cereal Figure.** From a magazine coupon offer. (Courtesy John C. Flavin, National Biscuit Company)

3C-10

3C-12

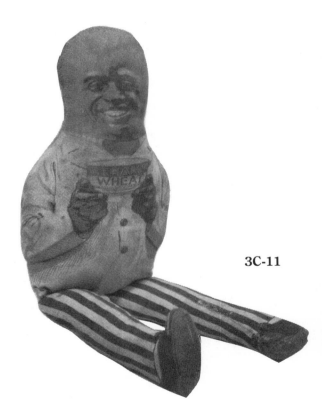

3C-11

3D-1

3D-3

3D-2

3D-1   **Dairy Queen of Texas, The DQ Kid and Sweet Nell, 13″.** The other character in this 1979 trio was Funfighter McDoom, easily recognized by the black patch he wears over his right eye. (Author's photograph. Courtesy Chase)

3D-2   **Dairy Queen of Texas, The Houston Oilers Cheerleader, 12½″.** To promote the Oilers, the Texas Dairy Queen Association distributed this doll marked with an oil derrick on the back. Another Chase Bag doll. (Courtesy Chase)

3D-3   **Dak Meat Company, Thor, 13½″.** A copy of the Dak trademark, a product of Denmark. Thor has a dark red-orange beard and looks just like a Viking should look. A Chase Bag doll. (Courtesy Chase)

3D-4   **Dutch Maid Noodles, Dutch Maid, 13″.** Lithographed cloth, white dress, blue vest, yellow hair, hands, and feet. This 1976 premium cost $1 with a product wrapper. (Weaver collection. Photograph courtesy the owner)

3E-1   **Eskimo Pie Ice Cream Novelties, Eskimo Pie Boy, 15″.** This lithographed cloth, flat sew-and-stuff doll was first offered in 1964 and was available until 1974 when the design was changed. The character has been the trademark of the company since the 1930s. A Chase Bag design. (Author's collection)

3E-2   **Eskimo Pie Ice Cream Novelties, Eskimo Pie Boy, 16″.** New design for the Eskimo Pie boy, 1975. Another product of Chase Bag. (Haag collection)

3D-4

3E-2

3E-1

3F-1

3F-2

3F-3

3F-1   **Faultless Starch Company, Miss Phoebe Primm, 12½″.** A 1978 reprint of a 1914 original. There was also a Miss Lily White of similar design. The two dolls were a premium for either six ten-cent-size package fronts or twelve of the five-cent size, plus eight cents in stamps. Marked on back of sash: **MISS PHOEBE PRIMM/FAULTLESS STARCH DOLL, KANSAS CITY, MO.** At bottom of panel: ©**1978 Faultless Starch/Bon Ami Company/Kansas City, Mo. 64101.** Reprint was manufactured by Chase Bag Company. Panel measures 14″ × 16″. (Author's collection)

3F-2   **Franklin Life Insurance Company, Benjamin Franklin, 13″.** Lithographed cloth, yellow vest, black coat, red pants. Marked **FRANKLIN LIFE/INSURANCE COMPANY** on back. Free for listening to the Franklin story promotion, 1970s. (Wiseman collection)

3F-3   **Frostie Root Beer, Frostie, 16½″.** Early 1970s, purchased in 1974, all-lithographed cloth. Manufacturer, Chase Bag. (Weaver collection)

3G-1   **Gold Medal Flour, General Mills, Girl, 7½".**
Brown and red plaid dress, apron imprinted with the
flour sack label. Label reads: **Eventually/Washburn
Crosby/GOLD/MEDAL/FLOUR/Why
not now?** Washburn Crosby was one of the small,
independent mills that merged to form General
Mills in the late 1920s. (Braden collection)

3G-1A   **General Mills, Betty Crocker, 13".** Lithographed, stuffed cloth, removable clothes. Came
with bake set of Betty Crocker dessert mixes,
cookie cutters, baking pans, etc. Red spoon
emblem on apron is the Betty Crocker logo. Betty
Crocker Products is a division of General Mills, as
is Kenner Products Company, manufacturer of the
dolls. (Catalog illustration courtesy Kenner)

3G-2   **Green Giant Company, Jolly Green Giant,
16".** "From the valley of the Jolly (ho-ho-ho) Green
Giant" comes this prestuffed, lithographed rag doll
in varying shades of green, 1960s. A Chase Bag
doll. (Rebekka Anderton collection)

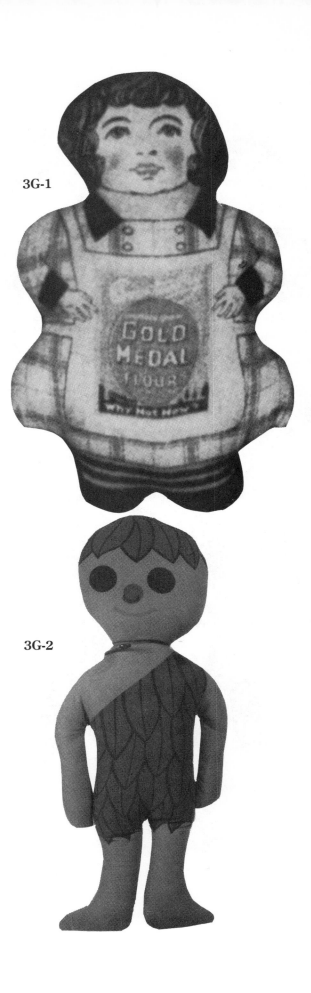

3G-1

3G-1A

3G-2

3G-4

3H-1

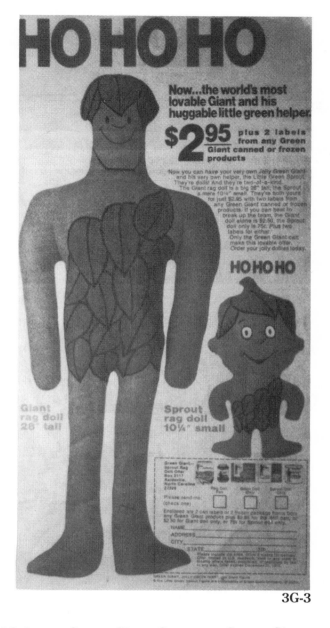

3G-3

3G-3   **Green Giant Company, Green Giant and Little Sprout, 28″ and 10¼″.** Both dolls were advertised in the Sunday comic sections of numerous newspapers. Mail-in offer expired December 31, 1973. From Chase Bag Company. (Author's collection)

3G-4   **Gillette Company, George Washington, 13″.** Screen-printed on cloth by Chase Bag for White Rain Shampoo as a Bicentennial commemorative doll. Other products of the company also featured the offer from 1974 through March of 1976. George is marked **The Gillette Co. 1974.** (Author's photograph. Courtesy Chase)

3H-1   **Hardee's Hamburgers, Gilbert Giddy-Up, 13½″.** Produced by Chase Bag Company, 1971. (Author's photograph. Courtesy Chase)

37

3H-2 **Henderson Glove Company, Indian Chief, 11″.** Printed in shades of brown. Some dolls are unmarked. (Braden collection)

3H-3 **Honeywell, Inc., Allergy Annie, 15″.** Lithographed cloth. Doll came with coloring book. Promotion used by Honeywell, the "Air Cleaner People." A Chase Bag doll.

3H-4 **Hot Tamale Candies Company, The Hot Tamale Kid, 16″.** Also available in 18″. Offered from 1967 through 1975. All brightly lithographed cloth. Mail-in order required candy boxtop and cash. Chase Bag doll. (Author's photograph. Courtesy Chase and Marion Weaver)

3H-2

3H-3

3H-4

3J-1

3J-2

3K-1

3J-1 **Jack Frost Sugar Company, Jack Frost.** Available in two styles. Pictured on the left is a doll purchased from a collector in 1967. On the right is a 1973 mail-in offer for one boxtop and $1.50. Chase Bag Company. (Sheinwald and Weaver collections)

3J-2 **Jensen, 8½".** Created for an advertising agency by Chase Bag Company. No other identification available. (Author's photograph. Courtesy Chase)

3K-1 **Kellogg Company, Goldilocks and the Three Bears.** Papa Bear is 13½", Goldilocks 13", Mama Bear 12", Baby Bear 10". Pictured is believed to be the 1926 second series. First series had different clothing, different sizes. On cereal bowls is printed **Kellogg's.** On each doll is the doll's name. Papa Bear holds a box of Kellogg's cereal.

3K-2 **Kellogg Company, Set of Four Animals, 11″ to 12½″.** Beautiful colors, printed flat for mail-in orders. These delightful, 1935 pillow-type pieces are pictured as a bonus and to illustrate the variety of items available from Kellogg's over the years. Recommended, even *required* reading on the subject, is Robison and Sellers' book, *Advertising Dolls*, 1980. (Author's collection)

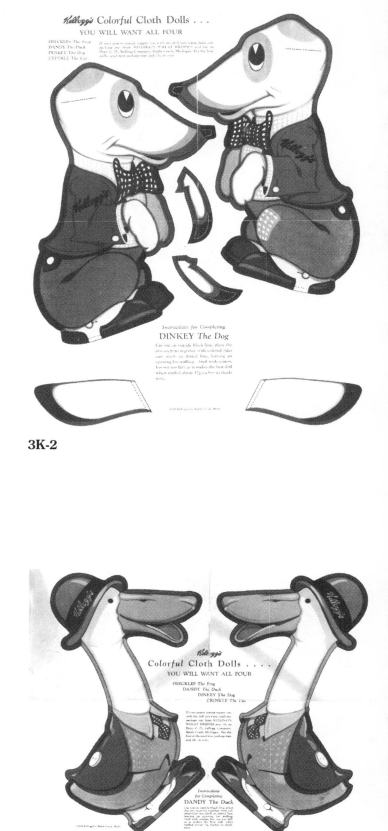

3K-2

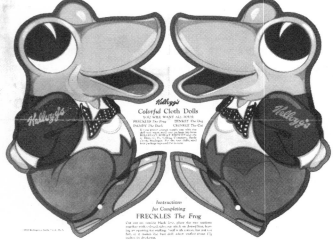

3K-3

3K-4

3K-5

3K-5

3K-3	**Kellogg Company, Three Fun Fair Clowns, 15″.** From Chase Bag Company, 1973. (Author's photograph. Courtesy Chase)
3K-4	**Kimberly-Clark Corporation, Patient Pat, 7″.** A trademark of the company translated into doll form by Chase Bag Company. (Author's photograph. Courtesy Chase)
3K-5	**Korn-Krisp Cereal, Miss Korn-Krisp, 26″.** Lithographed cloth. Has **"My Name is Miss Korn-Krisp"** printed across the front just below the waist. Compare this doll with other printed dolls of the early 1900s. Printed flat for home sewing, they were excellent for use as advertising premiums with just a bit of advertising copy added. Some, of course, were specially designed for the product. However, many companies used dolls already in their lines, adding logos and product names. (O'Rourke collection)

3L-1   **Long John Silver Restaurants, Peg Leg Long John Silver, 17″.** A Chase Bag Company doll. The Jolly Roger Restaurant also used a cloth pirate premium doll almost identical to this, with some slight clothing changes. (Author's photograph. Courtesy Chase)

3L-1a   **Libby's Foods' Libby.** Wears their slogan "Libby's, Libby's, Libby's" on her shirt. This 14″ talking, singing doll, produced by Mattel, Inc., ©1974. Large advertisement ran in the April 6, 1975, edition of *The Sunday News,* Detroit, Michigan, as well as other Sunday supplements across the country. (Courtesy Mira Walilko)

3MC-1   **McDonald Corporation, Ronald McDonald and Hamburglar, 17″.** Chase Bag made three styles of Ronald and two styles of Hamburglar. The Ronald pictured was purchased in 1971, Hamburglar in October of 1972. (Weaver collection)

3L-1

3MC-1

3L-1a

42

3M-1

3M-2

3M-3

3M-4

3M-1	**MD Bathroom Tissue, Georgia Pacific Corporation, Dorothy of Oz, Scarecrow, Tin Woodman, and Cowardly Lion.** One of many sets offered over the years by this company. The dolls pictured are (l to r) 18″, 16″, 18″, and 9″. Produced by Chase Bag Company, 1971.
3M-2	**MD Bathroom Tissue, Maisy and Daisy Twins, 17″.** Late 1960s through 1971. Doll pictured on left has one winking eye, one button eye. Doll pictured on the right has two buttons for eyes. Later dolls are a different size and have both eyes open. All-original blouses and jumpers are removable. Yellow yarn hair. Mail-in offer from MD Tissue. A Chase doll.
3M-3	**MD Bathroom Tissue, Caterpillar, Alice, Mad Hatter.** From *Alice in Wonderland.* Offered in 1974. Chase Bag Company dolls. Alice's skirt is missing. (Author's photograph. Courtesy Chase)
3M-4	**Mary Merritt Doll Museum, Official Mary Merritt Doll, 14″.** Red, white, and blue cloth, 1974 to the present. Chase Bag doll. (Weaver collection)

3M-5 **Mission Macaroni Company, J. P. Patches, 14″.** Offered through a Seattle television show for $2.50 and product wrappers. A Chase Bag doll. (Author's photograph. Courtesy Chase)

3M-6 **Morton-Norwich Products, Inc., Morton's Salt Girl, 15″.** One of three Mattel Shoppin' Pals™, ©1974. Yellow yarn hair, all cloth, flesh-colored face, legs, arms. Yellow plastic, sewn-on boots, cardboard umbrella, yellow raincoat. Carries tiny box of Morton's Salt. (Weaver collection)

3M-7 **Mohawk Carpets, Mohawk Tommy, 15″.** Early 1970s, Chase Bag Company. (Author's photograph. Courtesy Chase)

3M-8 **Myers Publishing Company, Lerner News-Boy, 12½″.** Chase Bag Company, 1970. There was also a girl and a dog. (Author's photograph. Courtesy Chase)

3M-5

3M-6

3M-7

3M-8

3N-1

3N-2

3O-1

3P-1

3N-1   **NETS, Nicky, 15″.** Chase Bag Company, 1974, an advertising premium. No company known. (Weaver collection)

3N-2   **Nestle Company, Little Hans, The Chocolate Maker, 13″.** Prestuffed rag doll premium by Chase Bag Company, 1970. Marked ©**The Nestle Company, Inc.** on right foot. (Author's collection. Courtesy the Nestle Company)

3O-1   **Sunbeam Corporation, Oster Super Pan, 18″.** 1972. (Rogers collection)

3P-1   **Peter Pan Ice Cream, Peter Pan, 18″.** Chase Bag Company, 1972. (S. Ricklefs collection)

3P-2 **Philadelphia Flyers Hockey Team, Freddie Flyer, 16″.** Represents Bobby Clarke, captain of the two-year Stanley Cup winners. Yellow hair, red shirt with large black *P*. Note missing tooth. Marked **Reg. Pa. #110 LARAMI CORP. PHI-LA. PA.** (Weaver collection)

3P-3 **Philadelphia Phillies Baseball Team, Phil and Phillis, 15″.** Trademarks of Veterans Stadium where the Phillies play ball at home. Seen on the scoreboard whenever there is a home run. Names are printed on hats. Dolls pictured were purchased in 1972. (Weaver collection)

3P-4 **Planters Peanuts, Standard Brands, Inc., Mr. Peanut, 22″.** Bright yellow and black, pre-stuffed, lithographed cloth. Trademark of Planters since the 1930s. The example pictured is 1960s. Chase Bag Company. (Zillner collection)

3P-2

3P-4

3P-3

3P-5

3Q-1

3Q-2

3P-5 **Princeton Partners, Thumbody Loves You, 13″.** From an advertising agency. This giant thumbprint doll was designed as a real messenger of good will with its large smile, "extended" right hand, 1972. Chase Bag Company. (Author's photograph. Courtesy Chase)

3Q-1 **Quaker Oats Company, Cap'n Crunch, 15½″.** Synthetic feltlike material. Marked with a large *C* on his hat. Sewn-on cloth label on his boot reads: **Exclusively made for/The Quaker Oats Company.** On the other side is: **Animal Fair, Inc./ Copyright 1978.** Illustration shown is from a cereal box. (Author's collection)

3Q-2 **Quaker Oats Company, Popeye the Sailor, 15½″.** All-lithographed cloth. Purchased for $1.75 from Puffed Quaker Rice, P.O. Box 2205, Reidsville, North Carolina 27320. Apparently this is a Chase Bag doll, although it does not appear on Chase's master list. (Weaver collection)

3Q-3   **Quaker Oats Company, Uncle Mose, 16″.**
This character is a part of the Aunt Jemima Family.
UNCLE MOSE is printed on back of collar.
Complete instructions for finishing doll are printed
on the flat, as well as **THE QUAKER OATS
COMPANY/ST. JOSEPH, MISSOURI/©1929.**
Uncut flat, 1929, is illustrated. (Author's
collection)

3Q-4   **Quaker Oats Company, Quaker Crackels
Boy, 17″.** Lithographed cloth, pale lavender suit
with green vest, gold buttons, brown shoes. Blond
hair, blue eyes, carries box of Quaker Crackels in
his hip pocket. According to a spokesperson for
Quaker, the cereal was discontinued in 1924. For
this reason, I identified this doll with that date in
the advertising section of my first book. Later, I
located an uncut flat of the doll very plainly marked
**THE QUAKER OATS COMPANY/CHICAGO,
ILLINOIS/©1930.** (Doll courtesy Ralph's Antique Dolls. Uncut flat, author's collection)

3Q-3

3Q-4

3Q-4

48

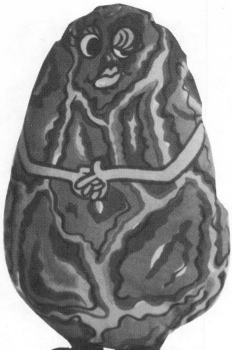

3R-1

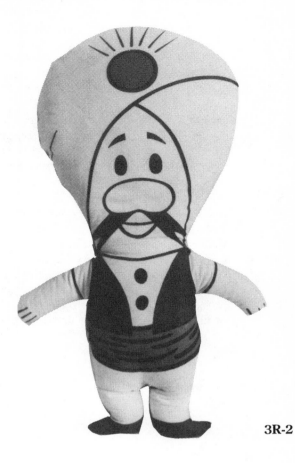

3R-2

3S-1

3R-1   **Ralston Purina Company, Raisin Bran Chex, Raisin Doll, 15″.** Lithographed cloth, mail-in offer, 1973. A Chase Bag doll. (Author's photograph. Courtesy Chase)

3R-2   **Riviana Foods, Mahatma, 15″.** A Chase Bag doll. (Author's photograph. Courtesy Chase)

3S-1   **Shamrock Oil Company, Little Leprechaun, 15″.** All cloth, produced by Chase Bag Company. (Gibbins collection)

3S-2   **Levi Strauss Company, Official Levi Denim Girl Doll, 17".** Produced by Knickerbocker Toy Company under license from Strauss, 1974. Doll and all clothes are blue denim. (Weaver collection)

3S-3   **Supreme Sugar Company, Miss Supreme, 15".** Doll was printed on the back of a 100-lb sugar bag. Logo on the front is a picture of blue, snowcapped mountain peaks and the words **Supreme Sugar/Reg. U.S. Pat Office.** There is no date. Below the logo is: **Supreme Sugar/Extra Fine Granulated Cane Sugar/New Orleans, Louisiana.** The model shown has been embroidered, apparently to enhance her appearance. (Wiseman collection)

3S-4   **Swiss Miss Lite Hot Chocolate, Swiss Miss, 16".** Sanna Division, Beatrice Foods Company. Removable clothes, all cloth, yarn hair. Offer expired December 31, 1980. Manufactured for Beatrice Foods by Product People, Inc., copyright Swiss Miss 1977. The original offer from a product package, also offered a childsize playhouse of heavy-duty, corrugated cardboard styled as a Swiss chalet is also shown. (Haag collection)

3S-4

3S-2

3S-3

3S-4

3T-1

3T-1   **Tastycake Bakeries, Tastycake Baker, 14″.**
Doll shown was purchased in September 1973
(dates may vary according to marketing areas on
many promotions). A premium coupon in a package of Tastycake cupcakes and $1 brought this
gem to your mailbox. A Chase Bag doll. (Author's
photograph. Courtesy Chase)

3T-2   **Tennis Menace, 13½″.** Manufactured for an
advertising agency by Chase Bag Company. There
was also a golf doll, a bowling doll, and another
unidentified sport doll. Printing on the doll reads:
"Voodoo Power, Curse and Cure, Are you SPELL-
BOUND by your opponent's dazzling form? Cast
your own SPELL with the T.M. Voodoo Doll . . .
why wait for FATE? PINPOINT his weakness.
. . ." Points of stress, such as "tennis elbow" and
"broken shoelace" are marked all over the doll.
There is even a warning: "CAUTION: The Voodoo
General has determined that this ritual may be
hazardous to your opponent." The instructions
continue, "you now possess the power to JINX
your foe. Get right to the POINT. JAB those pesky
PROBLEMS and PLAY tennis with a free spirit.
You now possess the POWER TO RELIEVE
YOUR ANXIETIES. BEWARE: Your opponent
may also own one of these DOLLS." (Author's
photograph. Courtesy Chase)

3T-2

3W-1   **Western Union Telegraph Company, Dolly-Gram, 6″.** Has raffia wig, stuffed velvet body and head, pocket in front for message. Marked **Dolly-Gram by/Western Union.** (Author's collection)

3W-2   **Wurlitzer Company, Funmaker Sprite, 15″.** In green suit, this doll advertised the Sprite Easy-Play Organs manufactured by Wurlitzer. A Chase Bag doll. (Author's photograph. Courtesy Chase)

3W-1

3W-2

4 Domestic Commercial Dolls

Virtually every doll manufacturer in every country in the world has produced at least one rag doll. Cloth dolls are very commercial. They make money for the manufacturer and show a tidy profit. Cloth dolls are usually easy and relatively inexpensive to design and make. They have strong purchase appeal because they are soft and cuddly and usually carry a relatively low price tag. The latter makes them attractive to manufacturers and buyers alike, particularly during economic downturns. Cloth dolls always sell.

This is not to say that all cloth dolls are good sellers. A poorly conceived or constructed doll would have approximately the same appeal as any other piece of shoddy merchandise. But in general, it is safe to say that rag dolls are good sellers.

Doll manufacturing is a very competitive business. Manufacturers vie for the services of top designers. They compete for licensing rights to popular names around which the aura of success already glows. Then they create dolls and wardrobes based on these characters. They seek out new designers and try to outguess their competitors. Their goal is a slice of the market pie, just as large a slice as can be obtained, of course, using all the merchandising resources at their command.

If a doll does not sell as well as expected the first year, a manufacturer may cancel the item, or they may try one more year before making the decision to drop the doll from their line. For this reason, cloth dolls are just as susceptible to sudden disappearance from the market as are other manufactured products.

The classic dolls, of course, seem to go on year after year. Raggedy Ann and Raggedy Andy are unequaled in their longevity and lasting appeal. These two characters created by author Johnny Gruelle were based on a doll his mother once made. They have been produced in dozens of forms and sizes by a bevy of manufacturers since Raggedy Ann was patented in 1915. See pages 366-367 in *Twentieth Century Dolls* for the full story.

They have appeared not only in a range of sizes in rag doll form, but also as commercial patterns for home sewing and as paper dolls in countless formats. They have been immortalized on china and plastic dinnerware, on silver and stainless tableware, on paper napkins, placemats, tablecloths, party favors, invitations, and even disposable diapers. A song has been written about them. A movie has been produced to relate their adventures. They are instantly recognized in nearly every country in the world and have provided many happy moments of play for millions of children. In short, they are commercial. Quite a career for a pair of refugees made from scraps.

Parallel to the continued success of Raggedy Ann and Raggedy Andy runs the story of a long line of commercially produced rag dolls of domestic and foreign origin. In the United States, there were the Martha Chase dolls, the Alabama Babies, the Columbian Dolls, the Philadelphia Babies, the advertising rags, the by-the-yard dolls, and dozens of others. From overseas came the Chad Valley dolls, the Steiffs, the Lencis, and the Dean's Rag Book Company dolls, among others. Rag dolls have always been considered desirable and highly satisfactory play toys, and their history affirms this assessment.

The Hallmark Rag Dolls

Hallmark Cards, Inc., long known for quality greeting cards, gift wrap, and party accessories, is also the source of some interesting rag dolls. Especially noteworthy is the fact that Hallmark set out to create a series of dolls that would be attractive to all collectors — from a grandmother buying a birthday gift to the most experienced doll collector. The Hallmark dolls have a definite appeal.

The list of dolls supplied by Hallmark and illustrated here begins with a 1971 entry, the familiar Raggedy Ann. Most of these dolls came in small sizes, with the 15″ Sasparilla the Witch being the largest I have found to date. All are discontinued at this writing. No rag dolls are presently being planned by Hallmark. The collector should bear in mind, however, that this could change if it should suddenly be decided that rag dolls would be a good seller next spring or this winter. *Que sera sera.*

The collector should note that the date given by Hallmark for a particular doll may vary from the date on the doll's tag. In addition, there were a variety of styles of tags used to mark these dolls and no explanation is available for these variations. All the dolls examined for this book have the name of the doll on the tag, with the exception of the Sasparilla witch. This doll's tag merely reads "Doll Toy," a designation given to all Hallmark rag dolls.

Where possible, I have attempted to indicate dolls and boxes that are not dated. For purposes of brevity, ND means "no date" and NB means "no box." Only a few of the dolls were retailed without boxes. Some, as we shall see, were never marketed.

Hallmark Rag Dolls

Everyday Dolls

Stock Number	Box	Description	Date on Doll	Company Date
75 PF 162-3		Raggedy Ann*		2-1-71
375 NP 50-1		Betsey Clark Boy		3-1-73
375 NP 50-2		Betsey Clark Girl		3-1-73
125 QS 140-5		Raggedy Ann*		4-1-73
125 QS 140-6		Raggedy Andy	1973	4-1-73
200 DT 27-1		Lucy		10-1-73
200 DT 27-2		Zeke	ND	10-1-73
200 DT 27-3		Charlotte		10-1-73
200 DT 27-5		Babykins		10-1-73
200 DT 27-6		Bessie		10-1-73
200 DT 27-7		Curly	ND	10-1-73
200 DT 27-8		Butch	ND	10-1-73
200 DT 27-9		Pam		10-1-73
200 DT 28-1		Kathy		10-1-73
200 DT 28-2		Ginny		10-1-73
200 DT 28-3		Linda	ND	10-1-73
200 QS 187-1		Little Lulu		4-1-74
200 QS 161-1		Raggedy Ann*		8-1-74
200 QS 162-1		Raggedy Andy		8-1-74
200 QS 163-1		Uncle Clem	1974	8-1-74
200 QS 164-1		Henny	1974	8-1-74
200 QS 165-1		Beloved Belindy	1974	8-1-74
200 PF 900-1		Buttons		6-1-75
200 PF 900-2		Bo		6-1-75
250 DT 900-3	ND	Ben Franklin	ND	10-1-75
250 DT 900-4	ND	Betsy Ross	ND	10-1-75
250 DT 900-5	ND	Martha Washington	ND	10-1-75
250 DT 900-6	ND	George Washington	ND	10-1-75

Famous Americans, Series I

400 DT 113-3	1979	Annie Oakley	February 1979	3-1-79
400 DT 113-4	1979	Chief Joseph	ND	3-1-79
400 DT 113-5	1979	Babe Ruth	ND	3-1-79
400 DT 113-6	1979	Amelia Earhart	ND	3-1-79
400 DT 113-7	1979	George Washington Carver	ND	3-1-79
400 DT 113-8	1979	Susan B. Anthony	February 1979	3-1-79

Famous Americans, Series II

400 DT 113-9	NB	P. T. Barnum	August 1979	8-1-79
400 DT 114-1	NB	Mark Twain	August 1979	8-1-79
400 DT 114-2	NB	Davy Crockett	August 1979	8-1-79
400 DT 114-4	NB	Clara Barton	August 1979	8-1-79
400 DT 114-5	NB	Molly Pitcher	August 1979	8-1-79

Holiday Dolls

200 VPF 2-4		Cupid		1976
100 SPF 8-4		Leprechaun		1972
200 SPF 1-1		Leprechaun		1977, 1978
350 SDT 380-2	NB	Leprechaun (7½″)	ND	1981
200 EPF 4-4		Barnaby		1977-1979
200 EPF 5-1		Bernadette		1977-1979
350 HDT 17-2		Sasparilla Witch (15″)	ND	1973
200 HDT 13-7		Scarecrow		1975
200 HDT 9-1		Scarecrow		1976, 1977
300 HDT 825-3	ND	Winifred Witch (7″)	ND	1978
100 TDT 13-1		Girl Pilgrim		1972
100 TDT 14-4		Boy Pilgrim		1972
200 TPF 16-9		Girl Pilgrim		1975
200 TPF 17-7		Boy Pilgrim		1975
200 TDT 3-1		Girl Pilgrim		1976, 1977
200 TDT 4-4		Boy Pilgrim		1976, 1977
300 TDT 826-3	ND	Indian Maiden	ND	1978
200 XDT 49-2		Elf		1973
200 XDT 51-2		Angel		1973
200 XDT 52-5		Drummer Boy		1973
250 XDT 50-5		Santa		1973
250 XDT 57-2		Snowman		1973
200 XPF 16-9		Santa		1975
200 XPF 17-7		Mrs. Claus		1975
300 XDT 828-3	ND	Santa Claus	ND	1978
300 XDT 829-6	ND	Drummer Boy	ND	1978
350 XDT 830-7		Snowman		1979, 1980

*Not included in this list furnished by Hallmark is a 5¾″ Raggedy Ann, NB, ND, Stock No. 150 TM 262. Although in doll form, this item was created as a gift trim. Other gift trims in doll form have been produced through the years. During the holiday season of 1983, for example, there were a number of Hallmark items available that could conceivably be included in a cloth doll collection.

Here is a partial list defining the codes used in Hallmark's stock numbers. The first three numerals in the stock numbers were the original retail prices.

EDT Easter Doll Toy
EPF Easter Party Favor
EMS An Easter doll designation (exact meaning not known)
EHD Easter Holiday Doll
DT Doll Toy
HHD Halloween Holiday Doll
HDT Halloween Doll Toy
VDT Valentine Doll Toy
VPF Valentine Party Favor
SPF St. Patrick's Party Favor
SDT St. Patrick's Doll Toy
TDT Thanksgiving Doll Toy
TPF Thanksgiving Party Favor

XDT Christmas (Xmas) Doll Toy
QS Special Raggedy Ann and Andy promotion (six dolls)
PF Party Favor
TM Gift Trim designation
NP Found on a Betsey Clark doll (exact meaning not known)

The Genesis of the Famous Americans Series

On the 159th birthday of Susan B. Anthony, Hallmark Cards, Inc., sent out a press release announcing a new series of dolls aimed both at the collector market and the general doll-buying public. Hallmark hoped the dolls, which went on sale February 15th, 1979, would provide a history lesson for youngsters and adults alike.

The challenge was to make the dolls out of a material other than vinyl and plastic. And Hallmark did just that. Half of the historical likenesses would be women because women have not always been included in the history books to the extent they deserve, Hallmark officials felt. In addition, interesting figures from all American minorities would be included. They, too, have often taken a back seat when it comes to having their achievements recognized.

Hallmark considered several alternatives before settling on its Famous American series. According to Tom Nocita, product manager:

> We thought of figures prominent in world history, and we thought of famous people in the fine arts and entertainment fields. We also considered American literary characters, such as Huck Finn, and we looked at the possibility of marketing dolls patterned after American heroes and heroines. We looked at all of them and eventually settled on a mixture of famous Americans — whether they be in sports, entertainment, politics, or the military.
>
> Each person must have an interesting story — something a little out of the ordinary, something that makes each one special. Then they must have a costume that readily identifies them, either by trade or by time period. We could have done Mary Todd Lincoln, but she doesn't have any unusual dress characteristics. The fashion in that era wasn't unique.

Each character was to have a familiar environment. Hallmark does not sell just a doll. It also sells a "house," a unique packaging technique that gives each cloth doll its own residence. Research on the package design was as painstakingly done as that for the characters themselves. George Washington Carver, for example, comes boxed in a facsimile of the Tuskegee Institute. A Hallmark designer fashioned the package from an actual photograph of the laboratory used by Carver. Inside each box is a brief historical reference for that particular doll.

Hallmark had plans in 1979 for another series of famous Americans, but whether by corporate design or marketing judgment, a decision was made not to market the second set through their regular retail outlets. These five dolls were later made available to collectors through an alternative market. The remaining dolls on Hallmark's list were never produced.

What were the plans for the series? Tom Nocita mentioned a few names in his press release that year. There was Juliette Gordon Lowe, founder of the Girl Scouts, John J. Audubon, famous ornithologist, and Harriet Tubman, the Black woman who led slaves to freedom via the famous Underground Railroad during the Civil War.

Fig. 4-1

None of these dolls were ever produced. And yet . . . it may sound contradictory . . . but it may be possible that somewhere, someone will find these dolls in an out-of-the-way shop or surplus store.

In fact, a dealer from a small Kansas town showed me three examples of the Juliette Gordon Lowe doll, Fig. 4-1. Each was marked **August, 1979, Made in Taiwan.** The dolls were not boxed and looked like the doll I had been told was never produced.

A call to Hallmark provided further information. Discontinued merchandise, I was told, is usually sold to a company that buys closed-out items and the like at a very low price. When sales of the first group of Famous Americans (Anthony, Carver, Earhart, etc.) did not live up to expectations, the whole project was cancelled.

Twain) were already in production when the decision to discontinue the line was made. Consequently, the entire lot, including Series I remainders and some holiday dolls, was disposed of to a surplus inventory dealer without boxes and with the explicit understanding that all Hallmark identification tags were to be removed. The inventory was subsequently retailed at prices somewhat higher than those charged by Hallmark in their shops.

Series I dolls and holiday dolls had been packed in boxes that should have been removed by the remainder agent. However, many, perhaps all, of these dolls apparently went out on the surplus market with boxes and labels intact.

As for the third series, which was to have included Lowe, Tubman, and Audubon, and maybe even Harriet Beecher Stowe, these were already in production when the low sales on Series I became apparent. In addition, Hallmark ran into some licensing problems with at least one of these characters. It was discovered, too late, that permission was needed from the Juliette Gordon Lowe Foundation. These dolls could not even be sold to a remainders agent and all were therefore destroyed — all, that is, except for a few floaters that had been used in the offices or by sales people as samples. A few had been funneled into the remainders market before word came down to destroy the lot. Thus a few collectors will be able to own a Juliette Gordon Lowe doll.

Incidentally, Hallmark was right in their assessment of these dolls insofar as collectors are concerned. They found that initial sales were to collectors, but that there was little interest demonstrated by the general public, a sad commentary on our modern values, perhaps. The collector market, although admittedly large, is not strong enough to ensure continued marketing of a product by a monolithic manufacturer who must sell millions of any item to keep it alive.

Hallmark is a huge corporation, divided into so many divisions and departments within those divisions, that it is often difficult to determine where a line was developed and by whom.

There is apparently no central filing system, no central morgue of original art, no comprehensive museum of company products. There is no central authority to coordinate or collate what the company is doing. Small attempts have been made, but the general overview is one of mass confusion.

The objective, on a daily basis, is to get the job done, to get it to the printer, or wherever, and hence to produce revenue. Understandable as that may be on an economic basis, it leaves much to be desired from an artistic or historical viewpoint. Hallmark has produced a huge volume of art in various forms over the years that may prove a valuable resource in the future as commentary on the lifestyle of Americans in the twentieth century.

4HM-1   **Famous Americans, Series I, 7″.** Susan B. Anthony, Babe Ruth, Annie Oakley, Amelia Earhart, George Washington Carver, and Chief Joseph. All six dolls were marketed in uniquely styled boxes. (Photograph courtesy Hallmark Cards, Inc.)

4HM-2   **Bicentennial Commemorative Series, 7″.** Benjamin Franklin, Betsy Ross, George Washington, Martha Washington. These were also boxed dolls. (Photograph courtesy Hallmark Cards, Inc.)

4HM-3a

4HM-3b

4HM-3c

4HM-3d

4HM-3e

4HM-3a-e Famous Americans, Series II, 7″. Davy Crockett, Clara Barton, Mark Twain, Molly Pitcher, and P. T. Barnum. Unboxed dolls were never marketed by Hallmark, but were made available through other sources. (Author's collection)

4HM-4a-d Holiday Dolls Series, 7″. The Little Drummer Boy, Santa, Indian Maiden, Winifred Witch. All boxed dolls. (Author's collection)

4HM-4a

4HM-4b

4HM-4c

4HM-4d

4HM-5

4HM-6

4HM-7

4HM-5   **Santa, 6″.** This item, 200 XTM 2111, is not on Hallmark's doll list. Stock codes and loop on top of head indicate its intended use as a Christmas trim. All lithographed. (Berg collection)

4HM-6   **Mrs. Santa, 6″.** White floss hair, peach cotton skin, red dress, red-white striped apron, 200 XPF 17-7. (Berg collection)

4HM-7   **Raggedy Ann, 5¾″.** Not on Hallmark's doll list, 150 TM 262, listed as a gift trim. (Author's collection)

4HM-8   **Raggedy Andy, 6″.** Face similar to 4HM-7. However, this doll, 125 QS 140-6, is on Hallmark's doll list, 1973. Hallmark tag with ©**Knickerbocker Toy Co. Inc.** (Berg collection)

4HM-9   **Raggedy Andy, 7″.** Has the traditional face, peach cotton skin, red-white striped socks, black shoes, red and white checked shirt. Hallmark tag shows copyright of Knickerbocker Toy Co., Inc. (Berg collection)

4HM-10   **Raggedy Ann and Raggedy Andy Handkerchief, 9″** square. Marked in the corner: ©**THE BOBBS MERRILL CO. INC.**/(the Hallmark crown)/**Hallmark** (in script). Date unknown. (Berg collection)

4HM-11   **Henny, 6″.** One of the characters from the books by Johnny Gruelle, 200 QS 164-1, 1974. Peach cotton, blue-white striped socks, tan shoes are integral part of doll. Wears removable light blue cotton suit with white collar, blue string tie, blue and white hat. (Berg collection)

4HM-8

4HM-10

4HM-9

4HM-11

4HM-13

4HM-12

4HM-14

4HM-12 **Uncle Clem, 6½″.** Another of the Raggedy characters, 200 QS 163-1, 1974. Dressed in red jacket, black belt, red and white plaid. (Berg collection)

4HM-13 **Beloved Belindy, 6″.** Raggedy character, 200 QS 165-1, dressed in green, orange, and white removable clothing, 1974. (Berg collection)

4HM-14 **Curly and Butch, 4″ and 5″.** These dolls, 200 DT 27-7 and 200 DT 27-8, have no bodies — only pieces of flat felt that are dressed. Something like putting three-dimensional clothes on a paper doll. (Berg collection)

4HM-15 **Linda and Zeke, 3″ and 4″.** From the Little Loves series. Both dolls, 200 DT 28-3 and 200 DT 27-2, have embroidered eyes, painted dot mouths, applied noses, and came packed in acetate cylinders. Shown are end pieces from their packages. (Berg collection)

4HM-16 **Sasparilla the Witch, 15″.** Six-piece doll with stitch-jointed elbows, shoes glued on, clothes sewn on, hat separate, purple dress, paper and cloth tags, 350 HDT 17-2, 1973. (Berg collection)

4HM-17 **Angel Cloth Ornament, 4″.** A trim, not a doll, but a nice addition to a rag collection, 175 QX 220-2. A bit of applied lace across feet. (Berg collection)

4HM-15

4HM-17

4HM-16

4HM-18

4HM-19

4HM-20

4HM-18   **Cupid, 5¾″.** Peach cotton, felt ears, pink felt wings, red cotton skirt, yellow-orange embroidery floss hair, stitched fingers and toes, 1976, 200 VPF 2-4. (Berg collection)

4HM-19   **Leprechaun, 6″.** Same construction as 4HM-18, 200 SPF 1-1, wears brown cotton boots, white dotted green shirt, green cotton hat with felt shamrock. Both dolls have unusual head and neck construction. Neck fastens about one-third of the way up the head in front to form a chin, 1977, 1978. (Berg collection)

4HM-20   **Buttons and Bo, 6″.** These dolls, 200 PF 900-1 and 200 PF 900-2, are of pale cream cotton with yellow legs and green shoes integral parts of dolls. Girl wears pink and white checked dress, rosebud pantalettes, white apron. Boy has pale blue cotton hat and pants, pink and white checked shirt, rosebud print tie, 1975. (Berg collection)

4HM-21 **Scarecrow, 6″.** Yellow-orange yarn hair, denim overalls, blue shirt, red print bandana, cream-colored cotton body. Date unknown, 200 HPF 13-7. (Berg collection)

4HM-22 **Scarecrow, 6″.** White cotton, dressed in checked shirt, green striped pants, burlap hat, green tie, 200 HDT 9-1, 1976, 1977. (Berg collection)

4HM-23 **Leprechaun, 7½″.** Green cotton doll, green felt hat, felt shamrock, boots, lapels, 350 SDT 380-2, 1981. Head is peach cotton, features are lithographed, hair and beard are yellow-orange embroidery floss. A finger puppet. Child's fingers fit in arms of doll. Cello-wrapped. (Author's collection)

4HM-24 **Snowman, 5½″.** White terry cloth, red pompon ear muffs, green felt holly, red-white striped scarf, 200 XDT 46-5, 1973. (Berg collection)

4HM-21

4HM-22

4HM-23

4HM-24

4HM-25

4HM-25

4HM-25 **Sweet Susannah, 12½".** A pillow doll, CK2022, 1977, sold in flat form as a Stitchin' Time Doll. Red-orange hair, pink bows, brown eyes, green rosebud-print dress. Only two items from the Children's Korner were made for this series. The other is Bosun Teddy, a bear dressed in a sailor suit. Doll is marked only ©**1977 HALLMARK CARDS, INC.** on the back. (Author's collection)

Kamar International, Inc.

"Love Comes in All Sizes"

Intelligence, wit, and imagination combine in the rag dolls created by Pascal Kamar for Kamar International, Inc. Since 1958, this company has constantly broadened and improved its line of natural-looking stuffed animals and rag dolls. The latest catalog includes hundreds of models.

Kamar International is a team composed of Pascal Kamar, president and designer, and Astrid Kamar, vice-president. The firm is probably best known for its excellent renditions of animals in a wide range of sizes and in a most realistic style.

The Kamar doll line is composed mostly of all-cloth dolls, although a few are shown with vinyl heads. The rag dolls are completely handmade and are beautifully dressed in quality fabrics. The characters are delightfully conceived and executed. There are witches and leprechauns, babies and toddlers, little girls and angels. There are Santas and elves, Indians and clowns. In short, there is something to delight any child or doll collector.

In each successive year since 1978, the dolls have taken an ever-increasing space in their catalog. In 1978, two pages sufficed. There were Ingrid, Jessica, Elizabeth, Mylene, and Chad, all traditional rag dolls with flat mitten hands, yarn hair, roundly stuffed heads, and embroidered features.

There was also Big Betty that year, a 23" girl dressed in gingham dress and matching bonnet, with her two small counterparts, 13" Bon Bon and 10½" Candy. New that year was Buster, the Happy Face Clown. Popcorn and Ann Marie, two 10" hand-crocheted numbers, topped off the list, along with a witch named Hazel, just 5" tall.

In 1979, the cast of Kamar characters was enlarged to include Van Dyke, a 13" Dutch boy dressed in green, a 6½" pixie named Crouton (in red or green), 6" Santa Cruz and 3" Santa Monica, and two angels, 6" Halo and 3" Twinkle. There were also two little girls in bonnets and matching dresses, 10" Ruthie and 7" Chicklet (in assorted styles).

Amanda in three sizes (11", 14", 15") was added in 1980, along with a 6" clown named Boots and a 12" clown called Bobbie. There was also a trio of little charmers named Mindy (7½"), Melody (7½"), and Bonnie (8½") plus a 7" witch called Harriet. Both witches, as any self-respecting witch should, have their own private means of transportation — regulation broomsticks.

In 1981, Amanda came in four sizes (10", 13", 16", 22") and Hazel the witch (may we call her Witch Hazel?) was listed at just 4" (seated on her broom, of course). An ever-growing list of new entries is evident this year: Jenifer, a 15" bonneted girl with golden yarn sausage curls; Tessie, just 10" with a darker version of the same hairstyle; Bonnie in 15" and 9" sizes; Laurie Lynn in three sizes (10", 13", and 16"); and Shirley, a 20" baby in delicately printed bonnet and dress with contrasting booties.

Spring Flower and Young Eagle, an Indian maiden and brave, both 10", were new in 1981, as was the pair of witches called Uglina (8") and Grotessa (16"). Another new character was McGregor the Leprechaun (13"), a handsome fellow dressed in traditional fey costume and wearing the shamrock, of course.

The pages of Kamar's 1982 catalog fairly bloom with the special smiles of their rag dolls. In addition to the old standbys, there were more than two dozen new models.

Leilani, 13", was available in a musical model as well as the regular rag doll. Also from the Islands were 8½" Ukelele and his 5½" counterpart of the same name. Hula, the female member of this group, also came in both these sizes. All wore big, wide smiles and appropriate costumes. (These latter dolls would make an excellent family of little Hawaiians for a display or collection.)

The body style of the Islanders was also evident in several other items in the Kamar 1982 line. There were Cowgirls Annie (7") and Calamity (12") as well as Bandit (12") and Wrangler (7"), their cowboy friends. There was a family of mainlanders, Lil Lu and Loko Junior (7") and Loko and Lulu (12"). In Kamar's Special Feelings™ line, there was 9" Gloria and 5" Glo, two angels, and 9" Zinger and 5" Zingy, two boy cupids. All wore deliciously happy smiles. The angels had halos and the cupids sported bows and arrows, all of the softest fabrics.

Barbara Ann, new and just 11", was available in regular or musical versions. Tenderly, 13", was made only as a musical doll. Tenay, a dark brown model of Bonnie, had the stitched toes found on all the barefoot dolls and came in both 10" and 15" sizes.

Four happy-faced scarecrows contributed to the overall appeal of the line. They were 10" Hoosier, 13" Buckeye, 15" Sooner, and 20" Husker. All wore properly patched clothes with "straw" peeking out their extremities. Eric and Erica, two 15" Dutch children, completed the 1982 offerings for Kamar.

Pascal Kamar has outdone himself and one can only wonder what the fertile imagination of this master toymaker will produce in the future. Surely, it will be something equal in appeal and collectibility to his past offerings.

4KI-1

4KI-2

4KI-3

4KI-1   **Gloria, 9″.** Orange yarn wig, yellow halo, pink body, blue bow. The 5″ doll is called Glo. (1982 catalog illustration courtesy Kamar)

4KI-2   **Uglina and Grotessa, 8″ and 16″.** White yarn wigs, red shoes, black clothes, white aprons, red ribbons on black hats. (1981 catalog illustration courtesy Kamar)

4KI-3   **Van Dyke, 13″.** Yarn wig, button eyes, embroidered mouth, green hat and overalls, red print shirt. (1981 catalog illustration courtesy Kamar)

4KI-4 **Buster, Bobbie, and Boots, 17″, 12″, and 6″.** Yarn wigs, embroidered eyes and mouths, applied noses, multicolored costumes. (1981 catalog illustration courtesy Kamar)

4KI-5 **McGregor Leprechaun, 13″.** Synthetic wig, green vest, brown hat and pants, red socks. (1981 catalog illustration courtesy Kamar)

4KI-6 **Hazel and Harriet, Witches, 4″ and 7″.** White yarn wigs, embroidered eyes and mouths, applied noses, stuffed cloth broomsticks. (1982 catalog illustration courtesy Kamar)

4KI-7 **Leilani, 13″.** Black yarn wig, tropical-looking print dress. Note stitched toes. Available as musical version or plain. (1982 catalog illustration courtesy Kamar)

4KI-4

4KI-5

4KI-6

4KI-7

4KI-8

4KI-9

4KI-10

4KI-8   **Barbara Ann, 11″.** Yarn wig, musical doll. (1982 catalog illustration courtesy Kamar)

4KI-9   **Annie, 7″.** Yarn wig, blue body, red bandana. The 12″ size is called Calamity. (1982 catalog illustration courtesy Kamar)

4KI-10   **The Islanders Family.** Lil Lu, 7″, Loko, 12″, Lulu, 12″, Loko Jr., 7″. All have yarn wigs. (1982 catalog illustration courtesy Kamar)

4KI-11 **Hoosier, Huckster, Buckeye, and Sooner, 10″, 20″, 13″, and 15″.** These scarecrows all wear red checked shirts, dark blue overalls, and red-orange hats. (1982 catalog illustration courtesy Kamar)

4KI-12 **Laurie Lynn.** Available in three sizes: 10″, 13″, and 16″. Blond pictured on left wears blue calico. Redhead in center wears yellow. Blond on right wears pink. (1982 catalog illustration courtesy Kamar)

4KI-13 **Spring Flower and Young Eagle, 10″.** Black yarn wigs, red dress, brown suit. (1982 catalog illustration courtesy Kamar)

4KI-14 **Jenifer and Tessie, 15″ and 10″.** Yarn wigs, embroidered features. Pink dress for Jenifer. Golden-yellow dress for Tessie. (1981 catalog illustration courtesy Kamar)

4KI-11

4KI-12

4KI-14

4KI-13

Miscellaneous Cloth Doll Manufacturers

4A-1

4A-2

4A-1   **Little Miss Muffet.** All original, applied felt features, orange yarn hair. One of the Nursery Tale Raggi line. Cloth tag on dress reads: **RAG-GI™/LITTLE MISS MUFFET.** On box:©**1969 Amsco/Toys, Hatboro, Pa./Mfg. in Hong Kong.** (Author's collection)

4A-2   **Meg and Jo, 16″.** Little Women dolls by Madame Alexander. All original, 1930s. Meg has red-brown mohair wig, brown painted eyes, thin white cotton dress with dark red flocked design and ricrac trim. Tag reads: **Meg/"Little Women"/COPY-RIGHT/MADAME ALEXANDER N.Y.** Jo has blond mohair wig, brown painted side-glance eyes, thin blue cotton plaid print dress trimmed with red band around skirt, white organdy apron. Her tag reads: **JO LITTLE WOMEN/MADAME ALEXANDER N.Y.** Both dolls wear white gauze combinations with pantalettes and embroidery-edged ruffles, replaced shoes. Bodies are of peach cotton, firmly stuffed. (Author's collection)

4A-3   **Early Alexander Rag Dolls.** A rare find is the group of early, well-preserved Alexander rag dolls pictured, most of which still boast their original costumes. The doll in the white replacement dress and the doll wearing only original underwear are unidentifiable since their dresses have been lost. Both have blue painted, side-glance eyes and blonde mohair wigs. Construction is identical to Beth and Little Dorrit. All have mask faces, painted features. Little Dorrit, front row, second from left, 16″, is all original with brown side-glance eyes, green cotton print dress with orange and white flowers, white organdy collar with orange ribbon, white binding on lower edge of dress, matching bonnet, one-piece organdy slip and pantalettes, shoes, socks, c.1930. Dress tag reads: **"Little Dorrit"/Madame Alexander/New York.** Beth of Little Women, front row right, 16″, has a red-brown mohair wig, brown painted eyes, off-white organdy dress with pink flowers, one-piece combination, white socks, black shoes. Dress tag reads: **"Little Women"/Beth/ COPYRIGHT PENDING/MADAME ALEX-ANDER N.Y.** Lady Doll, 24″, the tall doll in the back row has a red-brown mohair wig, painted blue eyes with very long lashes, very long, slender limbs. She wears an original brown cotton skirt, beige velveteen jacket, turquoise scarf decorated with dogs, olive green grosgrain ribbon ties on jacket, long beige stockings, black leather shoes, 1930s. Dress tag reads: **MADAME/ ALEXANDER/NEW YORK.** Tippy Toe, 18½″, back row left, has a blond mohair wig, possibly original checked dress, unmarked, c. 1925. (All six dolls from the Tardie collection. Photograph courtesy the collector)

4A-3a   **Little Dorrit, 16″.** Shows body construction of the majority of the early Alexander cloth dolls. This basic doll was dressed in a number of different costumes and wigs. Note that the face has darkened with soil in comparison to the body, which was probably protected by clothing. (Tardie collection)

4A-3

4A-3a

4A-4

4A-6

4A-5

4A-4   **Little Shaver, 16″.** All stuffed cloth, molded, painted features. All-original clothes, 1937. Cloth tag on dress reads: **LITTLE SHAVER/ MADAME ALEXANDER/NEW YORK.** Artist Elsie Shaver painted the cover picture for the 1942 Neiman-Marcus Christmas catalog. Alexander's Little Shaver was featured in their toy department that year. (Wiseman collection)

4A-5   **Alice in Wonderland, 16″.** Felt mask face, painted blue eyes, yellow yarn hair with red hairband, red and white cotton dress-panties combination, red and white socks, black shoes, c. 1923. Cloth tag on dress reads: **ORIGINAL/ ALICE IN WONDERLAND/TRADEMARK 304,488/MADAME ALEXANDER N.Y.** Red paper tag has quote on one side from book, beginning with "Curiouser and curiouser." On the other side is: **ALICE/IN/WONDERLAND/ TRADEMARK (curiouser quote)/A MADAME ALEXANDER/CREATION/REG. U.S. PAT. OFF.** (Weeks collection)

4A-6   **Alice in Wonderland, 22″.** Yellow yarn hair, painted blue eyes, pink cotton stuffed with cotton. Original red and white checked dress trimmed with red bias, white collar, attached bloomers, replacement pinafore, original shoes, socks, 1930s. Cloth tag on dress reads: **ORIGINAL/ALICE IN WONDERLAND/TRADEMARK REG. U.S. PAT. OFF./MADAME ALEXANDER N.Y.** (Busch collection)

4A-7 **Dionne Baby, 23″.** Brown human hair wig, painted blue eyes, lashes, closed mouth, fully jointed, all felt, original shoes, probably original clothes. A very early cloth Alexander, 1934-1940. (S. Ricklefs collection)

4A-8 **Marie Dionne, 21″.** Felt mask face, pink stockinette body and limbs, human hair wig, painted brown eyes with white highlights and red dots. Long, painted lashes, all-original pink batiste dress with silk ribbon roses, white ricrac trim, white batiste slip, flannel diaper, pink rayon taffeta coat with self-material ruching on neck and cuffs, matching bonnet with pink ribbon ties, crocheted pink and white booties. Gold paper tag on dress reads: **HUMAN HAIR.** Paper wrist tag reads: **THE DIONNE QUINTUPLET DOLLS/©1936 NEA SERVICE INC./ALL RIGHTS RESERVED/CHOOSE YOUR FAVORITE/ALEXANDER DOLL CO.-NEW YORK.** Inside the little booklet are poems about each Dionne child. Doll illustrated wears gold necklace with **MARIE** on it. (Courtesy Ralph Griffith)

4A-7

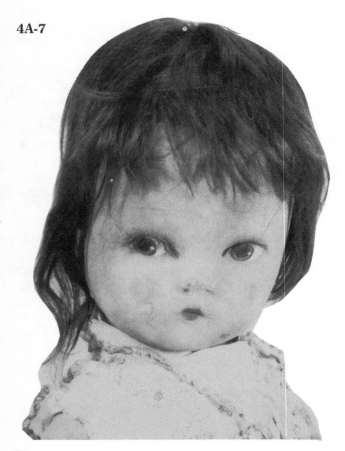

4A-7

4A-8

4A-8

4A-9

4A-8

4A-9   **Chubby Toddler, 27″.** Yellow yarn braids, blue painted, side-glance eyes, original yellow blouse-panties combination, blue apron, matching bonnet. Blouse has tag reading **Madame Alexander/ New York.** Doll is very chubby. Waist measures about 26″, head circumference is about 22″. (Courtesy Jayne Allen)

4A-10 **Indian Girl.** One of a large number of character dolls manufactured by Averill Manufacturing Company and advertised in *Playthings* from 1915-1920. Paul Averill Manufacturing Company, Averill Manufacturing Company, Georgene Novelties, Inc., and Madame Georgene Dolls are all a husband and wife team effort in doll manufacturing. From the variety shown here the collector can begin to comprehend the extent of the output of this manufacturer, which included a large number of cloth dolls in its line for many years. Cowboys and cowgirls, Dutch boys and girls, even a Grace Drayton doll called Chocolate Drop were a part of the line. After the couple left Averill Manufacturing Company, their dolls were produced by K and K Toy Company.

4A-11-14 **Character Cloth Dolls.** All are 13″, except 4A-12, which is 10″. Yarn hair, mask faces, painted features, all-original costumes (except 4A-12). These dolls date from the 1930s and 1940s. Tags on 4A-11 and 4A-13 read: **A/GENUINE** (script) **GEORGENE/DOLL/A Product of Georgene Novelties Inc./New York/Made in U.S.A.** (Mason and Young collections)

4A-10

4A11

4A-12

4A-13

4A-15

4A-15 **Kirget, 18″.** Yellow yarn hair, painted eyes with black button centers, oilcloth face, red flounced skirt, bonnet, blue ribbons, c. 1964. Dress tag reads: "KIRGET." Paper tag reads: **AMERICA'S/· BEST LOVED DOLLS/ARE MADE BY/ "GEORGENE"/PENN. REG. NO15.** Other side: **A "GEORGENE"/DOLL/ Georgene Novelties, Inc./New York, N.Y./ MADE IN U.S.A.** This doll still in original box. (Kittman collection)

4A-14

4A-16 **Hansel and Gretel, 12½″.** Floss hair, painted features, mask faces, pale peach cotton, all-original costumes, wooden shoes. Tags read: **A "GEORGENE" DOLL/"GRETEL" (or "HANSEL")/GEORGENE NOVELTIES, INC./New York, N.Y./Made in U.S.A.** Reverse same as tag for 4A-15. (Mason collection)

4B-1 **Soldier and Sailor, Bye Bye Kids.** Made by Bach Brothers, New York. Registered U. S. Patent Office. As shown in *Playthings* 1909 advertisement. (Courtesy *Playthings*)

4B-2 **Dolly Darling and Her Friends.** By Grace G. Drayton, 1916. Produced by Bentley-Franklin Company of New York. "Not since the coming of the Teddy Bear," reads the advertisement, "have any novelties been introduced that have met with such instant and widespread success as the quaint little creations shown herewith. They are sold made up complete and stuffed with clean white cotton ready for use. They may also be had sewed up ready to stuff." The line also included three Drayton animals — Pussie, Doggie, and Duckey. (*Playthings*, August 1916. Courtesy the magazine)

4A-16

4B-1

Dickie Darling
© G.G. Drayton 1916

Bobbie Bean Bag
© G.G. Drayton 19.16

4B-2

Uncle Sam

4B-2

4B-3

Bettie Bean Bag
©G.G. Drayton 1916

Dolly Darling
© G.G. Drayton 1916

4B-2

4B-3   **Dolly Darling, 16″.** By Grace G. Drayton, 1916. Manufactured by Bentley-Franklin. This same doll is shown as 4B-2. This doll's features, including clothing detail, hair, arms, and hat, are embroidered in black floss on closely woven tan linen and stuffed with cotton. Shading is in pink, otherwise all is the natural color of the fabric. This example may have been made from a kit. Six inches at the widest point. (Author's collection)

4B-4 **Sleepy Sam, 10½".** Yarn hair and lashes, sewn-on lids over painted eyes. Body is of cotton in tiny red and white checks. Dressed in original red and white striped cotton pajamas. Cloth tag on pajamas reads: **"SLEEPY SAM"/DESIGN PATENT 89359/I CAN BE UNDRESSED/MADE IN U.S.A./UNDER SANITARY/CONDITIONS/ GEO. BORGFELDT CORP./NEW YORK, N.Y.** (Page collection)

4B-5 **Bruckner Baby, 14".** All original, lithographed face and hair, blue eyes, blond hair, cheesecloth body. On shoulder of mask-face head is: **PAT'D JULY 9, 1901.** Closeup shows how the head is attached to the body. (Courtesy Stella Mae's Doll Shop)

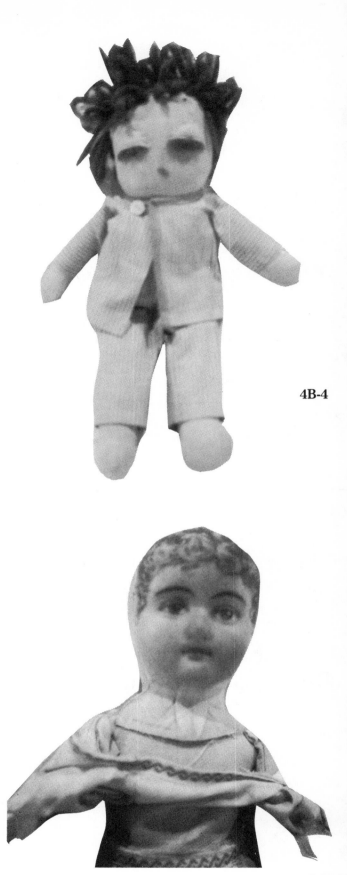

4B-4

4B-5

4B-5

80

4B-6

4C-1

4B-6   **Dollypop, 12″.** All original, lithographed face and hair, blue eyes, yellow hair, pink cotton body. Dress tag reads: **Bruckner/"Dollypop"/U.S. PAT. OFF. MADE IN U.S.A.** This doll and 4B-5 were both manufactured by Albert Bruckner, Jersey City, New Jersey. (Courtesy Gladis Antiques)

4C-1   **Chase Stockinette Doll.** "The celebrated Chase Stockinette Doll has always been made in the U.S.A. The best cloth doll ever made: raised features, jointed, washable, durable, repairable, handsome, flexible, sanitary, satisfactory, and lasting. Also, the Chase Sanitary Cloth Doll, a doll that can be given a bath in the tub." So read an advertisement placed in the January 1915 issue of *Playthings* by the M. J. (Martha) Chase Company of Pawtucket, Rhode Island. An April 1910 advertisement in the same periodical states the dolls are "durable, lifelike, hygienic, delight children, and enthuse mothers." It also states the dolls are "hand made by skilled art workers from the best clean cotton, specially woven stockinet and heavy, fine cotton cloth, making them practically indestructible. The faces are formed to natural features, beautifully hand-painted. They can be washed with warm water, keeping infecting germs from our babies." The Chase dolls were available in six sizes: 12″, 16″, 20″, 24″, 27″, and 30″. The ad also claims "our trade mark on every doll," although the mark was apparently not applied in a permanent manner since I have found many unmarked, authentic Chase dolls. The illustration is from a July 1915 advertisement in *Playthings*. (Courtesy the magazine)

4C-2   **Chase Boy, 18″.** Stockinette fabric, molded, painted features, blue eyes, applied ears, jointed hips and shoulders. (Zillner collection)

4C-3   **Chase Boy, 22″.** Pink sateen body, stitched fingers and toes, separate gusseted thumb, head of painted stockinette. Written on a piece of white cloth sewn to the underthings is: **Tommy Thomas 1908/Tommy Bryan 1941.** This doll was apparently a valued family heirloom. (Hafner collection)

4C-3

4C-2

4C-2

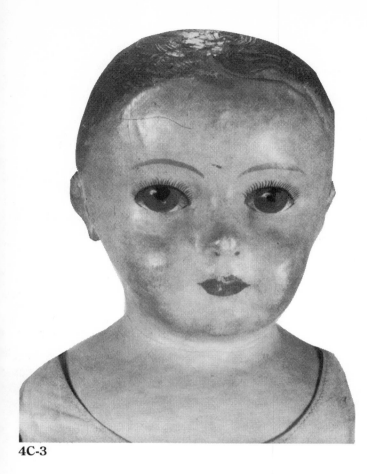

4C-3

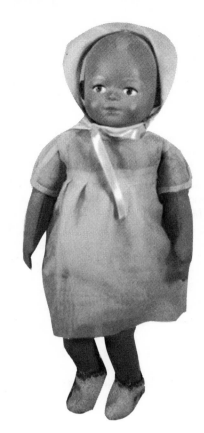

4C-5

4C-4

4C-4   **Modern Chase Boy, 16½″.** Redressed, unmarked vinyl-coated cloth, heavily stuffed, (Mason collection)

4C-5   **Modern Chase Baby, 13″.** Pale blonde hair and eyebrows, blue eyes, all painted. Original pale yellow organdy dress and bonnet, 1970s. (Rogers collection)

4C-6   **Modern Chase Girl, 16½″.** Blonde hair, blue eyes, all-original costume, 1970s. (Rasberry collection)

4C-7   **Mary Had a Little Lamb.** One of Grace Drayton's Hug-Me-Tight dolls. Produced by Colonial Toy Manufacturing Company who advertised they were "exclusive selling agents for those popular stuffed Doll Characters, created by the originator of the famous "Campbell Kids," the 'DRAYTON MOTHER GOOSE HUG-ME-TIGHTS,' retailing for 50 cents." Also prominent was "Made in America for Americans." Illustration is from a March 1917 advertisement in *Playthings.* (Courtesy the magazine)

4C-8   **Country Calico Miss, 15″.** Yarn hair, cloth mask face, red and white dotted outfit. Created by Country Calico, New Orleans. (Rogers collection)

4C-6

Mary had a Little Lamb.

(c) G. G. Drayton, 1916

4C-7

4C-8

4D-1

4D-2a

4D-2b

4D-1   **Dakin Dream Doll, 8″.** Orange yarn hair and beard, green eyes, stuffed cloth on wire armature, original blue coat, white pants, red and white striped shirt, yellow fisherman's hat. Marked: **DREAM DOLLS/©R. DAKIN & CO./SAN FRANCISCO CALIF./PROD. OF JAPAN.** (Vandiver collection)

4D-2a, b   **Disney Seven Dwarfs, 12½″.** Painted buckram faces, plush beards, c. 1938. Sleepy, 4D-2a, has painted blue eyelids. Clothes are part of body. Green shirt, brown shoes, orange pants. Grumpy, 4D-2b, has gold jacket, brown pants, black belt, black and white eyes. (Wiseman collection)

4D-3 **Disney's Snow White, 15″.** Buckram face, cloth body. Glued-on wig is missing. Original red dress with white organdy apron printed with Disney design and the words: **Snow White and the Seven Dwarfs.** (Author's collection)

4D-4 **Dollywood Defense Dolls, 12″ and 16″.** A popular World War II mascot doll by Dollywood Studios, Inc., of Hollywood, California. (March 1942 *Playthings* advertisement)

4D-5 **Dollywood Soldier, 16″.** Khaki-colored oilcloth body, limbs, and back of head. Face is peach muslin over a shaped mask. Painted cheeks and lashes, googly disc eyes. This doll, although not exactly like those shown in 4D-4, is so similar I feel it is probably one of the Studio's line. (Author's collection)

4D-3

4D-4

4D-5

4D-7-8

4D-6

4D-6   **Mrs. Dencla Rag Doll.** The only claim to fame I know of for this doll is that it appeared in a December 1919 *Ladies' Home Journal* article entitled "Christmas Dolls for the Kiddies," in which the Jessie McCutcheon Raleigh dolls were featured. The caption read, "Here Is a Rag Doll With Real Hair That Will Stand All Kinds of Rough Treatment." My research has brought to light no further information. (Author's collection)

4D-7-8   **Joan Walsh Anglund Children. 6⅜".** Lithographed cloth, flat stuffed. Boy has removable hat and red print bandana. Girl has removable skirt and hair bows. Although boy carries a 1958 copyright date, it is most probable they were both made about the time of the girl's copyright, 1975. Tag attached to girl reads: **Your smile is my sunshine.** Determined Productions. (Berg collection)

4D-9 **Dreamland Topsy Turvy.** A teddy bear at one end, a regular rag doll at the other. Quite a novelty. Introduced in the April 1907 issue of *Playthings*. Dreamland Doll Company. (Courtesy the magazine)

4D-10 **Dreamland Rag Doll.** "Made under strictest sanitary conditions, guaranteeing perfect cleanliness," according to the April 1907 *Playthings*. Dreamland Doll Company. (Courtesy the magazine)

4D-9

4D-10

4F-1

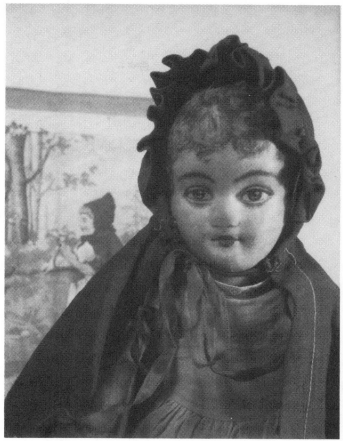

4F-2

4F-1   **Fairyland Rag Doll.** Available in seven sizes and nineteen styles. Dressed according to the latest fashions. New styles every year. Manufactured by Mary C. W. Foote, Plainfield, New Jersey. Distributed by George Borgfeldt & Company and A.S. Ferguson & Company, both of New York. (June 1904 *Playthings*. Courtesy the magazine)

4F-2   **Fairyland Red Riding Hood, 14″.** Lithographed features and hair, all original. Under curve of chin is: **Pat'd July 9, 1901.** This doll was received as a Christmas gift by its owner in 1906. The child's handkerchief, displayed in the background, is one of a set of twelve, each illustrating a different children's story. (O'Rourke collection)

4F-3   **Fairyland Red Riding Hood.** From the November 1907 Fairyland advertisement in *Playthings*. (Courtesy the magazine)

4F-4   **Fairyland Rag Dolls.** Seven sizes, twenty-two styles. Advertised in the November 1908 issue of *Playthings*. The company is now billed as Fairyland Doll Company, still in Plainfield, but they maintain a New York office on Broadway. Four of the twenty-two styles are shown. (Courtesy Playthings)

4F-3

4F-4

4G-2

4G-1

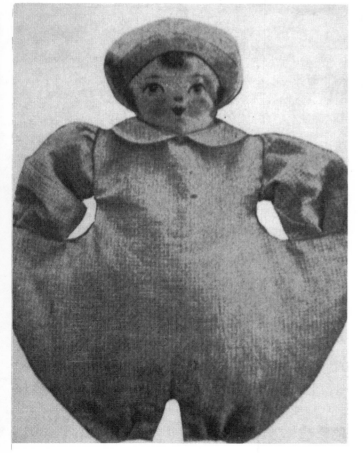

4G-1   **Kisses by Goldberger, 14″.** Acrylic hair, painted features. These are exclusively licensed greeting card and comic strip characters in doll form. Avalanche, the Modern Girl, K4501; Rotunda, Loves Cookies and Robert Redford, K4502; Chip — A Chip Off Any Block, K4503; and Odessa — Black Is Beautiful, K4504. Assortments of these dolls were packed, four pieces each for Avalanche and Rotunda, two pieces each for Chip and Odessa. The last two dolls are more difficult to locate. (1977 Goldberger Doll Company catalog)

4G-2   **Jane Gray, Kuddles, the Bed Time Dollies, 12″ × 14″.** Hand-painted, flat cloth, patented May 19, 1916, copyright Jane Gray Company. (January 1917 *Playthings*)

4G-3   **Jane Gray, Kuddles Rag Girl and Boy, 12″ × 14″.** Blue or pink checked gingham dress or romper trimmed with white, all soft-stuffed. Patents 49,586 and 1,206,483. Copyright 1917, Jane Gray Company. Hand-painted, hygienic heads. (April 1917 *Playthings*)

4G-4 **Jane Gray and the Kuddles Dolls.** The caption beneath this photograph reads: "Introducing Sarah Jane Veal of Georgia, originator of 'Georgia Kuddles'." (July 1917 *Playthings*)

4H-1 **Hasbro's Baby Sweet Dreams, Amanda.** Boy doll, Alfie, also available. Washable dolls in various shades of gingham check with yarn hair and embroidered features. (Hasbro 1978 catalog)

4H-2 **Kutie Kins, 10″.** Made of felt, hand-painted features, stuffed. Colors were guaranteed fast, noninjurious, and unaffected by moisture. Characters were Tom the Piper's Son, Red Riding Hood, Bo Peep, etc. Designed to retail for ten cents each. A. W. Hanington & Co., Inc., New York. (November 1915 *Playthings*)

4G-4

4H-1

4H-2

4H-3

4H-4

4H-5

4H-3   **Bo Peep.** One of the Kutie Kins "painted by a new process that produces startling effects." A. W. Hanington. (January 1916 *Playthings*)

4H-4   **Stella, the Wonderful Rag Doll.** Available in two sizes. Greatest feature, according to the advertisement, is the new "Stella" patented shaped face which, while indestructible, possesses pretty features and a good profile. E. I. Horsman Company. (1903 *Playthings* advertisement)

4H-5   **The Gee-Gee Dollies.** One of the soft Knock About dolls, a line of rag dolls by E. I. Horsman. Yarn hair, hand-painted faces, soft-stuffed. Designed by Grace G. Drayton and apparently named after her (first two initials). Trademark registered and head model copyrighted in 1912 by Horsman. Illustrations from April and May issues of *Playthings*. (Courtesy the magazine)

4H-6

4H-6   **Betty Buttons.** By Horsman. Shown with two esteemed friends in the 1964 Spiegel Christmas catalog. Blond yarn hair, button eyes, dress and shoes covered with buttons. Limbs could be buttoned into various amusing positions. (Courtesy Spiegel)

4H-7   **Little Lulu, 9″.** All cloth with yarn hair and red dress. Also available in 14″ size. By Horsman. (1975 Horsman catalog)

4H-7

4H-5

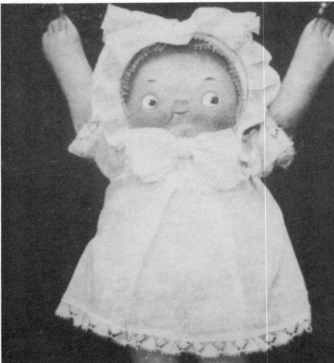

4H-8

4I-1

4H-8   **The Snuggables Angelove, 13″.** Pictured on the left is blond with pink print dress and bow. Right is redhead with yellow dress and bow. Copyright 1978 Hallmark Cards, Inc. Silk-screened on cloth. They "coo" when hugged. Washable. (1978 Horsman catalog)

4I-1   **Rosalind, 14″.** By Independence Toy Works, Brooklyn, New York. Printed-on dress in seven colors. Retailed for just ten cents. (July 1914 *Playthings*)

4K-1a-b **Kamkins, Kampke Art Dolls.** By Louise R. Kampes, Atlantic City, New Jersey. Two different faces, method of construction, and style of clothing are shown. Human hair and mohair were used for wigs. Dolls were completely handmade. Bodies are cotton and heads are heavy canvas-type fabric, molded and painted. "A Dolly to Love" was the slogan used in the advertising. Emphasis was on making the dolls sanitary and washable. Canvas was vulcanized to a rubber formula. Marks: **KAMPES/Atlantic City,** 1928. (O'Rourke collection)

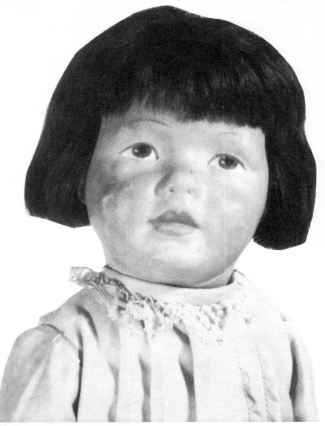

4K-1a

4K-1b

4K-1b

4K-1a

4K-1b

4K-2

4K-3

4K-2   **Raggedy Ann and Raggedy Andy.** Manufactured by Georgene Novelties. Tag on Black doll reads: **JOHNNY GRUELLE'S OWN RAGGEDY ANN AND ANDY DOLLS Copyright P. F. Volland Co., 1918, 1920...1945./ GEORGENE NOVELTIES/NEW YORK CITY/EXCLUSIVE LICENSED MANUFACTURERS/MADE IN U.S.A.** (Author's collection)

4K-3   **Gingerbread Man, 14″.** Furry fabric in appropriate gingerbread brown. Eyes white felt and black buttons, red felt mouth. **Joy of a Toy/Knickerbocker** on tag. (Rogers collection)

4K-4 **Hansel and Gretel, 15″.** Pink cotton fabric, black corduroy and red print clothing. On clothes tag: **Gretel™©/Rag Doll/1969 Knickerbocker Toy Co., Inc./Middlesex, N.J. 08346.** Same label on Hansel, except for name. (Meekins collection)

4K-5 **The Count.** A Sesame Street character, copyright Muppets©, Inc. Manufactured by Knickerbocker in Taiwan, Republic of China, 1970s. (Haag collection)

4K-6 **Happy and Joy, 13″ and 14″.** Designed by Ruth Moorehead, dressed in blue denims with their names in bright colors on the pockets. (1979 Knickerbocker catalog)

4K-4

4K-5

4K-6

4K-7

4K-8

4K-9

4K-10

4K-7   **Annie.** The Broadway star and cartoon character. Available in three sizes: 9½″, 16″, 23½″. Curly orange hair, bright red dress, a tiny Sandy tucked in her pocket. (1979 Knickerbocker catalog)

4K-8   **Story Dress Dolls™, 11½″.** Each with a different nursery rhyme or fairy tale illustrated around the skirt, dressed to fit the story. Pictured are Little Red Riding Hood, Cinderella, and Bo-Peep. (1979 Knickerbocker catalog)

4K-9   **Half-Pint and Tag-Along Clowns, 8″ and 16½″.** Clown faces, bright costumes. Tag-Along has yellow yarn hair. Half-Pint is a red-headed boy. (1979 Knickerbocker catalog)

4K-10   **Baby Kuddles, 14″.** Dressed in bib, bonnet, terry cloth outfit in three colors: pink, yellow, blue. (1979 Knickerbocker catalog)

4K-11 **Betsey Clark Rag Doll, 10″ and 14″.** Rag doll version of copyrighted character owned by Hallmark Cards, Inc. Dressed in pink calico dress, white and pink striped apron. Yarn hair, painted features. (1979 Knickerbocker catalog)

4K-12 **Holly Hobbie and Family.** Pictured (l to r): Holly Hobbie (9½″, 16″, 27½″, 34″), Carrie (9½″, 16½″, 27½″, 34″), Amy (9½″, 16½″, 27½″, 34″), Robby Hobbie (9½″, 16″), Grandma Hobbie (14″, 24″). All dressed in calico, patchwork, and striped country prints. All have yarn hair, painted features. (1978 Knickerbocker catalog)

4K-13 **Kruger Football Player, 17″.** Yarn hair, felt ears. Marked **K** in a blue circle and **TRADITIONAL/KRUGER/N.Y.C.** (Kirtley collection)

4K-11

4K-12

4K-13

4M-1

4M-2

4M-3

4M-1   **Tatters, 19″.** Talking rag doll by Mattel. Says eleven phrases, wears raggedy clothes (#5320). (1965 Spiegel catalog illustration)

4M-2   **Shrinkin' Violet (Violette), 12″.** Eyes close, mouth moves. Talking doll (#5383), 1964-1965. (Mattel catalog illustration)

4M-3   **Red Riding Hood and Wolf Turnover Talker.** One of the Talking Patter Pillows by Mattel (#5267). (Mattel catalog illustration)

4M-4 **Bedtime Baby, 12½″.** All cloth, yellow coveralls and bonnet, painted face (#3196). (Mattel catalog illustration)

4M-5 **Gramma, 20″.** By Mattel, 1970-1973. Dressed in cotton print dress, white cotton apron, pantaloons. Yarn hair, painted features and glasses. Also came in a 16″ size and a 19½″ talking model that said ten phrases. Created by Joyce Miller. Sold only at Sears. (1970 catalog illustration courtesy Sears, Roebuck and Company)

4M-6 **Hawaiian Hula Boy and Girl.** By E. E. Merrill, Los Angeles. Three sizes: 10″, 15″, 24″. Dolls were handmade of brown sateen with shiny black eyes. Patented and manufactured by Merrill. (November 1919 *Playthings*)

4M-4

4M-5

4M-6

4N-1

4N-2

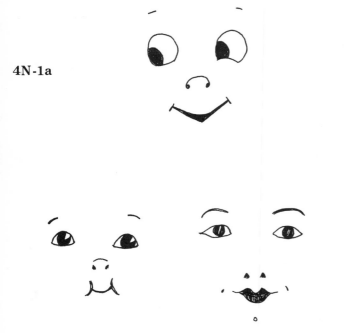

4N-1a

4N-1b   4N-1c

4N-1a-c **Nelke Dollies, 12″.** Knit fabrics stuffed with soft material. Hand-painted faces in a variety of expressions. Garments were sewn on. No pins were used. Manufactured by the Elk Knitting Mills Company of Philadelphia, Pennsylvania. (April 1918 *Playthings)*

4N-2 **Nelke Dolly, 8″.** Painted blue eyes, plush terry cloth fabric, all in one. (Hartwell collection)

4N-3	**Nelke Dollies.** "Assorted color unbreakable jersey cloth bodies, waterproof hand painted features," as shown in a Butler Brothers catalog for October 1928. The entire display of twenty pieces, including bears, cats, ducks, and dolls, had a retail value of $10, were 8″ tall on the average. An assortment of 13″ toys (five pieces) retailed at $5.

4N-4	**Cuddles, a Nelke Dolly, 10″.** One-piece patented jersey cloth body, hand-painted features and hair. Note the Kewpie-like facial expression. (September 1929 Butler Brothers catalog)

4N-5	**Slivers.** "Born in America" and produced by Novelty Doll Works, Kansas City, Missouri. (January 1915 *Playthings*)

4P-1	**Annabelle, 20″.** By Pauline. Brown yarn hair, embroidered features, name embroidered on apron. Ruth Glasser, Inc. (1980 catalog illustration courtesy Dolls by Pauline)

4N-3

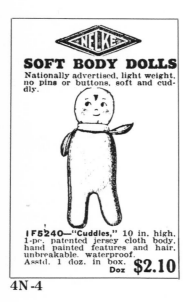

4N-4

4 N-5

4P-1

4P-2

4Q-1

4P-3

4P-2   **Elizabeth, 19″.** By Pauline. White yarn hair, embroidered features, red or blue checked gingham dress, white cotton apron. Ruth Glasser, Inc. (1980 catalog illustration courtesy Dolls by Pauline)

4P-3   **Jill, 15″.** Synthetic wig, painted features, crepe fabric over wire armature, wears pink velvet dress and shoes. Marked: **Made in Japan/Exclusively/for/Herman Pecker Co. Inc./NYC #737.** (Childhood doll of Delene Hafner)

4Q-1   **Tubbies.** By E. & G. Quakenbush, New York City. These dolls were apparently made of a special patented material that had been treated with rubber to make them washable and waterproof. They also advertised eighteen varieties of Tiny Tots for which they owned all rights. (July 1917 *Playthings*)

4R-1 **Shoebutton Sue, 15″.** Mate is Shoebutton Sam. Billed as "the 1920 Doll Sensation," she was all cloth, had painted features, shoebutton eyes, and removable clothing. She was "guaranteed to take your mind off your troubles." Doll retailed for $1.19. A Jessie McCutcheon Raleigh doll. (1921 catalog illustration courtesy Sears, Roebuck and Company)

4S-1 **Daisy Dollies, 12″.** Stuffed velvet dolls manufactured by Sackman Bros. Co. of New York City. The two examples shown have "patents applied for" and are "absolutely new." (1909 *Playthings*)

4S-2 **Alabama Baby, 26½″.** By Ella Smith of Roanoke, Alabama. Cloth with head, shoulders, and limbs painted with a waterproof paint. Painted-on shoes are blue with black detail. Body has been slipcovered to preserve it. Eyes are brown and cheeks are quite rosy, Ella Smith Doll Company, unmarked, c. 1912. (Mason collection)

4R-1

4S-2

4S-1

4S-2

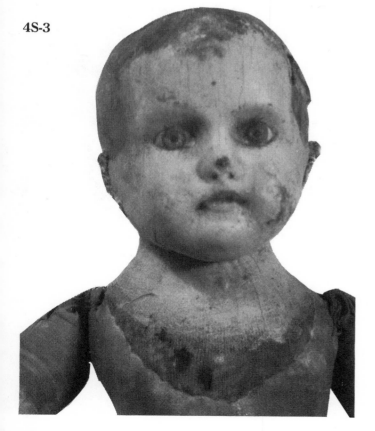

4S-3

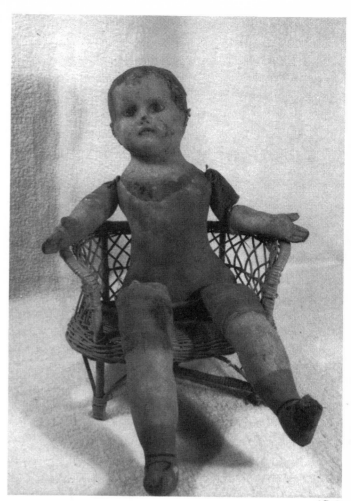

4S-3

4S-3   **Alabama Baby, 18″.** Painted hair, shoes, stockings, features. Stamped on front of body: **THE
ELLA SMITH/DOLL CO. MADE IN U.S.A./
THE ALABAMA INDESTRUCTIBLE DOLL/
PAT. NOV. 1919.** This doll was salvaged from a
wet basement where it had been stored for years,
which explains its sad condition. The special charm
of these old dolls still shines through despite the
deterioration. (Kirtley collection)

4S-4 **Li'l Souls, 6″, 7″, and 10″.** By Shindana. Curly black yarn wigs, black eyes, pink lips, stuffed bodies, all-original clothing. Coochy, Sis, Wilkie, and Natra. Manufactured by Shindana, Division of Mattel, Inc. (Hartwell collection)

4S-5 **New Li'l Souls, 16″.** Represent children of different cultures: Hispanic, Asian, American Indian. Manufactured by Shindana Toys, Inc., Los Angeles, California. (1979 catalog illustration courtesy Shindana)

4S-6 **Li'l Souls, 16″.** Advertised as "the only Black classic rag dolls on the market today." Manufactured by Shindana Toys, Inc., Los Angeles (1982 catalog illustration courtesy Shindana)

4S-4

New!
Li'l Souls Assortment

4S-5

Children will love these giant 16″ rag dolls, available in a three-doll assortment. They are the only black classic rag dolls on the toy market.
2035
Standard Pack: 12 (4 each of 3 different dolls) Weight: 13 lbs.
Package size: 17″ x 18½″ x 16½″
One-color chipboard, self-display package

2035

Li'l Souls Assortment

Shindana Toys Inc.

Shindana Toys, Inc., P.O. Box 71466, 6107 South Central Avenue, Los Angeles, California 90001

4S-6

4S-7

DOLLY DOLLYKINS

BOBBY BOBBYKINS

POLLY PIG-TAILS

4S-8

TOPSY

BABYKIN

4S-8

4S-7   **Character Girl Doll, 13½″.** Blond yarn wig, painted features, blue eyes, cloth mask face, all-original costume. Round paper tag reads: **Character/Doll/created by/Silk Novelty Corp./ N.Y.C./Made in U.S.A.** (S. Ricklefs collection)

4S-8   **Dolly Dollykins, Bobby Bobbykins, and Friends.** Six dolls from the series with Dolly Dollykins, Bobby Bobbykins, Polly Pig-Tails, Babykin, Bare Kid, and Topsy. Trademark registered by Frank A. Hays. Manufactured by Strawbridge & Clothier, Philadelphia, Pennsylvania. Advertised in the March and June 1910 issues of *Playthings*. (Illustrations courtesy the magazine)

Strobel and Wilken's American Art Dolls.
Widely advertised as the American replicas of "the
European article which sells at three or four times
the price." World War I had cut off the European
markets, at least temporarily, and American manufacturers were swift to fill the void. Strangely,
though the dolls were advertised as "waterproof,
indestructible, extra light weight, unbreakable,
lifelike, hand painted, and of entirely new construction," at no time was a direct statement made as to
the material used in their construction. As so often
is the case with such matters, it was clearly
necessary to locate one of the dolls in order to
solve the mystery. I was almost totally convinced
we were dealing with a line of cloth dolls. However, one does not print presumptions and
conjectures. The first dealer-friend I called agreed
with my opinion that the dolls must certainly be all-
cloth, even though he had never had one in his
shop. There were too many clues pointing in that
direction, he thought. I was happy to hear this.
However, I still needed more conclusive evidence.
Another phone call provided the answer. My
second dealer-friend had, indeed, handled one of
these dolls. It had come to him *sans* clothing, but
he distinctly remembered the doll and was happy
to share the information. The doll he had examined
was a very lightweight doll of somewhat lesser
quality than many of the European cloth dolls
collectors know. It was all-cloth, with a molded
masked face and painted head and features. There
was no felt involved in its manufacture. The body
had been made of a coarse material, something like
a twill. The head was seamed and the finish of the
face was a matte rather than a glossy finish.
Fingers had been stitched. He was not sure about
the toes. Returning to my original research material, I learned the Susie's Sister model was 17" tall,
had jointed arms and legs, and was dressed in
assorted colors, pleated cap, apron, shoes and
stockings. Each doll was packed in a separate
carton, and the retail price was a mere $2. As may
be seen here, the American Art Dolls were
expanded into a line of many characters, manufactured by Strobel and Wilken Co., Twenty-Third
Street, New York City, and West Adams Street,
Chicago, Illinois.

4S-9a

4S-9b

4S-9a **Susie's Sister.** American Art Doll, Strobel &
Wilken, New York. (*Playthings,* October 1915)

4S-9b **Faith.** American Art Doll, Strobel & Wilken, New
York. (*Playthings,* February 1916)

4S-9d

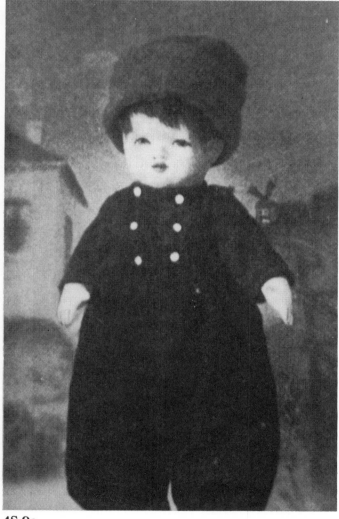

4S-9c

4S-9c   **Ulrich.** American Art Doll, Strobel & Wilken, New York. (*Playthings,* February 1916)

4S-9d   **Buddy.** American Art Doll, Strobel & Wilken, New York. (*Playthings,* February 1916)

4S-9e **Blanche.** American Art Doll, Strobel & Wilken, New York. (*Playthings,* March 1916)

4S-9f **Boy Scout.** American Art Doll, Strobel & Wilken, New York. (*Playthings,* March 1916)

4S-9f

4S-9e

4S-9g

4S-9h

4S-9g   **Liesel.** American Art Doll, Strobel & Wilken, New York. (*Playthings,* March 1916)

4S-9h   **Jimmy.** American Art Doll, Strobel & Wilken, New York. (*Playthings,* March 1916)

4S-10   **Mr. Twee Deedle.** Available in two sizes, all stuffed felt. Doll wears yellow coat with red trim, green pants, yellow shoes. According to *Playthings,* the *New York Herald* offered a prize of $2,000 for the best series of character subjects for their boy and girl readers. Mr. Twee Deedle was the winner and became a *Herald* cartoon character. The doll version of the character was manufactured by A. Steinhart & Bro. of New York. (*Playthings,* March 1911)

4U-1a-e   **Utley's New Rollinson Dolls.** Designed by Gertrude F. Rollinson. These dolls were advertised as "flexible, non-breakable, washable, and always salable." They were sold dressed or undressed, had painted or real hair wigs in assorted styles, were from 14″ to 28″ tall, were modeled from life and made of stockinette. The company's ads boasted, "our 1917 line surpasses anything ever shown in this country." Faces were both character and dolly types, made of stockinette, molded, then painted to duplicate lifelike children's features. There was no felt involved in the manufacture of these dolls. Faces were exceptionally three-dimensional. Made in America by The Utley Company of Holyoke, Massachusetts. Selling agents were Strobel & Wilken, as well as Louis Wolf, both of New York City. No names were given for the various models.

4U-1a   **Rollinson Doll.** Undressed, showing basic construction, The Utley Company. (*Playthings,* December 1916)

4U-1a

4S-10

114

4U-1b

4U-1c

4U-1d

4U-1b   **Rollinson Girl.** Long-curl wig, frilly white dress, The Utley Company. (*Playthings,* December 1916)

4U-1c   **Rollinson Boy.** Romper, short bobbed wig, The Utley Company. (*Playthings,* December 1916)

4U-1d   **Rollinson Child.** Fur-trimmed coat, white dress, The Utley Company. (*Playthings,* December 1916)

4U-1e **Rollinson Girl.** Long-curl wig, dressed in coat, hat, dress, The Utley Company. (*Playthings,* December 1916)

4U-2a,b **The Utley Fabco Doll, 14″ to 26″.** All-fabric dolls with jointed limbs, "beautiful eyes, nonbreakable, washable, any style wigs in mohair or human hair, all sizes." Construction shows clearly in the photographs, The Utley Company. (*Playthings,* December 1917)

4U-1e

4U-2b

4U-2a

4U-3

4W-1

4W-2

4U-3   **The Utley TUCO Doll, 14″ to 26″.** "The newest, most perfect doll ever made." With "jointed arms and legs, movable eyes, socket heads, natural flesh finish, washable, light weight, indestructible." Actually made of a material called "cloth papier-mâché." I would guess this material to be a combination of papier-mâché and cloth or perhaps a papier-mâché reinforced inside with cloth. Another method would be to construct the head of papier-mâché and apply the cloth to the outside where it could be painted with oils for a lifelike and durable finish. No clue to the actual method is given in the advertisements. (*Playthings,* February and March 1918)

4W-1   **Muslin Dolls.** By Weiler Manufacturing Company of Dunkirk, New York. Three styles, each 10″. Lithographed in five colors, stuffed with cork or sawdust. (October 1917 *Playthings*)

4W-2   **Sanitary Carriage and Bedtime Dollies.** By Weiler Manufacturing Company, Dunkirk. Printed on leatherette cloth and stuffed with "sterilized hair," these dolls were designed by Margaret Evans Price. The 10″ dolls sold for ten cents each. (June 1918 *Playthings*)

5 Foreign Commercial Dolls

The United States has long been one of the largest consumers of European goods. Whether it be wooden toys from Germany or rag babies from England, our vast continent with its ever-increasing population provides a market like no other in the world. Had it not been for the disruption of international trade caused by World War I, American production might have lagged for many more years. As it was, a huge volume of imported goods swelled our markets, for which many collectors are thankful today.

In addition to the major English manufacturers who exported to the United States, companies such as Chad Valley, Dean's, and Norah Wellings, cloth dolls were received here from several minor manufacturers. A few names are known to us. Others are identified only by the names of the importers who were the American distributors.

Fig. 5E-1

In the November 1907 issue of *Playthings,* an editorial about English cloth dolls stated that "each doll carries a toy of some type, a trademark of the English rags." Fig. 5E-1 shows a photograph from the editorial illustrating this characteristic. Also noted was the fact that the rag doll was a most popular English toy.

Though interrupted by a second worldwide conflict and severely diminished by economic depression, imports from England have continued in quantities ranging from flood to trickle. Furthermore, licensing arrangements have sometimes been carried out between manufacturers on both sides of the Atlantic, a fact that should give additional encouragement to the collector seeking something just a little different. With luck, it is possible to find nearly identical models, each bearing the label of a different manufacturer and country.

During World War I, England was flooded with refugees who had fled the devastation and horror of war in their homelands. Many projects were organized to provide work for these victims of war. One such undertaking was the manufacture of dolls and toys, many of which were artistically conceived and executed. These are dolls that collectors find most desirable.

In the January 1918 issue of *Playthings,* an editorial mentions a line of dolls created and produced by Belgium refugees living in England:

> E. I. Horsman Company are offering a genuine doll sensation in a wonderful line of felt dolls made in England by Belgium refugees. Sole selling rights have been secured and an excellent demand is confidently expected. There are about seventy-five characters in all, each one an absolute replica of the original, and each one a really artistic plaything.
>
> A few of the characters will give an idea of the scope of this line. There is the American "Sammy," the British "Tommy," the French "Poilu," the Scotch Highlander, Joffre, John Bull, Uncle Sam, Aviation "Tommy," French artillary officer, French cavalryman, British "Bobby," British Boy Scout and British Girl Scout, French and Belgium peasants, Alsatian Girl, Algerian, Old Professor, Latin Quarter artist, Harlequin, masquerade characters, etc. These dolls possess a peculiar charm and cover every character from grave to gay. The fidelity to detail is marvelous — for instance, the war medals on Joffre are exact reproductions of the originals.

Also at work were French and Russian artists who sought to support themselves by their dollmaking talents. In the November 1915 issue of *Playthings* were other dolls created by artists affected by the war. These were people we only know as J. Tozan, Poupelet, Piramonie, and Alexandronie, even though we have their works in a more permanent record. The well-known Russian artist, Sweika, was also reported as having contributed dolls to the effort. I know of no other source that mentions these artists.

With modern manufacturing techniques, the material of choice for dollmaking is usually vinyl or some other type of plastic. As a consequence, modern production of fabric dolls is somewhat less than that of the heyday of the cloth doll. Or perhaps, more correctly, the plural should be used since cloth has come to the forefront in times of economic emergency as well as during those shortages occasioned by war. Fortunately, a few companies still seem to produce cloth dolls and no doubt will continue to do so in spite of technological advances in the use of other materials. The tradition of the rag doll continues.

5E-1

5E-1

5E-2

5E-1   **Dolls Made by Belgium Refugees.** Seventy-five characters in the line, all felt, made in England, distributed in the United States by E. I. Horsman exclusively. (*Playthings*, January 1918)

5E-2   **Stockinette Dolls by Unknown British Manufacturer.** Importer advertised "BRITISH DOLLS, a complete new line for 1919. These stockinette character dolls are most unique and a complete departure from the usual rag doll." Two examples are shown from this line, unidentified by manufacturer. Since this importer, Meakin and Ridgway, Inc., of New York, represented several manufacturers, it is difficult to determine the origin of these particular dolls. Both dolls have molded, painted faces. (*Playthings*, January 1919)

5E-3   **East Indian Man, Gunga Din, 11½".** By
Farnell of England. This beautifully made doll
seems almost a portrait. All felt, painted features,
deeply molded. He is dressed in the traditional
garment of his people, with a red turban. Cloth tag
sewn on sole of right foot reads: **FARNELL'S/
ALPHA TOYS/MADE IN ENGLAND.** (Burger
collection)

5E-4   **Hottentot, 12½".** All cloth, a black knit material.
Black dyed rabbit fur wig, white button eyes, black
bead nose, embroidered red mouth. Wears red
wooden bead earrings, tan floss skirt, dark turquoise sash set off with a pearly button. The
Hottentot was a favorite doll in England for many
years. This particular doll once belonged to Mary
Margaret McBride and toured Europe with her in
the 1940s. (Burger collection)

5E-3

5E-4

5E-5

5E-7

Fig. 5E-6

5E-6

A & A PRODUCT
QUALITY
DOLLS
MADE · IN · ENGLAND

5E-5   **Picador and Matador, 16½″ and 19½″.** About 1939. Both have buckram faces and molded, painted features, all-original outfits. Picador has green velvet jacket, brown velvet pants, scarf, and patch pockets. Matador wears blue velvet pants, white shirt, black tie, yellow felt jacket, rose velvet cape lined in black, blue felt slippers (hat is missing). Quite a colorful pair. A similar doll was manufactured in England by H. G. Stone & Co. Ltd. (See *More Twentieth Century Dolls,* p. 693.) While the matador is nearly identical to Stone's, the bull shown in the illustration (by Knickerbocker) is completely different. (Sheinwald collection)

5E-6   **Character Girl.** By A & A Merchandising Company, Ltd. Mohair wig, molded-painted face, all cloth. Fig. 5E-6 shows company trademark. (*The Toy Trader and Exporter,* January 1944)

5E-7.   **Halfpenny Pocket Dolls.** The Halfpenny dolls are made in an old riverside warehouse located in Southwest England and are scaled for 1″=1′ doll houses. A variety of characters, children, and families are available. They are currently in production and available in the United States. (1981 catalog illustration)

5E-8 **Peasant Girl from Coleman's Peter Pan Series.** This kit for girls made a 16″ doll. Cecil Coleman, Ltd., England. (*The Toy Trader and Exporter,* September 1943)

The Chad Valley Dolls

CHAD VALLEY WORKS
HARBORNE, ENGLAND.

Fig. 5CV-4

COLEMAN'S TOYS for GIRLS

A Delightful Pastime for Miss Junior.

Cecil Coleman Ltd. have an original and fascinating Doll Set which is a simple and delightful pastime for Miss Junior. Full instructions and pattern are enclosed with every set which when finished is a Picturesque Peasant Girl. It stands 16″ high and is retailed to suit all pockets.

PETER PAN SERIES

5E-8

Many of this company's dolls of the 1920s were designed from drawings by Mabel Lucie Atwell, a popular illustrator of the period. Since Norah Wellings also worked for Chad for about seven years, some of the Chad Valley dolls are similar to the later Norah Wellings dolls (or vice versa). Also, some of Dean's dolls look like Norah Wellings dolls. So, look for labels, buttons, etc., or match unmarked dolls to marked, authenticated examples or to catalog illustrations.

5CV-1 **Chad Valley Girl, 19″.** Sold to author as Lillabet, a diminutive used for Princess Elizabeth, now Queen Elizabeth II. This doll, however, is not like other Princess Elizabeth dolls I have seen from Chad Valley. She has all-original wig and costume, dark reddish-brown mohair wig, brown painted eyes, felt mask face, pink cotton body (stuffed very hard), pink and blue linen dress and hat with mother of pearl buttons. Cloth tag sewn to front of dress reads: **MADE IN ENGLAND.** Cloth label sewn to bottom of right foot reads: **HYGIENIC TOYS/MADE IN ENGLAND BY/CHAD VALLEY CO. LTD.** She also wears blue felt slippers, white socks, and white, lace-trimmed full slip and panties, all original. (Author's collection)

5CV-1

5CV-1

5CV-2

5CV-2

5CV-2   **Chad Valley Girl, 17″.** Represented to me as either Shirley Temple or Princess Margaret. I am amused that some dealers seem to need to make a very nice doll into a personality to enhance its salability. This very nice doll is of stuffed pink velveteen with felt mask face. Wrists are delineated by winding thread around the lower arm to create a joint. She is dressed in all-original outfit of yellow organdy, yellow velvet sash and hair bow, lace-trimmed cotton combinations, white felt Mary Jane slippers, white ankle socks. Whether or not she is a personality remains to be seen. Sewn to the sole of the right foot is a red and white cloth label that reads: **HYGIENIC TOYS/REGD. DESIGN/MADE IN ENGLAND BY/CHAD VALLEY CO. LTD.** Note that although this doll is smaller than 5CV-1, it has much larger feet. (Author's collection)

5CV-3   Chad Valley Girl, 11½". Glued-on blond mohair wig, painted side-glance eyes and rosebud mouth, pink muslin body with stitched fingers, felt face. All-original clothing, black and white combination blouse and panties, dark blue felt jumper. On left foot is: **THE CHAD VALLEY CO. LTD.** (an emblem with two lions and crown mark) **BY APPOINTMENT/TOYMAKERS TO/H. M. THE QUEEN.** On right foot and sewn into clothing are cloth labels: **HYGIENIC TOYS/ MADE IN ENGLAND BY/CHAD VALLEY CO. LTD.** (Courtesy Close To Your Heart Antique Dolls)

5CV-4a, b   **Chad Valley Girls.** Chad Valley made a Princess Elizabeth doll that was the subject of an article in the July 18, 1938, issue of *Playthings*. Shortly thereafter the firm must have gone into war work as I can find no advertisements for these dolls in *Playthings* during the early war years. It was not until October and November of 1943 that advertisements appeared again. These two dolls date from those issues. Fig. 5CV-4 shows heading used on ads and replica of firm's crest. (Courtesy *Playthings*)

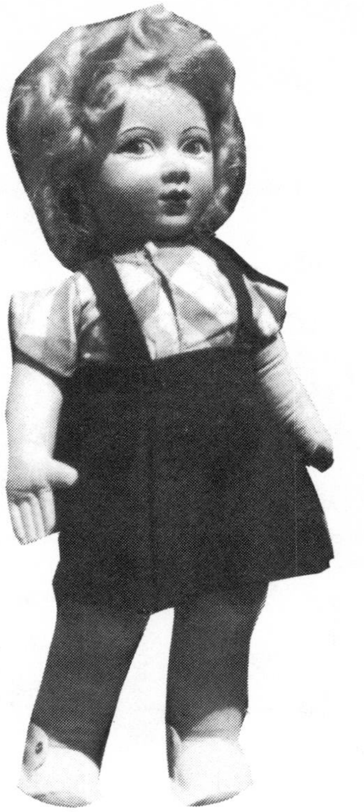

5CV-3

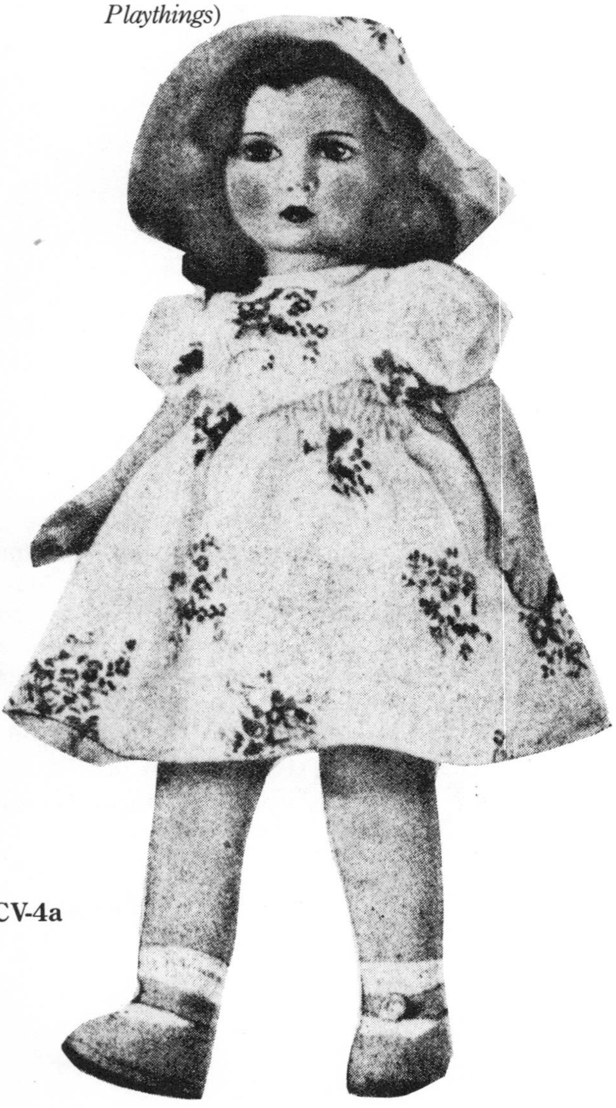

5CV-4a

5CV-4b

The Dean's Rag Book Company Dolls

Shortly after the turn of the century, Dean's Rag Book Company began printing dolls and toys on cloth and have continued the practice for many years. In 1980, Dean's announced they would reprint a series of designs from their past, beginning with the 1912 Peggy and Teddy, designed by Grace G. Weiderseim. The firm's production has been as varied as one could wish, ranging from the tall, thin dolls of the Playmate series, to the shorter, plush dolls such as Ronnie. Dean's distributor in the United States is the Horsman Doll Company.

TRADE  MARK.

DEAN'S
HYGIENIC

5DR-1

Fig. 5DR-1

5DR-1

5DR-1   **Dean's Velvet Girl, 14″.** Molded stockinette face, lithographed features, blond mohair curls attached in three places. Hooded coat is blue velvet with white "fur" trim and is removable. Panties are tacked to white muslin body. Blue velvet legs match coat. Metal tag on inside back of left leg. Dean's was established in 1903. This doll c. 1920s. (Author's collection)

5DR-2 **Dean's Man and Woman.** From *The Toy Trader and Exporter,* an English trade journal, January 1939 issue.

5DR-3 **Dean's Rag Girl, 40″.** One of the Playmate series. From *The Toy Trader and Exporter,* January 1940 issue.

5DR-4 **Dean's Ronnie.** One of their most popular dolls (according to Dean's own advertising copy). Produced in art silk plush in assorted colors, this doll was lightweight and soft. From *The Toy Trader and Exporter,* March 1940.

5DR-5 **Dean's Playmate, "Chums," 40″.** One of a series of lifesize dolls. The advertising copy read, "this range includes Air Force, Army and Navy dolls." From *The Toy Trader and Exporter,* March 1940.

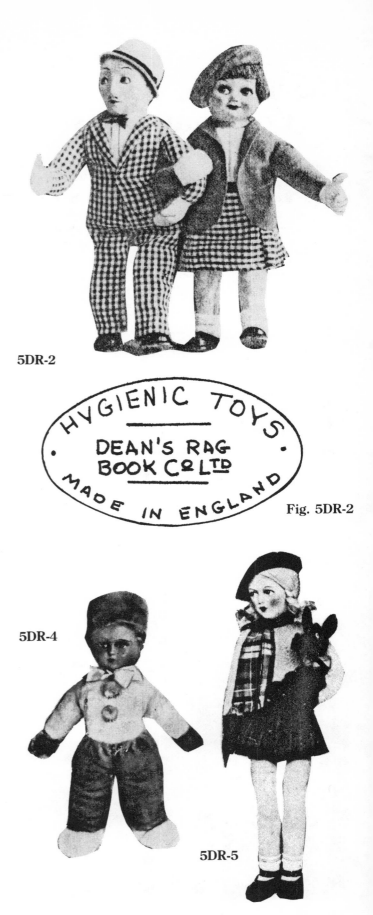

5DR-2

Fig. 5DR-2

5DR-4

5DR-5

5DR-3

5DR-6

5DR-6   **Dean's Peggy and Teddy.** Reprints of 1912 cloth dolls designed by Grace G. Weiderseim (Drayton). These two are the first of a series begun in 1980 to reprint old Dean's dolls. Available as kits or finished dolls. (From a Dean's 1982 catalog sheet)

5DR-7   **Dean's Mignonne, 15″.** Designed by Pauline Guilbert. First printed early 1900s. Instructions in five languages are printed on the sheet, an indication of the extent of Dean's world trade.

The Norah Wellings Dolls

Norah Wellings and her brother, Leonard, began making toys and dolls in 1926 at the Victoria Toy Works in Wellington, Shropshire, England. They also had an office on Regent Street in London. Nora designed the dolls. Leonard was the business manager. Together they were responsible for a great number of dolls that were sold all over the world. Many of their dolls were sold as souvenirs aboard oceanliners carrying tourists overseas. Most popular, perhaps, was the little velvet sailor, usually marked with the name of the ship on which it was sold. The dolls were marked with sewn-on labels stitched to the wrist or sole of a foot. (Fig. 5NW-1.) Labels were cream-colored or black and stitched on all four sides. Since the majority of the Wellings dolls were souvenir items or adult toys and never played with, many are found in relatively good condition today. Fig. 5NW-2 shows company trademark.

5DR-7

MADE IN ENGLAND
BY
NORAH WELLINGS

Fig. 5NW-1

Fig. 5NW-2

5NW-1 **Wellings Man in Fez, 10½″.** All velvet, painted side-glance eyes, tan face and shirt, red fez and pants, yellow felt shoes, two tiny wooden buttons finish shirt. Cloth label is sewn to sole of left foot. (Burger collection)

5NW-2 **Wellings South Sea Islander, 16″.** Black mohair wig, inset brown glass eyes, red painted mouth, white teeth defined with black lines. Brown velvet body, head, limbs. Doll is dressed in raffia skirt with grosgrain ribbon at waist. Torso is bound in multicolored raffia. Wooden bead necklace, yellow celluloid earrings, yellow and red ankle bracelets, yellow wrist bracelets. Cloth label is sewn to sole of right foot. (Author's collection)

5NW-1

5NW-2

5NW-3

5NW-4

5NW-5

5NW-3   **Wellings Dutch Boy, 13½".** All velvet including mask face, brushstroke painted hair, blue side-glance eyes, red rosebud mouth, pink hands and head. Clothes are integral part of body. Blue tie and pants, yellow shoes, green cap, green patch on knee, silver buttons. Green cloth label with golden-yellow lettering sewn to sole of right foot. (Author's collection)

5NW-4   **Wellings Sailor, 14".** Applied ears, velvet suit, cloth label sewn to sole of left foot. Clothes are integral part of body. (Zillner collection)

5NW-5   **Wellings Sailor.** This photograph comes from the old Kimport files. The file envelope had this notation written on it: "#605, German Sailor, $1.25, several." It seems to follow that this fellow, made by Wellings, was intended to represent a German sailor and had originally been designed for sale on a German oceanliner. Note the open, toothy smile and the all-white hat. (Courtesy Kimport)

5NW-6 **Wellings Little Bo-Peep.** From an advertisement in *The Toy Trader and Exporter,* February 1939.

5NW-7 **Wellings Scotsman and Scottish Lassie.** From *The Toy Trader and Exporter,* July 1939.

5NW-8 **Wellings Harry the Hawk.** From *The Toy Trader and Exporter,* March 1940. Advertisement reads: "Harry the Hawk, Norah Wellings are responsible for this line which is produced in association with the Royal Air Force Comforts Fund. An exceptionally interesting series of R.A.F. mascot dolls under the title of 'Harry the Hawk.' This line should prove an outstanding success as it is designed to serve a very worthy cause."

5NW-6

5NW-7

THE TOY TRADER for July, 1939

5NW-8

5NW-9

5NW-10

5NW-11

5NW-9   **Wellings Dollymine.** From an advertisement in *The Toy Trader and Exporter,* March 1940.

5NW-10   **Wellings Girl.** From the January 1941 *Toy Trader and Exporter.* Apparently another in the Dollymine line.

5NW-11   **Wellings Girl.** From the January 1941 issue of *The Toy Trader and Exporter.* I believe this to be another in the Dollymine series.

5NW-12 Wellings Baby, 10″. Pressed-felt face, inset eyes, flesh-colored velvet body, all-original christening dress and bonnet. Body and legs are one, with stitching delineating the hip joints. Doll was purchased in Miami Beach, Florida, in the early 1940s. Babies are not common in the Wellings line. (McLaughlin collection)

5NW-13 Wellings Welsh Girl, 8½″. Black mohair braids, painted blue eyes, stitched fingers, stockinette mask face, red velvet body and dress, blue and white gingham apron and scarf. Cloth label sewn to foot. Round paper wrist tag has **WELSH GIRL** on back. (Hoy collection)

5NW-14 Wellings Palace Guardsman, 14″. Felt construction, painted features, stitched fingers, all-original felt uniform, "fur" hat. (Kaufman collection)

5NW-14

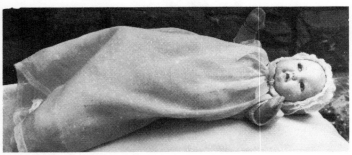

5NW-12

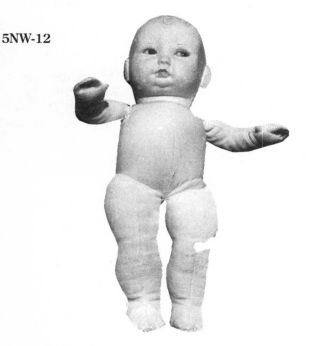

5NW-12

5NW-13

The Kaethe Kruse Dolls

Doll collectors often wish for the lost opportunity to speak with dollmakers of long ago. To be able to discuss dollmaking methods and ideas with these people would be pure delight to many of us. Consequently, I was elated to find an article written by Kaethe Kruse that had been published in the November 1912 issue of *Ladies' Home Journal.* In her own words, this beloved dollmaker tells the story of the origin of the famous German dolls (Fig. 5HK-1):

It happened thus: My husband did not wish to buy any dolls for our children. He disliked extremely the stiff, cold, breakable dolls. On the other hand the character dolls left very little play for the imagination of the child, I found out too. I have always believed that a mischief doll must be able to be everything: a little Princess and a beggar's child; a little mischief and a little angel.

My eldest two girls stood with eyes full of expectation before me and wanted a doll. So I took a towel, wrapped a potato into it, pulled the four corners and made them into two hanging members and then filled the body with sand. The face was made by primitive lines upon the potato head, drawn by burnt-off matches. This miserable performance immediately won the entire love of the two little mothers. They liked it because it was soft and lifelike, a sand body that nestled in the arms of the doll mothers. The little head fell to the side and always demanded to be thought of and to be protected. The effect of the hanging limbs is to them droll. Indeed with all their hearts did the children love these dolls; they were their playmates most of the day, and were taken lovingly with them to bed at night.

From this towel doll to the present Kaethe Kruse doll there are five years of thought and work. The idea was to make a nose out of material, two ears of material, and yet have no seams. I made repeated attempts to paint the head with washable paint, and at last one day my efforts were crowned with success. The form held a faultless little nose, and two little ears sat firmly on the little head, and the head itself, loosely and slantingly sewed on, peeped as sweetly out into the world as I could have wished it. I must confess that my husband, a sculptor, gave me some assistance.

There was an exhibition of homemade toys in Berlin to which I was invited, and I sent my children's dolls. From that day on the triumphal march began, and neither the dolls nor I know how it happened, for they were thought out only for my own children, were made only for them. They were a success because I had simply made a doll that was unbreakable and washable, and yet was a pretty doll. Each doll carries my name and number on the sole of the left foot.

Today requests for my dolls come to me from every country in the world. I now have assistants in my work. Every doll we make is a little different. The human hand cannot make exactly the same thing twice, and everything on and about the doll is hand work. How the little head is set on — this way or that — whether the hair or the eyes are painted light or dark, the rounding of the face and body, how the tiny feet stand — everything makes a different impression and gives to the doll a different character, and yet they have something in common.

Each doll goes through my hands at least twenty times. I think this is the secret of their success: not the technical solution — a man might have discovered that — but to create a baby, an innocent, sweet, foolish little thing! — this was only possible for a woman, a mother, who several times has held in her arms a loving, heavenly doll.

A note at the end of the article foresees reader inquiries with this statement:

NOTE: As these dolls are the special work of Frau Kruse, and are copyrighted, it is not possible for *The Ladies' Home Journal* to issue patterns by which they may be copied.

By 1914 the popularity of the Kruse dolls was greater than ever. Again the *Ladies' Home Journal,* in the January issue, carried an article by Frau Käthe Kruse (note the change in spelling). This time suggestions were made for expanding children's collections of dolls in an article entitled "Playing with the Christmas Doll" (Fig. 5HK-2):

With a new doll at Christmastime little girls are made the happiest of happy little beings, since the newcomer frequently adds one more to the collection of other years, and now there is quite a family for the little mother to train.

What fun it would be to have a school in a corner, if only some one at home will provide a few tables and benches which might easily be fashioned from boxes!

In the illustration they are all attention to the teacher, and we can almost hear the one in front with the hand raised saying "Present" to the morning roll call.

The two little tots with their baskets are off on a picnic, taking with them some crackers, cakes and candies for luncheon. Their pet lamb (a toy), of course, goes along. They are wearing pretty white muslin dresses and are allowed on this special occasion to carry their best silk parasols.

Two of their little friends are very anxious about the big gander (a toy) that has been lost and is now being driven home. Michel, with his pointed cap, feels very big in his suit like Father's.

"Let's play ball" is suggested by the wee mites pictured below.

Here Gretchen and Hans are talking things over. "What shall we do today?" asks Gretchen. They are ready for anything, and so we leave it to their little mother to make the day full of fun for them — perhaps a ride in their express wagon if the day is fine.

What a busy time they are having at their morning bath in the picture at the bottom of the page, washing in the basin and slipping on their clothes! A toy bureau with an inexpensive china set would enable one to make this seem almost real.

We had a hint that Kathe Kruse regarded her dolls as almost real when, in the first quotation, she admitted that neither she nor the dolls knew quite how their fame had come about. The little stories she wrote about each of the doll groupings pictured in the 1914 *Ladies' Home Journal* reinforces my feelings that she had a wonderful imagination and a special sensitivity to children, both of which are also evident in her dolls.

A further note at the bottom of the 1914 article reads:

NOTE — These hand-made stuffed dolls are manufactured of waterproofed material which is colored to a remarkably natural flesh tint. The dolls are very lifelike in character, smooth in finish and practically indestructible as toys. Inquiries will be gladly answered by the Editors.

I would venture to guess that someone at *Ladies' Home Journal* had definitely fallen under the spell of these very special childlike dolls, as have many doll collectors of more recent years.

Although the Kathe Kruse dolls are now made of modern vinyl and plastic with fabric covering, there remains a cloth doll line. Designed by Frau Kruse's daughter, Hanne, these dolls have terry cloth bodies and clothing with flat, painted faces and are guaranteed machine washable.

The Wonderful Kruse Baby Dolls

The Story of the Origin of the Famous German Dolls
As Told by Their Originator, Frau Kaethe Kruse

Playing With the Christmas Doll

By Frau Käthe Kruse

IT HAPPENED thus: My husband did not wish to buy any dolls for our children. He disliked extremely the stiff, cold, breakable dolls. On the other hand the character dolls left very little play for the imagination of the child, I found out too. I have always believed that a mischief doll must be able to be everything; a little Princess and a beggar's child, a little mischief and a little angel.

My eldest two girls stood with eyes full of expectation before me and wanted a doll. So I took a towel, wrapped a potato into it, pulled out the four corners and made them into two hanging members and then filled the body with sand. The face was made by primitive lines upon the potato head, drawn by burnt-off matches. This miserable performance immediately won the entire love of the two little mothers. They liked it because it was soft and lifelike, a sand body that nestled in the arms of the doll mothers. The little head fell to the side and always demanded to be thought of and to be protected. The effect of the hanging limbs is to them droll. Indeed with all their hearts did the children love these dolls; they were their playmates most of the day, and were taken lovingly with them to bed at night.

FROM this towel doll to the present Kaethe Kruse doll there are five years of thought and work. The idea was to make a nose out of material, two ears of material, and yet have no seams. I made repeated attempts to paint the head with washable paint, and at last one day my efforts were crowned with success. The form held a faultless little nose, and two little ears sat firmly on the little head, and the head itself, loosely and slantingly sewed on, peeped as sweetly

out into the world as I could have wished it. I must confess that my husband, a sculptor, gave me some assistance.

There was an exhibition of home-made toys in Berlin to which I was invited, and I sent my children's dolls. From that day on the triumphal march began, and neither the dolls nor I know how it happened, for they were thought out only for my own children, were made only for them. They were a success because I had simply made a doll that was unbreakable and washable, and yet was a pretty doll. Each doll carries my name and number on the sole of the left foot.

TODAY requests for my dolls come to me from every country in the world. I now have assistants in my work. Every doll we make is a little different. The human hand cannot make exactly the same thing twice, and everything on and about the dolls is hand work. How the little head is set on—this way or that—whether the hair or the eyes are painted light or dark, the rounding of the face and body, how the tiny feet stand—everything makes a different impression and gives to the doll a different character, and yet they have something in common.

Each doll goes through my hands at least twenty times. I think this is the secret of their success: not the technical solution—a man might have discovered that—but to create a baby, an innocent, sweet, foolish little thing!—this was only possible for a woman, a mother, who several times has held in her arms a loving, heavenly doll.

NOTE—As these dolls are the special work of Frau Kruse, and are copyrighted, it is not possible for THE LADIES' HOME JOURNAL to issue patterns by which they may be copied.

WITH a new doll at Christmastime little girls are made the happiest of happy little beings, since the newcomer frequently adds one more to the collection of other years, and now there is quite a family for the little mother to train. What fun it would be to have a school in a corner, if only some one at home will provide a few tables and benches which might easily be fashioned from boxes!

In the illustration they are all attention to the teacher, and we can almost hear the one in front with the hand raised saying "Present!" to the morning roll call.

THE two little tots with their baskets are off on a picnic, taking with them some crackers, cakes and candies for luncheon. Their pet lamb (a toy), of course, goes along. They are wearing pretty white muslin dresses and are allowed on this special occasion to carry their best silk parasols.

Two of their little friends are very anxious about the big gander (a toy) that has been lost and is now being driven home. Michel, with his pointed cap, feels very big in his suit like Father's. "Let's play ball" is suggested by the wee mites pictured below.

HERE Gretchen and Hans are talking things over. "What shall we do today?" asks Gretchen. They are ready for anything, and so we leave it to their little mother to make the day full of fun for them—perhaps a ride in their express wagon if the day is fine.

WHAT a busy time they are having at the bottom of the page, washing in the basin and slipping on their clothes! A toy bureau with an inexpensive china set would enable one to make this seem almost real.

NOTE—These hand-made stuffed dolls are manufactured of waterproofed material which is colored to a remarkably natural flesh tint. The dolls are very lifelike in character, smooth in finish and practically indestructible as toys. Inquiries will be gladly answered by the Editors.

5HK-1

5HK-1   **Hanne Kruse Frottee Baby, 30 cm.** Washable dolls for babies and small children, designed by Frau Kruse's daughter, Hanne. (1968 Kruse catalog illustration)

The Steiff Dolls

When the name Steiff is mentioned, many collectors automatically think of teddy bears or hedgehogs named Mecki and Mucki. Relatively few realize the variety of dolls made by this well-known manufacturer. The Steiff production began when Fraulein Margarete fashioned toy animals of felt mill ends and scraps. Her earliest dolls apparently date from about 1894, although the animals were made several years earlier.

The Steiff dolls cover a wide range of characters. There are Keystone Kops and English Bobbies, nursery rhyme characters and musicians. There is even an entire circus of performers and animals. One of the most unusual sets is the Teddy Roosevelt on Safari in Africa diorama. Every aspect of the life of this popular American was newsworthy, and merchandise associated with his exploits proved marketable and profitable. Settings such as the safari and circus were shown complete with tents, animals, and equipment of every sort in trade advertisements of the early 1900s.

Also advertised were Bavarian children and Dutch twins as well as a Dutch couple. There was Private Sharkey, Sergeant Kelly, and Private Murphy, all United States soldiers. There was a strange little boy named Billy, who is oddly reminiscent of the then-popular Billiken. All of the dolls were named, although it is often difficult for collectors to discover their names if tags and other identification are missing. One can only hope to find old catalogs or advertisements where names and illustrations are shown together.

Once again, I am indebted to generous collectors for valuable information. One collector in particular has shared an impressive collection and array of photographs with each doll carefully described. The Kutz collection is a microcosm of the world of Steiff dolls, representing production from a wide period and illustrating the remarkable diversity of the dolls.

Styles change as years pass. Reflected in the appearance of the new Steiff dolls is the technology of the period as well as an attempt to retain some of the traditional values of former years. Illustrated is a photograph taken from a 1974 Steiff catalog, showing seven models offered that year. There is Gabi (19), Gitte (20), Tina (21), Uwe (22), Jackie (23), Dolly (24), and Romy (25). The dolls are of velvet plush with thick wigs of synthetic furlike fabrics, plastic button eyes, and their own special personalities. (5ST-22)

5ST-1

5ST-2   5ST-3

5ST-1 **Bellhop Pull Toy, 9″.** Red suit and cap, sound box under seat activates as cart moves, black bead eyes. (Kutz collection. Photograph courtesy Clarence A. Kutz)

5ST-2 **French Soldier, 9″.** Navy jacket, red pants and cap, blue glass eyes. French tri-color bow. (Kutz collection. Photograph courtesy Clarence A. Kutz)

5ST-3 **Swiss Soldier, 6″.** Green uniform, yellow Alpine cap with feather, brown glass eyes. (Kutz collection. Photograph courtesy Clarence A. Kutz)

5ST-4

5ST-5

5ST-6

5ST-7

5ST-4 **Italian Fascist Youth, 7″.** Black shirt, gray shorts, black tasseled hat, brown glass eyes. (Kutz collection. Photograph courtesy Clarence A. Kutz)

5ST-5 **Man, 13″.** May be representative of a waiter in a Biergarten (note the apron). Applied hair and moustache, bright blue glass eyes. (Kutz collection. Photograph courtesy Clarence A. Kutz)

5ST-6 **Man, 16″.** Formal evening attire, hat lined with silk. Doll is quite worn. Note paint is off one shoe; blue glass eyes. (Kutz collection. Photograph courtesy Clarence A. Kutz)

5ST-7 **American Indian, 16″.** Decorated orange vest, brown leatherlike fringed pants, blue-gray striped cotton shirt, brown moccasins, tan woven strip hangs down front (as a decoration?), pupil-less brown glass eyes. (Kutz collection. Photograph courtesy Clarence A. Kutz)

5ST-8, 9 **Church-Going Pair, 9″.** Each carries a prayer-book. Girl has green dress, red print blouse, black shawl and headscarf, white apron, brown glass eyes. Boy has straw hat, black coat, brown lederhosen, short socks, brown glass eyes. (Kutz collection. Photograph courtesy Clarence A. Kutz)

5ST-10 **Lady, 12″.** Unusually sharp chin. All in black and white, trim at bottom of skirt is velvet, brown glass eyes. Umbrella not original with this doll. (Kutz collection. Photograph courtesy Clarence A. Kutz)

5ST-8

5ST-9

5ST-10

5ST-11

5ST-13

5ST-12

5ST-11   **Girl, 16″.** Red felt skirt, vest and cap, red shoes, white cotton blouse, blue glass eyes. (Kutz collection. Photograph courtesy Clarence A. Kutz)

5ST-12   **Musician, The Drummer, 15″.** Fine brass helmet with red plume, brass cymbal in right hand, fine leather belt around waist has mountaineer equipment, axe, and rope. Boots are hobnailed with tiny Steiff buttons. Navy jacket has red epaulettes, gray and oxford-striped cotton trousers, blue glass eyes. (Kutz collection. Photograph courtesy Clarence A. Kutz)

5ST-13   **Musician, Bass Fiddler, 11″.** Very plump, mounted on wooden base, Steiff buttons down jacket front, brown felt jacket, black suit and shoes, black pupil-less eyes. (Kutz collection. Photograph courtesy Clarence A. Kutz)

5ST-14 **Musician, Trumpet Player, 16″.** A very thin fellow mounted on wooden base. Hip joints allow him to bend. He is all black except for brass earmuffs across top of head under hat, black pupilless eyes. (Kutz collection. Photograph courtesy Clarence A. Kutz)

5ST-15 **Little Girl, 11″.** Blue print cotton dress, knit socks, blue pupil-less eyes. (Kutz collection. Photograph courtesy Clarence A. Kutz)

5ST-16 **Mushroom Man, 10″.** Red mushroom-cap hat is removable, blue felt top, cream-colored britches, green shoes, pupil painted on glass eyes. (Kutz collection. Photograph courtesy Clarence A. Kutz)

5ST-14

5ST-15

5ST-16

5ST-17

5ST-18

5ST-19

5ST-20

5ST-17   **Uwe, 15″.** One of the first flat-faced felt dolls by Steiff, 1960s, blue suit, red checked shirt, plastic eyes. (Kutz collection. Photograph courtesy Clarence A. Kutz)

5ST-18   **Devil Hand Puppet.** Red felt, black fur trim, black glass eyes, 1970s. (Kutz collection. Photograph courtesy Clarence A. Kutz)

5ST-19,20 **Max and Moritz Hand Puppets.** Comic characters by Wilhelm Busch, Germany. Preceded Hans and Fritz, made in 1970s. Black pupil-less glass eyes. (Kutz collection. Photograph courtesy Clarence A. Kutz)

5ST-21 **Bubi, 8″.** Multicolored terry body, washable, brown plastic eyes, 1980. (Kutz collection. Photograph courtesy Clarence A. Kutz)

5ST-22 **Steiff 1974 catalog.** Photo showing seven dolls offered that year.

5ST-23 **Group of Character Dolls.** By Steiff. From advertisement in *Playthings*, February 1912.

5ST-24,25 **Private Sharkey and Sergeant Kelly, U. S. Soldiers.** The sergeant wears a blue uniform. The private wears khaki with all equipment. Also included in the group was Private Murphy (not shown) in the same style with equipment. (*Playthings,* 1909)

5ST-24

5ST-25

5ST-21

5ST-23

5ST-26

5ST-27

5ST-28

5ST-26	**Hubertus and Anthony.** Two dolls from the 1909 Steiff line. Also included were Alida and Olaf, all in at least two sizes, 10″ and 20″. (*Playthings,* October 1909)
5ST-27	**Brownie Policeman and the Kentucky Donkey.** Stuffed with corkdust, extremely lightweight, made of wool and silk, plush and felt, according to advertisement in *Playthings,* April 1905 issue.
5ST-28	**Steiff Characters.** This group won a grand prize in St. Louis in 1904 and Brussels in 1910. Closeup shows detail. (*Playthings,* February 1912)

5ST-29   Closeup of 5ST-28.

5ST-30   **The Steiff Circus.** A page from the March 1911 issue of *Playthings* shows the variety of characters included in the circus line.

5ST-31   **Fraulein Margarete Steiff. From a 1909 issue of *Playthings*.**

5ST-29

5ST-30

5ST-31

The Lenci Dolls

The story of the Lenci dolls is long and somewhat complicated. Created by Enrico and Elena Scavini in 1919, these dolls came into international prominence between 1920 and 1922. Lenci, the name chosen for the dolls, a diminutive of Elena, was Madame Scavini's pet name from early childhood.

The Lenci dolls were never inexpensive, with their prices reflecting their quality. Advertising of the day took special note of their artistically conceived design, the quality of materials and workmanship used in their manufacture, and the amount of handwork required to complete each doll. The dolls were extremely popular among those seeking well-made, high-quality dolls for play. (Collectors would come to appreciate these same attributes in later years.)

As is the case with any successful product, there were soon imitators in the marketplace. Many such manufacturers sold their look-alikes at a fraction of the prices attached to the Lencis, a fact that seems to have affected the sale of the Lencis only marginally.

Those who desired the better dolls were quick to observe the differences, and the better shops were eager to supply their needs. The dolls quickly became status symbols, along with other top-quality imported lines such as the Kaethe Kruse and Chad Valley dolls.

Nevertheless, the lower-priced Lenci look-alikes found a ready market, suited, as they were, to the buying capacity of a larger segment of the population. The style of the Lencis was copied on a worldwide basis. In addition, their stylistic influence may be seen in the costumes and faces of dolls with heads of composition, papier-mâché, and felt-finished papier-mâché offered in the late 1920s.

For the most part, the Lenci dolls were made of felt, although some woven cloth was used in body construction. In addition, buckram and other stiffening materials were used to back the outer fabric. Costumes were of felt and organdy, ingeniously combined to achieve remarkable effects.

Wigs were of mohair, with tufts sewn in by hand around the hairline, and the remainder finished in the usual wig fashion by sewing strips of hair tufts around and around the head. A few wigs were of felt cut in narrow strips for a special effect.

Lencis range in height from the 4″ miniatures to the 48″ Poupee Salon, or display figures. The most common sizes are the 18″ children, the 8½″ and 9″ foreign-costumed dolls, and the 13″ children. This is not to say that many of the other sizes are so unusual as to be considered rare (although some are rare, of course), but rather that the play sizes are usually more common.

There are at least twenty different labels and marks for the Lencis and literally hundreds of different styles, models, or numbers, as they are called in the trade.

205—Matelda Green
204—Matelda Red
107—Corin
106—Colette
313—Samantha
201—Clo Clo Green
202—Clo Clo Blue
311—Rossella
312—Melania
203—Susanna

5L-1-5 **Lencis from Kimport.** With the exception of 5L-1, these dolls appear to be from the Mascottes or Miniatures lines. 5L-1 was designated Lenci Girl on her Kimport envelope and priced at $9.95. The other four dolls retailed for $5.95, indicating a difference in size. 5L-2 is called Roman, 5L-3 is Lenci Tulip Girl, and 5L-5 is described as Girl in Silk. All were marked genuine Lencis. (Photographs courtesy Kimport Dolls, Inc.)

5L-6-10 **Lenci Competitors from Kimport.** The first three dolls in this group could pass for Lenci Mascottes, while the last two would never be mistaken for the real thing. All were offered in direct competition to the Lencis in Kimport's *Doll Talk* magazine. (Photographs courtesy Kimport Dolls, Inc.)

5L-1

5L-2

5L-3

5L-4

5L-5

5L-6

5L-7

5L-8

5L-9

5L-10

5L-11

5L-13

5L-12

5L-11 **Lardeguo, 19″.** Black mohair wig, classic Lenci side-glance eyes, marked **Lenci/Made in Italy** and **Firense,** the Italian name for Florence. On the hang tag is **Lardeguo.** (Kaufman collection)

5L-12 **Lenci-type with Basket of Fruit, 18″.** All original, this doll wears wooden clogs and beads. Her hand is attached to the basket in such a way that while her head turns, the basket remains stationary. Quite a nice little feat of engineering. Doll is unmarked, but an identical one has been found with the tag of a Brazilian doll manufacturer, which ties in nicely with Coleman's statement that former Lenci factory employees established new companies to make similar dolls, and some went to Argentina to do so. Thus, although this doll is not a genuine Lenci, it is related to the original. (Author's collection)

5L-13 **Unmarked Lenci, 16″.** Mohair wig, jointed shoulders, hips, neck, felt-trimmed organdy dress, felt shoes. Note the typical Lenci fingers. This doll is almost identical to one shown by McKee (See *Lenci Clothes,* p. 81) except the lower lip of this doll is painted the same shade of rose as the upper lip. (Zillner collection)

5L-14 **College Girl, 17″.** Unmarked slim girl, felt head and limbs, pink cotton body, stitched toes, three separated fingers and two stitched together. All-original outfit is of felt. Lace-trimmed panties, camisole, bra, long socks, felt moccasins. Original Tosca mohair wig, painted brown side-glance eyes, closed painted mouth with dark rose upper lip and pale, glossy pink lower lip. (See *More Twentieth Century Dolls*, color section.) (Author's collection)

5L-15 **Lenci Lady Doll, 23½″.** Unmarked, original mohair wig, painted side-glance eyes, shaped bosom, stitched fingers and toes, turning head, jointed shoulders and hips. Feet are highly arched for high-heeled shoes. Doll appears to be from the 165 series, possibly a 165/30 or 165/33 as shown by Coleman (see *Fabulous Figures of Felt — Lenci*, p. 67). (O'Rourke collection)

5L-14

5L-14

5L-15

5L-16

5L-17

5L-16   **Lenci-type Girl, 7″.** Curly mohair wig, painted features, pressed-felt body, original clothes, holds felt ball. Tag on foot reads: **MADE IN ITALY.**

5L-17   **Lenci-type Minstrel, 10″.** Mohair wig, painted features, stiff cloth body and limbs, mask face, felt clothing, knit tights. **Galafe/Made in Italy** on tunic tag. **Made in Italy Expressly/for A. Harris & Co.** on additional tag. **Giocalioli Artistici/ Galafe/Florence/Made in Italy** on paper label attached to cape. (Gibbins collection)

5L-18   **Lenci-type Dolls.** From a 1928 catalog advertisement. Two sizes: 11″ for $1.19, 15″ for $1.95. Offered on the same page were two felt dolls with composition heads, painted features, mohair wigs, made to look as much like the Lencis as possible. These sold for 49¢ and 95¢ respectively in the same sizes.

5L-19   **Lenci-type Dolls.** From the December 31, 1928, Butler Brothers catalog. Although the heads of these models are of papier-mâché and composition, the dolls are included here to illustrate the influence of the Lenci designs on the doll trade, as well as the supreme effort on the part of other manufacturers to compete with the Lencis.

5L-18

5L-19

"I could write a book about that" is a commonly used phrase, meaning, of course, that there is much to say about a particular subject. Dorothy Coleman has done just that with respect to the Lenci dolls. Her book, *Fabulous Figures of Felt — Lenci*, delves deeply into the subject and is recommended reading for serious cloth doll collectors, particularly those with a special interest in the Lencis.

One point made by Coleman is that the Lenci dolls were varied in size, characterization, and construction. They were also usually marked. However, there are cases of authenticated unmarked Lencis. This is not to say that every unmarked felt doll that resembles a Lenci *is* a Lenci, since several companies made excellent copies and placed them on the market in direct competition. In other cases, there is no question the dolls are merely poor imitations of the originals.

Kimport Dolls, Inc. has been importing dolls since the 1930s and most of their records are intact. They distributed both Lenci dolls and Lenci look-alikes. In their collector's magazine, *Doll Talk,* Vol. 3, No. 6, March-April 1940, I found these paragraphs:

> This was another "close out" of which we availed ourselves, all of the 9″ size in Italian-costumed Lencis that were this side of the ocean. There are wide-eyed girls of Castilrotto wearing a red silken snood under the broad brimmed hat and carrying under one arm the cutest blue keg with a spigot — and brave lads of the same village with a trumpet, and peacock feather in each jaunty hat! You will love this pair, or Maria alone, the most irresistable of all the surprised-looking little folk this artist has produced. Others are in other garb; they'll be favorites, no matter what else you have; price $7.50 each. Materials are as perfect as the styling of their quaint, wee garments and their dumpy, appealing little selves!

5L-a

A charming description of these little costumed Lencis and certainly a commentary on what has happened to their value in the intervening years. There followed two more paragraphs about the Lenci look-alikes:

> Aristocratic dolls like the Lencis have kinfolk who bear a family resemblance but who wear crash and calico instead of fine wool and crisp organdie. And that's a lucky thing, too, for the little girl or thrifty adult who wants to stretch her limited budget to cover the map of troubled nations.
>
> So, we can offer a real Italian-made girl with round eyes and mouth depicting the same happy, though baffled expression, 8″ tall at $1.95.

In the early days, all illustrations in *Doll Talk* were drawn by Ruby Short McKim, one of the founders of Kimport, since photographs were too expensive to reproduce. (Fig. 5L-a.) It was common for Kimport to send out tiny (1½″ × 1¾″) photographs of dolls they thought customers would like — a kind of personalized catalog service. Or in response to a customer's request for more information about a doll mentioned in the magazine, a photograph would be sent.

Duplicate photographs were carefully filed in tiny envelopes with information about each doll written on the front. Regretfully, not *all* the information a collector or researcher would like to have was recorded. Often there was no size noted, but usually there was a retail price given, which is almost as interesting to the average collector, especially those who happen to have examples of these exquisite little dolls tucked away in a collection.

The Lenci dolls were produced in a period of Art Deco influence. The variety of styles is extensive, and it is sometimes very difficult to distinguish between Lencis and some of their contemporary competition. The dolls were marked with metal buttons, cloth labels, the name stamped on a foot, or a combination of two or more of these elements. The collector is urged to study the literature and to view as many verifiably authentic dolls as possible. Even with the best preparation, it is possible to go astray.

Adding further to the research on the Lenci dolls is a recent book, *Lenci Clothes,* by Carol A. McKee. The unique features of the Lencis are fully explored by McKee, who discusses body structure, underwear, and costuming in detail. Instructions are given for reproducing a variety of original costumes. Color photographs allow the reader to compare reproductions to originals, a device that should prove encouraging to the fledgling or timid seamstress who may wish to attempt such a project. The book is definitely recommended reading, in my opinion.

Throughout history, wars have created major disruptions in the affairs of man. Social orders, political structures, industrial complexes all have crumbled before the onslaught of the chariot or the tank. After the havoc of three wars, Madame Lenci left her factory to others. The Garella family took over operations in the late 1930s, and a nephew of the original family continues the business today.

The New Lencis

The new Lencis hit the collector market of 1978-1979 with great impact. Collectors were both amazed and delighted with the prospect of being able to add new Lencis to their collections. Produced from the original molds at the Turin (Torino) factory, this latest production featured the same fascinating use of felt and organdy that had been the trademark of the Lencis for so many years.

Although much of the factory had been destroyed in the extensive bombings during World War II, the Garellas maintained production through the 1950s and for the following two decades. Production during those years, however, seems to have been of different types of dolls using materials other than the traditional felt and organdy. For example, I know of a baby doll with composition head and limbs, stuffed cloth body, and original clothing, marked on both feet with the familiar Lenci signature, c. 1950. (See *More Twentieth Century Dolls,* pp. 925-926.)

When and how the decision was made to return to the traditional designs and styles is not known. One might surmise that the burgeoning collector market offered an attractive outlet for the wares of a struggling manufacturer. While the designs of these new Lenci costumes are in strict accord with those of the past, it is sometimes difficult to find exact duplicates of original costumes.

The new Samantha, #313, for example, seems to have been dressed in an interpretation of the costume worn originally by the 165/6 Miss Sweet-Flower. The older styles appear to make much more intricate use of seaming and piecing of the felt colors. They also reflect the little girl styles of the 1920s and 1930s, with the shallow-yoked, full-skirted dresses, whereas the new Lencis display a decided leaning toward the 1940s styles and even later influences. Wigs on the new dolls are decidedly different since they seem to be of the new synthetic materials. The old dolls had mohair wigs almost exclusively.

In other words, technology and economic factors have been at work in the production of the new Lencis. They are different in some ways from the older dolls, but still remarkable, beautiful, and highly desirable both as play dolls and as additions to the best collections.

The Anili Dolls

When Lenci left her factory in the 1940s, she could no longer use her own name for dolls because the new owners held the rights to the name. After the war, Lenci and her daughter, Anili, began producing the last dolls Lenci designed, marketing them under the daughter's name.

Elena's experience with a huge factory employing hundreds of workers had left her feeling less than enchanted with such a large operation. She convinced Anili that their new company must remain small so that they might have close artistic control of their products. Elena was actively involved in the manufacture of the Anili dolls until a few years prior to her death in 1974. The dolls are still being produced under Anili's direct supervision.

Although they have been available in a few select shops in Europe for many years, the supply of dolls has always been very limited because of the small size of the factory and the diversity of its production. Anili, following her mother's example, not only designs dolls, but children's and women's clothing as well as the fancy-dress costumes so popular in Italy at Carnival. Only in the past few years have these dolls been available in the United States through the Pittsburgh Doll Company. Only four hundred dolls per year are available in this country.

Anili dolls do not roll off the assembly line. Each doll is made entirely by hand by a few highly skilled women working meticulously in a small Turin factory. Basic features are colored by one of the women, but Anili completes the painting of the eyes and lips. She also signs and dates each doll. None of the dolls is brought to completion if Anili should happen to be out of town. They await her return for the finishing touches and final inspection. Because each doll is made to order by hand, no two are exactly alike. Expressions, shades of wig and fabric, eye color, and placement of decoration all may vary slightly. Each doll is a small work of art.

Anili dolls are costumed in colorful felt and organdy, sometimes in combination with silky materials or cotton, trimmed with the traditional Lenci flowers and felt appliqué and occasionally a bit of maribou. Only the finest materials are used, a fact that sometimes limits production as the workers await delivery of a special Swiss organdy or a dyed-to-order felt.

The dolls have pressed-felt faces and wigs of either mohair or synthetic. The limbs are also made of felt. Bodies are sometimes of felt, but usually cotton. All the heads turn, although those of the Grugnettos are quite stiff.

For the most part, four molds have been in use. However, a fifth design has been discovered quite recently and is scheduled to go into production soon. All Anili dolls may be considered limited editions in the usual understanding of the term. Since a mere four hundred dolls enter the country each year, based on eighty different models, none of the Anili dolls will ever reach a very large edition. The following is a description of the Anili dolls. (Note that with the additional use of the Liz mold on the Midinette doll, there are five basic configurations plus two variations. This list does not include the recently discovered mold that has not yet gone into production.)

The Grugnetto. A 23″ child with disc-jointed legs. This doll can sit and stand alone; it has two faces, pouty and slightly smiling.

The Caricatura. A 17″ toddler-type with a childlike face, stiff legs. This doll can stand alone.

Liz. A slim, 17″ adult, face is similar to the one used for the Gish Sisters in the early Lenci line. This doll has soft legs and cannot stand alone.

The Miniatura. A 12″ younger, more childlike version of Liz. A slim doll with soft legs.

The Midinette. The 23″ version of Liz.

The Cenerentola. A 27″ version of Grugnetto with soft limbs.

5A-1 **Ivan and Katinka, 23″.** Grugnetto faces. Ivan wears black felt pants, boots, and hat trimmed with maribou plus white tunic, red-orange felt jacket with vivid felt flowers. Katinka wears orange felt skirt trimmed with vivid felt flowers, black vest, magenta headdress trimmed in gold, white cotton blouse, white organdy veil. (Photograph courtesy Pittsburgh Doll Company)

5A-2 **Monello (boy) and Fioraia (girl), 17″.** Caricatura faces. Toddler-types, dressed in typical felt costumes. Boy wears cotton shirt. (Photograph courtesy Pittsburgh Doll Company)

5A-3 **Harlequin, 17″.** Liz face. Dressed in light blue felt with colored bars to form plaid, blue hat with feather, white collar and trim. (Photograph courtesy Pittsburgh Doll Company)

5A-1

5A-2

5A-3

5A-4

5A-5

5A-6

5A-4	**Sabrina, 12″.** Miniatura face. Comes dressed in assorted colors of felt with white cotton sleeves, panniers, mob cap, felt flower trim. (Photograph courtesy Pittsburgh Doll Company)
5A-5	**Aurora, 23″.** Slim bed doll-type, Liz face, Midinette line. Wears pale pink organdy. (Photograph courtesy Pittsburgh Doll Company)
5A-6	**Catalog Sketch.** By Joyce Kintner. Illustrates variety of costuming available in the Anili dolls. (Catalog illustration courtesy Pittsburgh Doll Company)

Miscellaneous Foreign Dolls

Dolls have been imported into the United States from many countries, including Germany, Italy, France, Ireland, and Lebanon. Many foreign manufacturers that were responsible for large shipments of hard dolls either made few or no cloth dolls, or merely did not ship them to this country. Some of the familiar foreign makers, however, do occasionally sell cloth dolls.

Collectors are often prone to think of foreign cloth dolls in terms of a few major manufacturers whose wares were, in many instances, far superior to the rest. A careful examination of foreign-made fabric dolls, however, reveals that many created by the lesser factories rate notice, too. For this reason, I have attempted to show a cross section of such dolls, thus offering a word of encouragement to the collector. Avoid passing over these secondaries without serious examination and consideration. Treasure does not always wear a sign proclaiming its worth.

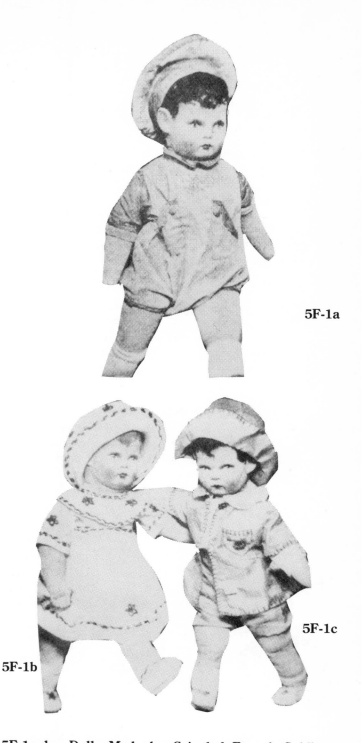

5F-1a

5F-1b

5F-1c

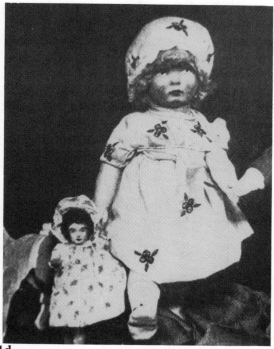

5F-1d

5F-1a-d **Dolls Made by Crippled French Soldiers.** These dolls are made in the tradition of such manufacturers as Chad Valley, Dean's, Norah Wellings, Kathe Kruse, and Madame Lenci. These all-cloth dolls with molded felt faces and painted features were made by crippled soldiers who might otherwise have remained idle, dependent on others for their support. Many countries developed special programs to provide work for war victims. (*Playthings*, June 1918)

5F-2   **Les Cadenettes, C. R. Club Dolls from France.** Club is the maker's name, not an organization. In the line of Club's all-cloth dolls were Citronnelle (80 cm) in white ruffled dress, Campanule (55 cm) in marinier and pantalon, Cytise (55 cm) in flowered or cotton dress, and Camomille (80 cm) in striped or embroidered dress. This manufacturer is known for the quality of its products. (C. R. Club 1977 catalog illustration)

5G-1,2   **German Character Men.** Excelsior-stuffed bodies, felt heads and limbs, mohair upholstery fabric wigs sewn as part of head construction, brown glass eyes, applied ears and noses. Doll 5G-1 has human hair moustache, printed velvet vest, plaid pants sewn as body. Doll 5G-2 wears black and white checked suit, brick-red felt vest. Both have mitten hands with fingers indicated by machine stitching and are all original. Doll 5G-2 has coarse pink cotton body with limbs pin-jointed at shoulders and hips. Shoes on both dolls are sewn as part of body construction. See Fig. 5G-2, picturing front and back of lapel tag from 5G-2. (Author's collection)

5F-2

5G-1   5G-2

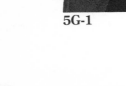

5G-1

5G-2

156

Fig.5G-2   Oval tag attached to the lapel of a doll identical to 5G-2. (Courtesy Paul Johnson and Ralph's Antique Doll Museum.)

5G-3

5G-4

5G-3   **German Goebel Clown, Oskar, 42 cm.** Stuffed cloth with felt features. All Goebel dolls are extremely well marked with sewn-in labels, tags, etc. (1976 Goebel catalog illustration)

5G-4   **Two Little German Girls, 15″.** Obtained in Germany during the U. S. occupation, yarn wigs, painted and stitched eyes, embroidered mouths, hard-stuffed bodies of stockinette. Shoes are sewn-on felt. Dresses and hats are satin and jersey. Completely handmade, one-of-a-kind dolls. (Patterson collection)

5G-5   **German Velvet Boy Character Doll.** Manufactured by H. Josef Leven of Sonneberg, Thuringia. From *The Toy Trader and Exporter,* January 1939.

5G-6,7   **German Boy and Girl, 10″ and 9¾″.** Handmade dolls with molded-painted wigs and features. Bodies are of cloth, stuffed firmly, then painted. Clothing is all original, handmade from wool. (Adame collection)

5G-8   **German Peasant Girl, 15½″.** Floss curls, mask face with molded-painted features, all-original outfit, red apron and bodice, green hat trimmed with varicolored braid, white peasant blouse, black skirt, shawl, and shoes. Skirt and apron are hand embroidered. Doll also wears a cross. (Patterson collection)

5G-5

5G-6   5G-7

5G-8

5G-9

5I-1

5G-9　**Tyrol Man from Germany, 14″.** Mohair curls, embroidered features, hard-stuffed muslin body and limbs, stockinette face. Dressed all original in old wool and crepe. All handmade doll and clothes. (Patterson collection)

5I-1　**Irish Man, 9¾″.** All handmade with floss wig, hand-painted features. Body is wire armature covered with padding and hand-knitted covering. Clothing is all hand-knitted or hand-loomed wool. Cloth label sewn into the sweater: **KIMPORT DOLLS** (in oval) **/Independence Mo/This doll/ was made in/Ireland** (the latter typed on the label). I have on file a 1976 brochure from Liston's International Dolls, Pencara, Mill Road, Corbally, Limerick, Ireland, that reads: "Irish Handmade Character Dolls. These dolls come in two sizes 7″ and 11″. Completely handmade, beautifully finished with moulded faces, handpainted in oils and dressed in the finest of Irish materials. Real collectors items." In this brochure is shown, in addition to several other characters, a doll quite similar to this one. It is easy to suppose that the 1976 Donegal Man of the brochure is a descendant of the 1939 doll pictured here. (Author's collection)

5L-1   **Lebanese Woman.** Stockinette face and hand-painted features. This doll is completely hand-made. Note the detail of the costuming. (Photograph courtesy Kimport Dolls)

5L-2   **Lebanese Woman.** Kob-Kab on her feet. She is from Beit-El-Dine, the country of President Camille Chamoun. (Photograph courtesy Kimport Dolls)

5L-3   **Lebanese Couple.** The woman is dressed in the style of the eighteenth century. The man wears seventeenth century garb. These dolls were made in sizes from 10 cm to 23 cm. (Photograph courtesy Kimport Dolls)

5L-1

5L-3

5L-2

5L-4

5N-1

5O-1

5L-4   **Lebanese and Syrian Sheikh of the Mosque, 10 cm to 23 cm.** These dolls sold for $3 to $4. Note this doll's crudely rendered hands and compare them with the hands of 5L-1. (Photograph courtesy Kimport Dolls)

5N-1   **Norwegian Couple.** Felt with molded, hand-painted faces. Clothing is also of felt and is decorated with hand embroidery. This type of doll is one of the classics from Europe. Various models were marketed in the United States for many years. (Photograph courtesy Kimport Dolls)

5O-1   **Bangkok Pair, 13″.** Handmade, embroidered features, floss hair, silk clothing, gold-colored metal bracelets, rings, and ankle bells. (Terry collection)

50-2   **Oriental Child, 8″.** Handmade, black yarn hair, embroidered features, printed cotton outfit, red shoes, unmarked. (Reeves collection)

50-3   **Egyptian Woman, 9″.** Black yarn hair, stockinette face, painted features, wire armature, carries knitted basket on head, wears bead-trimmed shawl, dowry money is sewn to print dress, oilcloth wrappings on feet.

5P-1, 2   **Polish Boys, 5″ and 5½″.** On the left is Dancing Maciek with stuffed cloth body, felt and oilcloth clothing representing everyday dress, raveled wool hair. Doll on right comes from the Zakopane district (a mountainous area), stuffed with straw or excelsior, felt head, hands, and feet. Both dolls were two of many dolls brought home by the owner's father from his travels. The dolls were used as Christmas tree ornaments. (Walilko collection. Photograph courtesy the collector)

50-2

50-3

5P-1   5P-2

162

5R-1

5R-2

5R-3

5R-1 **Russian Artist Dolls.** Moorish Man and Russian Poetess. Created by Sweika, apparently a well-known artist of the time who was a refugee living in New York City when these dolls were illustrated in *Playthings,* November 1915.

5R-2 **African Child.** Created by an artist named Piramonie. Illustrated in the same *Playthings* article as 5R-1.

5R-3 **Russian Tea Cozy, 10″.** Another classic, this Russian tea cozy doll has a mischievous smile, stockinette head and hands. It is difficult to date these dolls since they were available over a long period of time. Kimport's *Doll Talk,* a publication filled with talk of dolls from the world over, has this to say about the Russian Tea Cozies:

> In the humble homes of Russia's countless peasants, the samovar, steaming, hissing and warming, is the center attraction of the main room. Around it gather the "Gossip" and her friend whom the villagers laughingly call "The Soaker" because of her ability to "soak up" such quantities of tea; the "Coquette," a mischievous twinkle in her eyes; the rich "Merchant's Wife" as placidly proud as any dowager queen; and far in the corner the shy little "Farmer's Daughter." Of course, the scene is imaginary, but it could well be true, for the Russians do love their tea and they love to drink it in company that makes the long evenings go faster with tales and jolly songs. It is especially fitting that these distinctive characters, made by humorous Russian artists, should harbor under their voluminous skirts the padding to make them efficient tea-cozies, as well as effective collection dolls.

From this description, it seems apparent that the tea cozy dolls were created to represent many different character types. The doll shown here may be the Coquette mentioned. Also, since the tea cozies were all handmade, each face is slightly different from all others. (Photograph courtesy Kimport Dolls)

5R-4 **Russian Tea Cozy, 20″.** Skirt padded to accommodate a teapot. This doll is unusual in that her skirt has a built-in wooden display section, fitted with miniature wooden barrels, a tub, baskets filled with chestnuts, rose hips, bran, tiny apples, and tea in a hamper. There is a lantern and hot peppers, onions, a ham and some bacon hanging on the walls. The doll's wig is of some sort of fiber. The head, arms, and body are of padded cloth. The lips are pursed as though she is ready to cool the tea in the cup in her right hand. She wears a cloth kerchief on her head and a calico dress covers her torso and the display area with the double front doors. (O'Rourke collection)

5R-5 **Russian Shepherd, 15½″.** All cloth with fiber wig, painted, molded features and unjointed body. He is all original and dates from about 1920. (Kaufman collection)

5R-6 **Russian Vera, 11″.** Purchased from Kimport in January 1966. Stockinette, blond mohair wig, painted features, nicely molded, pink cotton blouse, white apron with red trim, blue print skirt, blue babushka on her head, and brown cloth shoes. (Mason collection)

5R-4

5R-5

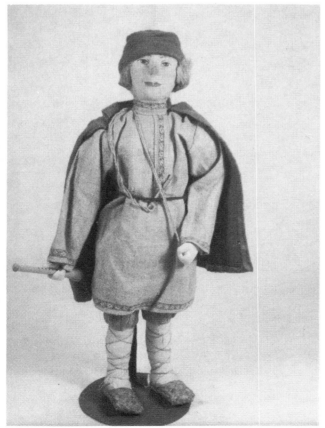

5R-6

5R-7

5M-1

5M-1

5R-7 **Russian Eskimo, 7″.** Mask face with molded, painted features, wire armature, hard-stuffed cloth with felt parka, carved wooden boots. Cloth tag sewn on front of left pant leg reads: **MADE IN SOVIET/UNION/8066** (or **VOSS**) **SAMCED.** (Author's collection)

5M-1 **Peasant Girl, 17″.** Completely handmade of excelsior-stuffed cloth. Face has stockinette cover, features are molded, then painted, hair is pale blond floss. The costume is beautifully detailed with braid, embroidery, and medallions to recreate what must be an outfit worn for special, festive occasions. (Adame collection)

5M-2 **Peasant Girl, 16½".** Handmade, her fingers are wire, padded and covered with stockinette, features are embroidered on stockinette face, hair is black yarn. Doll is dressed all original in red felt hat, red wool skirt hand-embroidered with flower designs, lace-trimmed organdy apron, and rust-colored silk shawl trimmed with fringe. (Adame collection)

5M-3 **Dutch Boy, 12".** Excelsior-stuffed body, glass eyes, embroidered features. Clothes are integral part of body. Doll is all-mohair fabric except for velvet face, felt stockings and shoes, velvet hands with red thread to indicate finger separation, c. 1910. (Perry collection)

5M-2

5M-2

5M-3

166

6 Photographic Faces

Early in this century, dollmakers began to apply the principles of photography to the production of some very realistic-looking rag dolls. At the same time, many companies were advertising dolls with lithographic faces. To avoid confusion, it is essential that the collector understand the difference between the lithographic faces and the photographic faces.

A lithographed face may be one drawn by an artist or it may be a face taken from a photograph. Those designated as having photographic faces can only come from one source — a photograph or image obtained by aiming a camera at a subject and capturing the likeness on a photographic plate or film.

For further explanation, I quote from *Webster's New World Dictionary of the American Language* (1970):

Lithography. The art or process of printing from a flat stone or metal plate by a method based on the repulsion between grease and water: the design is put on the surface with a greasy material and then water and printing ink are successively applied; the greasy parts which repel water absorb the ink, but the wet parts do not.

Photography. The art or process of producing images of objects upon a photosensitive surface (as a film in a camera) by the chemical action of light or other radiant energy.

Photogravure. A photochemical process by which photographs are reproduced on intaglio printing plates or cylinders; a print made from such a plate.

Thus, the true photographic-faced dolls must have faces that are obviously photographs of real people. Usually children and babies were the subjects used.

Although the Dreamland Doll Company in 1905 advertised that their dolls were the first such dolls, many other doll manufacturers quickly came to market with their own versions of the same. As is the case with any innovation or gimmick styled to attract attention and therefore the public's money, use of the photographic face spread throughout the industry in a few short seasons.

We may never be able to determine with any certainty which company actually made the first photographic-faced doll. We can, however, enjoy, compare, study, and learn about these interesting dolls that burst onto the market with such fanfare and were gone in so short a time.

Two companies located in Detroit, Michigan, vied for a share of the market with their trade advertising. The Rouech-Bowden Company, doing business at 49 West Larned Street in Detroit, advertised a photographic face on a new line of dolls in *Playthings.* They registered a trademark for the Playtime Dolls, which were advertised in the June and August 1906 issues as the "most natural Doll ever made; Faces photographed from life..." Their June advertisement was particularly appealing. It showed six of their dolls posed as though descending a staircase with the slogan, "This is a new line. If the faces don't talk to you, write us." The dolls were made in a variety of sizes from the best materials to retail at popular prices.

In the July 1907 issue of *Playthings,* the E. B. & E. Company of Detroit also advertised photographic-faced dolls. These dolls were touted as having "faces natural and lifelike." Their Happyland brand was a very complete line for distributors. An interesting note: This company also published illustrated postcards and novelties. Evidently the opportunity to print dolls' faces using their standard equipment (printing presses) represented a move into a new market for the company. No street address for the firm was given in the advertisement.

In 1907, the E. I. Horsman Company was also celebrating their new line of dolls:

Babyland Rag Dolls (Improved for 1907) with new and beautiful LIFELIKE™ faces. The Babyland is the original high-grade rag doll...in addition to the original face designs, which have long been distinguishing features of the 'Babyland' line, we take pleasure in announcing to the trade that we have perfected a new and beautiful series of LIFELIKE faces and our customers have the choice of either style.

By 1909, Horsman was using its advertising space to show six of their line of rag dolls with the lifelike faces as well as one doll with the Stella patented face. A March 1910 advertisement states: "Horsman now offers forty varieties of 'Babyland' Rag Dolls" and refers to them as "the pioneer rag dolls of America," a statement founded more in the fancy of some copywriter than in fact, since more than a few rag dolls preceded these in America.

The George Borgfeldt Company advertised the line of

photographic-faced dolls produced by the Dreamland Doll Company, a third name in the roster of companies located in Detroit. As early as 1905, the Dreamland Doll was advertised as "a new idea that surpasses any rag doll on the market. The faces of these dolls are photographed from life, thus giving them a natural, life-like expression. They are well made, dressed in dainty, up-to-date styles." The advertisement goes on to say that the 13″ doll was made to sell for fifty cents retail. The 14½″ retailed for one dollar.

In 1907, the industry was patting itself on the back for the development of the photographic face. Dolls were certainly improved. All seemed to agree on that. Here is part of an editorial stressing that point from the November 1907 issue of *Playthings:*

It was in the neighborhood of fifteen years ago that the rag doll industry might be said to have had its beginning in America, and from that time until today it has made rapid strides. Of course it is to be supposed that the first dolls were rather crude in appearance, that is, in comparison to the modern rag doll, but nevertheless, they were sufficiently charming to take a good firm hold upon the American child, and every year they sell in large quantities.

We say that rag dolls are improved every year; well, perhaps this is true, but in some cases the improvement is so slight as to be hardly recognizable, such as a better grade of materials, daintier dresses, more substantial construction, or some other minor detail, all of which go toward making the rag doll nearer to perfection. Manufacturers declare that the present-day rag doll is already perfection, and probably this is true to all purposes.

For years and years these soft dollies with their prettily painted faces were turned out by the thousand, and then there suddenly came a great change, a new sort of rag doll appeared, something totally different from the original variety. This was the doll with the photograph face, as everybody knows, the face photographed from life.

Of course, there were many little girls who thought it great fun to have something that her neighbor did not possess, and the new dolls were well received. On the other hand, however, there were many tots who had been playing with the old time rag dolls for so long that they could not see their way clear to give them up for anything else.

The writer has visited some of the factories where these fascinating playthings are made, and the most noticeable feature was the cleanliness of everything, for the makers of such well known varieties as the "Babyland," and "Fairyland," dolls guarantee absolute cleanliness. This, of course, is a very strong point in favor of the rag doll, for in these days anxious mothers intend that everything must be boiled before it gets into baby's hands. It would hardly do to boil a beautiful rag doll, so the makers see to it that the boiling process is not necessary.

The regular dolls that come to us from abroad, whether they be of French, German or some other nationality, are all white, but not so with rag dolls. There are cute little colored ladies, and an especially pleasing number of a doll called "Dinah," made to represent the cook. Another very cute doll is the Babyland "Topsy-Turvy," being a white and a colored doll combined. Little sailor boys are very desirable, and look mighty cute in the natty uniforms. Red Riding Hood is among the most popular of rag dolls and she looks just like the one in the story, with her little red cape and basket.

A feature of comparatively recent date is the rag doll to be dressed and undressed, and that, of course, allows the little owner to change dolly's costume as often as she pleases. When the Teddy Bear craze was at its height a manufacturer introduced a novelty in the form of a Teddy Bear and rag doll combined. When the child tired of the bear she could reverse the clothes, and then appeared the doll.

Such was the world of rag dolls in the year 1907, according to one copywriter, at least. Many collectors would be willing to debate a few points made in this article. For example, just how crude does one judge the earliest rag dolls to be? Were the Izannah Walker dolls crude? Should the Columbian dolls be considered crude? Or the Martha Chase dolls, or the Philadelphia Babies, or any of the handmade, homemade rag babies so loved by collectors today? I think not, but then perhaps crudity, as beauty, is in the eye of the beholder. Perhaps, too, collectors prefer to see the beauty in even the most crudely made old cloth doll.

6-1

6-1

6-1   **World War I Soldier, 16″.** Unmarked. Here is an example of a lithographed face for comparison with the actual photographic faces shown in subsequent illustrations. This doll is all original, dressed in a World War I army uniform complete with leggings fitted with tiny buttons. (O'Rourke collection)

Group of cloth dolls from the author's collection. All are illustrated and described elsewhere in this book.

Lady Doll of 1850, all original and complete with lacy underthings and cap. These very old, one-of-a-kind dolls are highly prized by collectors. (Mongeon collection. Photograph courtesy the collector)

Early Cloth Girl, 25″, all original clothing, hair and features are hand painted with artist's oils. (Rasberry collection)

Hester — 1860, 29″, sewn with chain-stitch machine, has features painted in artist's oils. (Rasberry collection)

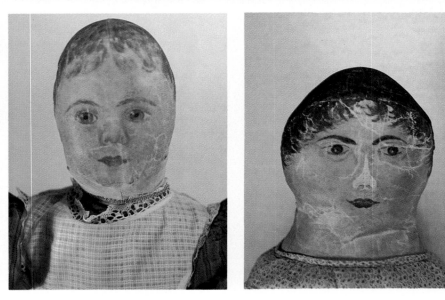

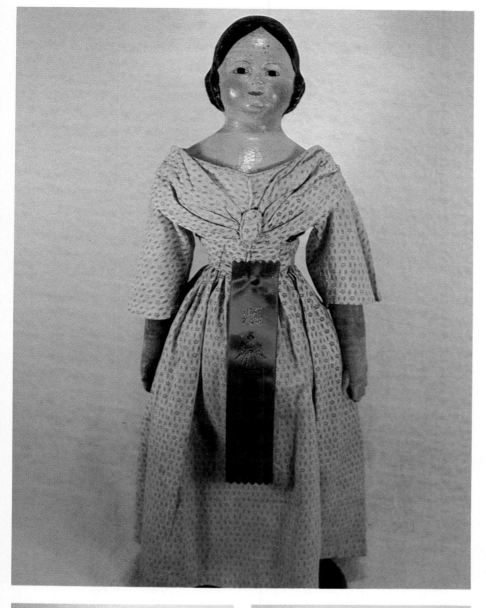

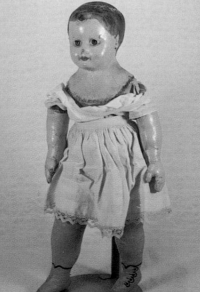

China-type Cloth Woman, 22½″, probably was molded from a china or papier-mâché head. An excellent example of a very rare type. (Rasberry collection)

Early Cloth Woman, 20″, probably all original. Features are hand painted, as is the hair. (Rasberry collection)

Chase Girl, 18″, painted feet and legs to simulate shoes and stockings. Original dress (not shown) is yellow dotted Swiss. (Rasberry collection)

The Little Children™ of R. John Wright are represented by these three charming examples. Shown (left to right): Jesse, Lillian, and Peter. All are 17″. (Photograph courtesy the artist)

Meg and Jo, Little Women dolls by Madame Alexander. These 16″, all original, 1930s cloth dolls are among the earliest from the very popular dollmaker. (Author's collection)

Chad Valley Girl, 19″, sold to author as Lillabet, a diminutive for Princess Elizabeth, now Queen Elizabeth II. Although well marked as to maker, doll bears no positive identification as Elizabeth and is different from other known Princess Elizabeth dolls from this maker. (Author's collection)

Lenci Boy, 20″, all original and a blue ribbon winner. This doll is an excellent example of the finer Lencis. (Rasberry collection)

Bed Doll Lady, all original, dressed completely in lace, has embroidery floss hair and fetching side-glance expression, molded mask face, painted features. (Author's collection)

SFBJ Lady, 18½″, in all original dress, marked *SFBJ* on metal disks on shoulder joints. (Rasberry collection)

Spanish Dancer and Musician, 34″, 1920s bed doll types with caracul wigs and highly detailed costuming. (Rasberry collection)

Shirley Temple, 18″ and 27″, are favorites of Judi Ward's customers. Faces are painted on the cloth. (Photograph courtesy the artist)

Lenci-type with Basket of Fruit, 18",
probably made in South America by
expatriate former Lenci employees.
(Author's collection)

Navajo Woman, completely handmade, dressed in velveteen and cotton sateen. (Author's collection)

174

Bruckner Child, 7", a much-loved
and played-with example. This doll
is all original, missing an arm, and
well marked. (Author's collection)

Irishman, 9¾", representing a man
from Donegal, all handmade with
floss wig, hand-loomed fabric. Date
on tag: 1939. (Author's collection)

The First Gerber Baby, 8″, pillow-type doll dressed in printed-on pink dress. Boy wore blue. Gerber is still searching for a boy to complete their archives. (Photograph courtesy Gerber Products Company)

Dean's Rag Book Lithographed Doll, 14″, marked on right foot. (Rasberry collection)

The Reely-Trooly Dollies, 8¼″, cloth and paper. These are two of six with paper faces and limbs glued to cloth shapes. (Author's collection)

Hartwell Sean and Libby Rose, two babies from Babyland General Hospital created by Xavier Roberts. Hartwell Sean wears new clothes provided by his adoptive mother. Libby Rose is in her original outfit. (Photograph courtesy Alice Wardell)

"Bathtime," lifesize, prize-winning group by Dianne Dengel. Her dolls reflect attention to detail, an apparent love of children, and her display experience. Note old woman and boy in background. (Photograph courtesy the artist)

Loma Lee, a Calico Lady, 17″, by Cynthia Harvey "Goose" Winston. Hand-painted features, yarn hair, button joints at hips and shoulders. Costume is integral part of doll's construction. (Photograph courtesy the artist)

The Grugnetto, #1 Pierrot, 23″, is made with the pouty face shown as well as a smiling face. An Anili doll, in the true Lenci tradition, this Pierrot wears quilted velveteen with organdy collar. (Photograph courtesy Pittsburgh Doll Company)

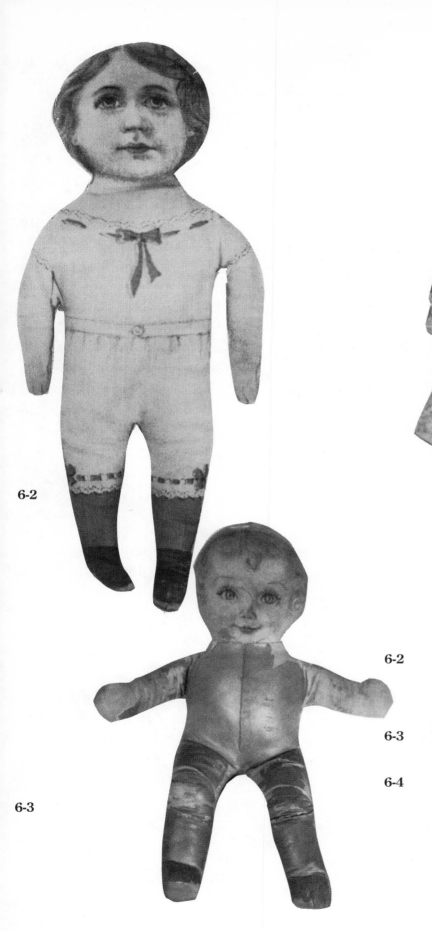

6-2

6-3

6-4

6-2 **Lithographed Girl, 7″.** Unmarked, typical of the early dolls with printed-on underwear, stockings, and shoes. Note the similarity to some of the advertising dolls of the period. This is not a photographic face. (Author's collection)

6-3 **Lithographed Baby, 12″.** Unmarked, an unusual baby doll. Most of the dolls of this type were older children. (O'Rourke collection)

6-4 **Dreamland Girl, 13″, 14½″.** Dreamland Doll Company, distributed by Borgfeldt. (From September 1905 *Playthings*. Courtesy the magazine)

6-5   **Happyland Rag Doll.** By E. B. & E. Co. of Detroit. Featured a photographic face, "natural and lifelike." Like many of the photographs taken from very old advertisements, this is not as clear as I would like. (July 1907 *Playthings*. Courtesy the magazine)

6-6   **Babyland Topsy-Turvy.** A photographic face times two. The topsy-turvy style was very popular. However, this doll is relatively rare. It is usually found as a white and black together. Horsman retailed these dolls for $1. (From *Playthings*, 1907. Courtesy the magazine)

6-7   **Babyland Baby, 14″.** By Horsman, 1910. Note that this is the same face used on one of the Topsy-Turvy heads in 6-6. The owner purchased the doll in its original box, at a sale of old warehouse goods labeled 1910. The doll is all original as shown. (Potter collection)

6-5

6-6

6-7

178

6-7

6-9

6-8

6-8 **Henrietta, the Crying Rag Doll.** Mentioned in an editorial in the November 1907 *Playthings*. However, no manufacturer's name was given. Claim was made that Henrietta was the first rag doll with a cryer. (Courtesy the magazine)

6-9 **Babyland Boys, Old and New.** By Horsman, 1907. On the left is the older, hand-painted face type. On the right, the new photographic-faced doll. Both types were available, depending on customer preference and price. (From a November 1907 *Playthings* editorial. Courtesy the magazine)

6-10 **Babyland Girl.** With the new photographic face. This girl matches the boy, 6-9. (November 1907 *Playthings*. Courtesy the magazine)

6-11 **Babyland Girl Rag Doll.** Improved for 1907 with "Life-like Faces™," said the advertisement in the March 1907 *Playthings*. (Courtesy the magazine)

6-12 **The Babyland Rag Doll Trademark.** From the June 1910 issue of *Playthings*. (Courtesy the magazine)

6-10

6-11

6-12

6-13a

6-13b

6-13c

6-13d

6-13a-e **Babyland Rag Dolls.** New Styles for 1909 from Horsman. From a 1909 advertisement in *Playthings*. All had the "Life-like" faces and retailed for $1 each. By 1911, Horsman was advertising that they had forty styles in this line of dolls, ranging in retail price from 25¢ to $5. (Courtesy *Playthings*) (Courtesy *Playthings*)

6-13a **Cy, the Farm Boy.** No. 220C.
6-13b **Golf Boy.** Hand-knitted sweater, No. 230B.
6-13c **Golf Girl.** No. 230G, hand-knitted sweater.
6-13d **Bo-Peep.** No. 220BP.
6-13e **Sunbonnet Sue.** No. 220SB.

6-13e

6-14a,b,c Playtime Photographic-Faced Dolls. By Rouech-Bowden Company of Detroit, Michigan. As advertised in *Playthings,* August 1906 issue. No further description was given for the three dolls illustrated. (Courtesy the magazine)

6-15 Playtime Photographic-Faced Dolls. By Rouech-Bowden Company. Part of the line-up shown in their June 1906 advertisement in *Playthings.* (Courtesy the magazine)

6-14a

6-14b

6-14c

6-15

7 Novelties, Personalities, and Other Dolls of Interest

Because of the economical nature of their manufacture, rag dolls often lend themselves to projects ranging from the sublime to the ridiculous, with a wide variety of categories in between. Some might even be said to reflect the seamier side of life (no pun intended).

Fund-raising projects sponsored by churches, clubs, and other organizations have produced some excellent handcrafted dolls with artistically painted or embroidered features. Others have been amateurishly conceived and executed — entirely forgettable specimens worthy of the worst connotations of the phrase *rag doll,* albeit all were no doubt produced with the best of intentions. (Commercial manufacturers, as well, are subject to similar fits of bad taste, whether in hard dolls or soft, fabric ones.)

Since the object of this book is to give an overview of the subject, a few dolls are shown here without editorial comment even though some collectors would not wish to include them in a personal collection. To dismiss such dolls would be to ignore a facet of the rag doll story that illustrates the incredible appeal of the medium to a wide range of people for as wide a variety of reasons. All of which only serves to point up the words collectors live by: One person's trash is another person's treasure.

Grouped together in this chapter are a number of dissimilar dolls whose only commonality is that each is unusual, offbeat, or just a bit different in some way from the other categories included in this book.

Multifaced dolls might have been listed elsewhere, along with the other dolls from the same manufacturer. I have elected, however, to show them here since their numbers are sufficiently small to enable collectors to classify them as unusual or even rare. By-the-yard dolls, those representing comic strip characters and other personalities, bed dolls or flappers, souvenir dolls, iron-ons, all are in the minority when compared with the overall doll production of any given year. Their smaller quantities have therefore landed them in this catchall chapter, where they seem, indeed, to be at home.

In no way can this chapter be considered a definitive work on the subject of unusual cloth dolls. Any time a writer attempts to define a subject, that subject seems to expand in inverse proportion to the amount of information on hand. Immediately upon publication of any book, a flood of letters washes over the land, channeling across an author's desk, dropping a rich silt of new information along with photographs and offers of assistance in the expansion of the former work.

Thus, readers help in the research of a subject, often expressing great satisfaction in being allowed to participate. All of this, of course, is true of any subject. An author has much to be grateful for in the generosity and cooperation of knowledgeable reader-collectors who are willing to share the fruits of their own experience with others.

Though not an example of the categories covered in this chapter, the Lerner Newsboy shown here is an excellent example of the sharing of collectors. In 1975, Mira Walilko sent this sketch of her Lerner Newsboy so that I could record the information for a future book (Fig. 7-1, to be exact). The actual doll can be seen in the chapter on advertising dolls.

Handwritten notes around figure:

Rag Doll - Polyester stuffing; cotton, printed.
12" high; 9" across widest part of the body. -

3/5/75

LERNER NEWSBOY

← flesh colored

Researched! Can photograph 4 U, if you'd like it for the next book.!

color of questions marks; colors as shown.

Design continued on the back with the following on the back of the shirt.

© 1970 Myers Publishing Company

main office, Chicago, Ill; Family's owner's name; Lerner

OUT PA EXT

Fig. 7-1

Dolls with a Mission
The UNICEF Rag Dolls

Some of the most charming of specialty dolls to be found are those manufactured by Aurora Products Corporation of West Hempstead, New York (a division of Aurora Plastics of Canada, Holland, and England), under license from the United States Committee for UNICEF. The United Nations Children's Fund is the only United Nations agency charged with devoting all its efforts and resources to helping the world's children.

UNICEF works in over one hundred developing countries in Africa, Latin America, and Asia. In partnership with the governments of those countries, it builds permanent health services, improves the nutrition of children and expectant mothers, raises educational standards, strengthens family welfare services, and provides emergency relief and rehabilitation when natural or manmade disasters threaten the lives of children. UNICEF is financed entirely by annual voluntary contributions from governments, organizations, and individuals.

The sale of Uniworld Toys is one of the many fund-raising enterprises the agency has developed.

The Uniworld Toy philosophy quoted from the box in which the doll was marketed is as follows:

Uniworld Toys are a whole new way to learn about life. First, they're fun. But more important — each Uniworld Toy is designed to help teach values like brotherhood, understanding, and cooperation.

Every Uniworld Toy is developed in concert with the U.S. Committee for UNICEF, to help your child broaden his horizons and exposure to the whole world around him.

Around the world, others look different, dress differently, and live in a way that's not familiar. But basically, we're all very much the same.

The philosophy of Uniworld Toys is to teach this lesson while your child has fun.

Cooperation between nations must start with children who understand each other.

Baby Many-Face is actually three dolls in one. She looks like a cute, cuddly Korean baby in a blanket, but flip the blanket and she becomes a bouncy baby from Nigeria wrapped in mother's iborun. Flip again and she's a merry Mexican baby in mother's rebozo. Each native costume is authentic and the dolls are soft-stuffed to be cuddly bedtime favorites.

Mary Many-Face is a sweet Israeli miss dressed in her native costume trimmed with bright coins and beading. With a flip, she becomes a girl from Chile in poncho and skirt decorated with pictures of llamas. Over her shiny, dark pigtails she wears her native hat. A second flip and she's from Thailand in a bright, flowered dress and matching hat. "Mary shows (the children) that even though each child is different in many ways, all over the world they are basically the same," reads the story on the box.

To indicate the impact the sale of these dolls has on a worldwide scale, UNICEF adds this information to the Mary Many-Face box: "With its share of the price of this toy, UNICEF can buy enough BCG vaccine to protect 13 children against tuberculosis."

The Baby Many-Face box reads: "With its share of the price of this toy, UNICEF can buy enough seed to grow 1600 tomato plants for a village food program."

7UN-1

7UN-2

7UN-1 **Uniworld Baby Many-Face, 11″.** All printed cloth. Box gives size as 12″. Doll is designed like a book, with pages that flip to change the doll's clothing. As a result, three babies are represented in one doll. A cloth tag sewn in reads, **ALL NEW MATERIAL/100%/New Polyester Fill/ REG.PA#262/6043-011.** On the reverse of the tag is: **BABY MANY FACE™/© 1973/Aurora Products Corp./W. HEMPSTEAD N.Y./U.S. AND FOREIGN PATS. PEND.** (Author's collection)

7UN-2 **Uniworld Mary Many-Face™, International Mini, 12″.** All printed cloth, 1972. Doll is constructed of a design similar to UN-1. Represents three little girls of different countries. A cloth tag on the right foot reads: **MARY MANY FACE™/ Aurora Products/Corp/West Hempstead/ N.Y./U.S. and Foreign/Pats. Pend.** The reverse of this tag is: **All New Materials/100% New/Polyester Fiber/Reg. PA 262/6041-011/Made in Taiwan.** On the box is printed: **Distributed under license from the U. S. Committee for UNICEF.** (Author's collection)

185

Rag Dolls by the Yard

The Saalfield Publishing Company

The Saalfield Publishing Company of Akron, Ohio, was a leading source of by-the-yard fabric dolls designed to be completed by the home needleworker. In a 1909 double-page advertisement in *Playthings,* dozens of cloth items were shown. There was Goldenlocks, a large blond doll in her underwear, printed in five colors on a square of muslin measuring 25″ × 34″. This is a different doll than the 1913 example called Golden Locks shown by Walker and Whitton (*Playthings by the Yard,* 1973). Wholesale price for the large Goldenlocks was twenty-five cents.

There were several dolls with the Drayton faces offered in the same ad. Dottie Dimple, printed in five colors on a 16½″ × 18″ square of muslin, was fifteen cents. Baby Boy and Baby Girl, on separate 12″ × 15″ squares in five colors, were ten cents each. A Topsy Turvy Doll in four colors on a 22″ × 32″ square cost thirty-five cents.

Also offered was the Greenaway Doll in five colors on a 17½″ × 18″ square for twenty-five cents (Fig. 7-2). The Japanese Kimono Doll on 16½″ × 18″ square cost twenty cents (Fig. 7-3), and Red Riding Hood in five colors on 17½″ × 18″ square was available for twenty cents. There were other items in cloth shown in this ad that do not qualify as items for this book and are mentioned only to point out how Saalfield covered the market with a variety of styles.

The company published many other dolls printed on cloth over a period of several decades. There were, among others, Dolly Dear, Mammy, Dottie Dimple, Little Mary, Baby Blue Eyes, Fritz of the Katzenjammer Kids, and a complete Rag Family. There was also an 8″ Tiny Traveler Series.

One of Saalfield's noble experiments proved unpopular in the long run. In their muslin book line they introduced the Cut-Out Series which included four titles: Dolly's Sewing Bee, Baby's Menagerie, Baby's Home Pets, and Babies of All Nations, all with a picture and verse on each page. When the child tired of the book, the illustrations could be cut out, sewn together, and stuffed to make dolls and toys. There were even clothes for the dolls. The only problem was that from constant handling the books often became too tattered to make into toys and thus part of the value of the design was lost. These books measured 9¼″ × 11¼″, were printed on good muslin, and cost sixty cents each wholesale.

Other early publishers of dolls printed on cloth were The Arnold Print Works, Art Fabric Mills, and the Cocheco Manufacturing Company. More recently, ABC Fabric Company, Lowenstein Fabrics, and Spring Mills, Inc., among others, have kept the home needleworker supplied with a variety of by-the-yard dolls and toys. As we shall see, a growing number of the older designs are being reproduced in kit and finished form.

On another note, many advertising premium dolls were sold or given away in to-be-completed form, printed on squares of muslin or other fabrics. Many of these pieces are included in the chapter on advertising dolls. Similarly, the Harold Lloyd doll, which was distributed as a flat, has been included with the personality grouping in this chapter.

Saalfield's Dolly Dear, a popular doll, was printed on a 21″ × 36″ piece of cloth. It made a 24″ doll and two "doll's dolls" just 7″ tall. The price was twenty-five cents, and Saalfield published the design into the 1930s (Fig. 7-4).

Fig. 7-2

Fig. 7-3

Fig. 7-4

The Arnold Print Works

The Arnold Print Works of North Adams, Massachusetts, was a prolific publisher of a wide variety of designs, many of which were created by Charity and Cecilia Smith. These two women, who were sisters-in-law, created the Arnold Cat that was so popular in the last decade of the nineteenth century. There followed a number of other animal designs that originated with the Smiths, too.

Arnold was also responsible for a jointed rag doll, a Gibson Girl doll, Little Red Riding Hood, Pitti Sing, and Pickaninny (later called Blossom). There were Palmer Cox Brownies en masse and a large contingent of toy soldiers (Our Little Soldier Boys). Evidence of the Arnold offerings may be found in contemporary advertisements. Many of the dolls and animals advertised in the trade journals and children's magazines of the period are being reproduced today, both in sew-it-yourself form and as finished toys.

The Toy Works of Middle Falls, New York, has faithfully reproduced selected items from the old Arnold line. The flats, called the Museum Collection, are marketed in see-through wrap, fastened with a cardstock top that tells the following story:

> The Toy Works has faithfully reproduced this piece from a select collection of 19th century American Folk Art dolls and animals. This art form began in 1886 with the introduction of E. S. Peck's Santa (the first commercially produced cloth doll in America), gained popularity with the Arnold Print Works' Tabby Cat in 1892, and revived by The Toy Works in 1974. Our antique reproductions are hand-printed on natural fabrics in New York State, employing a sophisticated screening technique to capture the design subtleties of our 19th century predecessors. Our prints are sold in both kit form (sew-it-yourself) and hand-finished (sewn and filled with natural fibers).

All selections are taken from examples in the Toy Collection of the Museum of the City of New York, which commissioned the reproductions. Each flat carries three trademarks (Fig. 7-5).

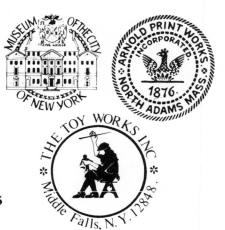

Fig. 7-5

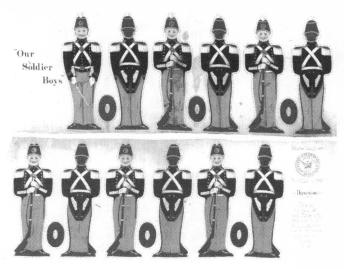

7APW-1

7APW-1 **Our Soldier Boys, 8½".** Top row wears red jackets, light blue pants. Bottom row has dark blue jackets, light blue pants. Printed on the flat is: **Patented July 5, 1892 and October 4, 1892.** The circle trademark of the Arnold Print Works and the title are both given here. Overall length of each piece of muslin is 23½"; 1892. Note: This set differs from the description given by Walker and Whitton in colors of uniforms. The set they describe has some all-blue uniforms, with others having navy jackets and red pants or light blue jackets and red pants. Measurements given here are for actual image size, excluding seam allowances designated by dashed lines around the figures. Walker and Whitton show 8½" as the size of the soldiers in their illustration. Remember that finished sizes may vary even more. Instructions printed on the flat describe the method of finishing the bottom of each soldier: "Cut thick, heavy paste board oval, to fit bottom piece, then sew together." (Author's collection)

7APW-2 **Sew-It-Yourself Blossom.** Issued in 1892 as Pickaninny, this reprint was copyrighted in 1977 by The Toy Works. Available in blue dress with pink hat or pink dress with blue hat. (Author's collection)

7APW-3 **The Improved Foot Life Size Doll, 9″ to 30″.** Sold flat, advertised as being "more easily put together than any other doll on the market." (From *Playthings,* September 1909)

7APW-2

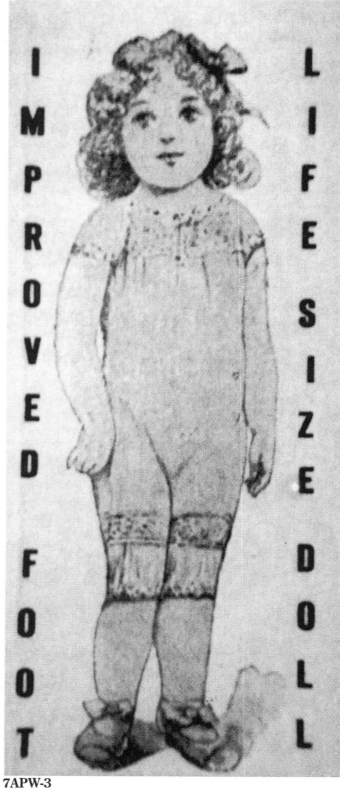

7APW-3

7APW-4

7APW-5

7APW-4 Jointed Rag Doll, 15″. Touted as "the latest thing in doll land" in the April 1911 *Playthings* advertisement. Elms and Sellon were distributors for the Arnold products. (Author's photograph. Courtesy the magazine)

7APW-5 Semidrest Gibson Patent Doll. Designed by Edward T. Gibson, this doll was described in a September 1912 *Playthings* advertisement of Elms and Sellon, Distributors, as a "No-Break, life-size doll." Designed and patented by Gibson. "Printed in beautiful oil colors," it was jointed so it would assume a seated position and came with directions for making the doll as well as a skirt that was fastened to the body, but hung free. Shoes were painted-on, high-button style. (Author's photograph. Courtesy the magazine)

7APW-6 Another "No Brake" Life Size Doll, 9" to 30". Also spelled No-Break. Designed and patented by Edward Tinkham Gibson and distributed by Elms and Sellon. Advertised in the August 1911 and September 1912 issues of *Playthings*. (Illustration courtesy the magazine)

7AFM-1 The Improved Life Size Doll, 20" and 30". Designed and patented by Edgar G. Newell, February 13, 1900. Printed in eight colors on heavy drill cloth. Distributors were Selchow and Righter, New York. (Author's photograph. From *Playthings,* September 1908. Courtesy the magazine)

The Art Fabric Mills

The Art Fabric Mills of New York City produced fabric dolls based on a patent obtained by its president, Edgar G. Newell. The patent date, February 13, 1900, appears on the foot of each Life Size Doll. Other dolls were produced by this company, among them Foxy Grandpa, Uncle, Billy, Newly Wed Kid, and Buster Brown.

The distributor for the dolls was Selchow and Righter, who subsequently took over the company and continued the business. Sears, Roebuck and Company, as well as Montgomery Ward, distributed the dolls. In the Montgomery Ward Catalog No. 70, there are three Art Fabric dolls listed. One is 32", another is just 20", and the third is their Topsy.

The dolls were advertised as printed in oil colors on heavy sateen and were to be cut out, sewn, and stuffed. In a September 1909 *Playthings* advertisement, an Improved Life Size Doll, 2½' when made up is shown. The improvement apparently had something to do with an updated printing process. The dolls were said to be lithographed in eight colors on standard heavyweight drill cloth. Wholesale price of the 30" Life Size Doll was $4 per dozen. The advertisement also suggested dressing the doll in a child's discarded clothing, which would enable the child to dress and undress the doll, thus improving skills in those areas in the course of play.

7APW-6

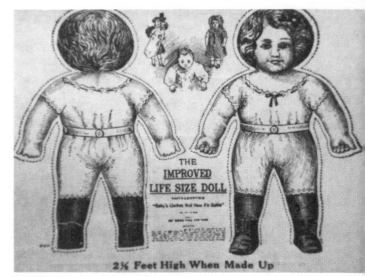

7AFM-1

7AFM-2

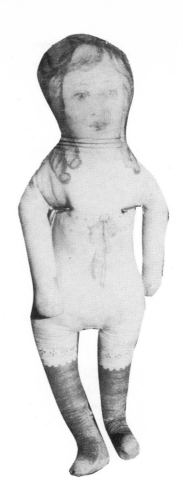

7AFM-4

7AFM-3

7AFM-2   **Foxy Grandpa, 11″.** Also available in a 20″ size. From a character drawn by cartoonist Carl Schultze for many Sunday newspaper supplements. Doll was designed and patented by Mr. Schultze. Stuffed stockinette head with painted features, yarn hair fringe around a bald head, straw hat, felt suit and tie, 1903. One set included Grandpa plus two 9″ grandsons.

7AFM-3   **Life Size Doll, 24″.** Wears old child's dress, hoists her skirt a bit to show her printed-on shoes, stockings, and underwear. On shoe bottom is: **Art Fabric Mills/Pat. Feb. 13, 1900.** (O'Rourke collection)

7AFM-4   **Life Size Doll, 26″.** This doll has long lithographed curls, and has apparently been played with very hard. As a consequence its printing has worn badly. Barely discernible on the bottom of one foot are two words: **Pat.** and **1900.** (O'Rourke collection)

191

The E. I. Horsman Company

The E. I. Horsman Company of New York City is well known among doll collectors of all ages and for dolls of just about all materials. The dolls of this company are among the best commercially made rag dolls.

In the field of by-the-yard, to-be-sewn dolls, Horsman was a leader if not in quantity, certainly in quality of manufacture and design. In the June 1906 issue of *Playthings,* their newest rag dolls were discussed:

> Children always love to make things and they also love dolls, therefore the new line of cloth dolls just placed on the market will be just the things for them. These come in sheets to be cut out, sewed together and then stuffed with some soft material. There are three sizes of the boys and three sizes of the girls, done in very pretty colors, and they will appeal very strongly to the young ones. Each one of these fascinating little dollies has a catchy name, such as "Bobby Bright," "Daisy Darling," "Little Fairy," etc. They will retail for 5, 10 and 25 cents each, and are destined to become excellent sellers during the Holiday season.

Strangely enough, the manufacturer of these marvelous new dolls was not mentioned. Fortunately, the company was identified directly beneath two examples of the new line described in the article.

Tommy Trim and Daisy Darling were chosen to represent the group that included Willie Winkie, in addition to the others named. These dolls were continued from 1903 to about 1917 or 1918. They were very successful in Horsman's line.

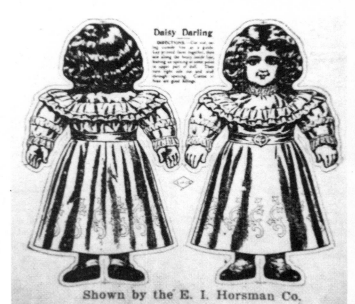

7EIH-1

7EIH-2

7EIH-1   **Daisy Darling.** Available in three sizes. From *Playthings,* June 1906. (Author's photograph. Courtesy the magazine)

7EIH-2   **Tommy Trim.** Available in three sizes. From *Playthings,* June 1906. The line also included Willie Winkie, Bobby Bright, and Little Fairy. (Author's photograph. Courtesy the magazine)

192

The Toy Works

In addition to the Blossom doll shown earlier, the Toy Works of Middle Falls, New York, has issued two 36″ dolls called Sybil and Jasmine, done in a stylized fashion with printed-on clothes of rather outlandish design and high color. In addition, this firm has introduced some original designs by a designer named Hudson Talbott.

The Talbott designs include a Little Red Riding Hood, the reverse of which is, of course, the Big Bad Wolf. This doll is 14″ tall and available in both kit and finished form. Another Talbott design is a 14″ Sinterklaas (Santa Claus) wearing a tall headpiece, carrying a small lighted tree, and steadying a large bag of toys with his other hand. Talbott has also produced some toy designs for the Toy Works line. These include animals, birds, and even fish.

7TW-1

7TW-1 **Sybil and Jasmine, 36″.** Both dolls are remarkable for their uniquely designed clothes as well as the unusual body shapes. The designs are handfinished by The Toy Works — and just as well, since the construction of the dolls does not lend itself to mass production. (Illustration courtesy the manufacturer)

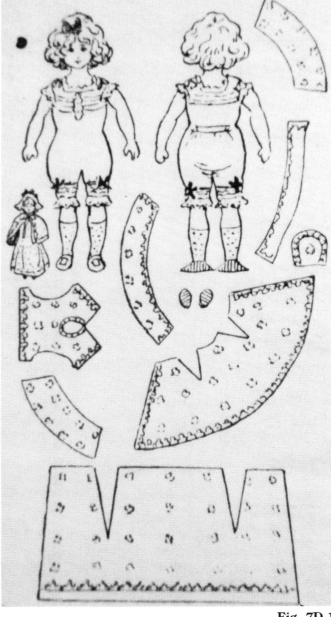

Fig. 7D-1

The Dean's Rag Book Company

The Dean's Rag Book Company of London was established in 1903 by Henry Samuel Dean. They used Horsman as their United States distributor and did a good business in this country. In the April 1908 issue of *Playthings,* the company received a complimentary writeup about their new line:

> An entirely new line of cloth dolls in sheets has just been placed upon the market by the manufacturers of Dean's favorite rag books, and if they find the popularity that the books did then there will be an enormous business done in them. The first illustration (see 7D-1) gives a good idea of how the dolls look before they are cut out. The children love to cut out these dolls and stuff them, and it is an inexpensive as well as harmless, amusement, at the same time being more or less instructive.

With each doll is supplied a variety of different costumes, representing several nations. One of the cutest of the lot is the Japanese doll. The sheets are printed on good heavy cloth, and lithographed in many bright colors. The second illustration (see 7D-2) shows the "fournations" dolls and they are particularly attractive. The third picture (see 7D-3) shows how the dolls look when completed. Cloth dolls on sheets need no introduction to the American toy trade, for they are already well and favorably known; but this new line is something quite out of the ordinary. Made in the same excellent style as the rag books, and offered to the trade at attractive prices, they should find a steady sale. Goods of this kind are always in demand at holiday time, but they have a pretty good sale all the year round.

Fig. 7D-2

Fig. 7D-3

Modern by-the-Yard Dolls

Many of the items available in yard goods departments and stores feature animals of one sort or another. Though in the minority, the by-the-yard doll can still be found occasionally. Valtex Fabrics, Spring Mills, Inc., ABC Fabrics, Lowenstein Fabrics, Manes Fabrics Company, and Cranston Print Works Company are among the publishers of by-the-yard dolls and toys.

As with any other piece of merchandise, by-the-yard dolls are subject to discontinuance based on the state of the market. On the other hand, many of these designs continue for years. Such designs follow fashion trends, the popularity of characters, as well as other influences. Seasonal items reappear with regularity, expressing time-proven themes in classic or new design. A trip to a fabric store in September might reveal a world of Christmas designs in addition to the popular character dolls of the moment and an abundant display of Halloween items.

Raggedy Ann, though a perennial favorite, seems at the moment to have taken a back seat to Strawberry Shortcake™, although Raggedy Ann may be back soon, as strong as ever. Perhaps the new to-be-sewn lines will feature E.T. or another, as yet unknown character or personality.

Since buyers for stores have tastes that vary, it is well to check out more than one store. Some stores may carry one or two lines that are not available elsewhere. Stock may be added monthly as new designs are announced by the mills. Ducking in the fabric store each time a trip to the shopping mall is necessary often proves a worthwhile habit for the serious collector.

While the doll collector is browsing through the fabric shop, there is another item to check, too. Whether a collector is interested in dolls, paper dolls, rag dolls, or even toys, there may be yard goods available printed with designs reflecting those interests. I have found Raggedy Ann and Raggedy Andy prints, paper doll prints (complete with tabs), and a lovely montage of collectible dolls from early bisques and chinas to the later compositions. This latter design has also been found in gift wrap. Many sewing projects may be completed using such fabrics: skirts, shirts, blouses, children's clothing, as well as projects such as lining an antique trunk or covering a box or notebook.

Wandering down the aisles of the fabric shop, the collector who is also a dollmaker, or would like to become one, should watch for the tiny prints so necessary to doll costuming. Very small designs are easier to find than they have been during other periods of our fashion history. However, it is a good idea to purchase a yard or two when appropriate prints are found. Very often when the bolt is empty, that pattern will not be reordered.

Dollmakers ought to be aware of proper proportions when selecting a fabric for doll clothing. An otherwise excellent doll can easily be spoiled by the choice of a fabric with a design too large for the size of the doll for which it is intended. Tiny checks, narrow stripes, minute flowers, and microscopic paisleys are desirable for doll clothing. The overall appearance of the doll is at stake.

7MY-1-4   Strawberry Shortcake™ and Her Gang. Produced by Spring Mills, Inc., ©1980, American Greetings Corporation. Pattern No. 5709, Strawberry Shortcake™, 20″. Pattern No. 5715, Apple Dumplin'™, 15¼″. Pattern No. 5718, Blueberry Muffin™, 19¾″. Pattern No. 5710, Huckleberry Pie™, 20¼″. Sizes shown are flat, unfinished measurements, but do not include the seam allowance. These characters may be found on greeting cards and many other items. I suggest that the collector who plans to cut and sew the designs take time to trim out the copyright declaration as well as the character's name and either attach them to the doll or include them in the stuffing near the opening. In this way, should a future collector wish to authenticate a doll, the information will be available. (Author's collection)

Strawberry Shortcake™

Apple Dumplin'™

LEAVE OPEN FOR STUFFING

LEAVE OPEN FOR STUFFING

LEAVE OPEN FOR STUFFING

INSTRUCTIONS
1. CUT OUT FRONT AND BACK ALONG THE OUTER EDGE
2. PLACE FRONT AND BACK RIGHT SIDES TOGETHER
3. STITCH ALONG STITCH MARKS LEAVING END OPEN FOR STUFFING
4. CLIP EDGES, TURN RIGHT SIDE OUT AND STUFF
   BLINDSTITCH OPENING

Blueberry Muffin™

Huckleberry Pie™

LEAVE OPEN FOR STUFFING

LEAVE OPEN FOR STUFFING

© SPRINGS MILLS INC. © 1981 AMERICAN GREETINGS CORPORATION   PATTERN 5710

© SPRINGS MILLS INC. © 1980 AMERICAN GREETINGS CORPORATION PATTERN #5710

196

© SPRINGS MILLS INC. 468

7MY-5 **Christmas Doll, 11½″ and 20″.** Copyright © Spring Mills, Inc., Pattern No. 468, undated, but purchased in September 1982. Doll is dressed in bright red and green, has yellow pigtails. (Author's collection)

7MY-6 **Welcome to the World of Strawberry Short-cake™.** Copyright ©1982 American Greetings Corporation, Spring Mills, Inc. Pattern No. 5730. Included on a single flat are six 6″ dolls: Huckleberry Pie, Raspberry Tart, Blueberry Muffin, Angel Cake, Lime Chiffon, and Plum Puddin'. All are trademarks of American Greetings Corporation. (Author's collection)

7MY-7 **Strawberry Shortcake™ Set.** Four dolls: 10½″ Strawberry Shortcake and Huckleberry Pie, 7⅜″ Apple Dumplin, and 4¾″ cat named Custard. All names are trademarks of the American Greetings Corporation. This is Pattern No. 5728. (Author's collection)

7MY-8 **Stitch Witch.** Pattern No. 7685. Copyright ©Spring Mills, Inc. Undated, purchased September 1982. Measures 20¼″. (Author's collection)

7MY-9 **Scarecrow Sam.** Pattern No. 7684. Copyright ©Spring Mills, Inc. Undated, purchased September 1982, 18¼″. (Author's collection)

7MY-10 **Christmas Angels from Around the World.** A V.I.P. Screen Print. Copyright ©Cranston Print Works Company. Undated, purchased September 1982. Eight 6″ dolls may be made from this panel. (Author's collection)

7MY-11 **Nativity Scene.** Seven dolls from 7″ to 8″ tall, plus a 4¾″ × 3½″ wooly lamb. Copyright ©Manes Fabrics Company. Undated, purchased September 1982. (Author's collection)

7MY-12 **Santa Claus, 8½″ and 16½″.** Another 2¾″ Santa motif appears twice on the panel. No copyright or date on this piece. Purchased on the secondary market in the summer of 1982. Walker and Whitton date this piece 1969. (Author's collection)

7MY-13 **Mr. and Mrs. Santa and Snowman.** A V.I.P. Screen Print. Copyright ©Cranston Print Works Company. Undated, purchased September 1982. This very large panel (36″ × 45″) makes three 15¼″ dolls. Printed in traditional bright Christmas colors. (Author's collection)

"Huckleberry Pie"

Raspberry Tart"

Blueberry Muffin"

INSTRUCTIONS:

1. CUT OUT THE FRONT AND BACK ALONG THE OUTER EDGE.

2. PLACE THE FRONT AND BACK RIGHT SIDES TOGETHER AND DUE TO THE SMALL SIZE OF THESE CHARACTERS, YOU MUST PAY SPECIAL ATTENTION TO STRETCHING THE FABRIC TO MATCH THE LINES.

3. STITCH ALONG STITCH MARKS, LEAVING THE OPEN END FOR STUFFING.

4. CLIP EDGES, TURN CHARACTER RIGHT SIDE OUT AND STUFF LIGHTLY FOR BEST RESULTS.

5. BLINDSTITCH OPENING.

INSTRUCTIONS:
1. CUT OUT FRONT AND BACK ALONG THE OUTER EDGE
2. PLACE FRONT AND BACK RIGHT SIDES TOGETHER
3. STITCH ALONG STITCH MARKS, LEAVING OPEN END FOR STUFFING
3. CLIP EDGES, TURN DOLL RIGHT SIDE OUT AND STUFF.
4. BLINDSTITCH OPENING

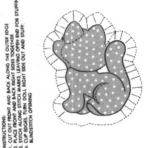

Angel Cake"

SUGGESTION FOR USE: THESE LITTLE CHARACTERS MAY BE USED YEAR ROUND AS LITTLE COLLECTIBLES, ALSO FOR USE IN MAKING A MOBILE FOR A CRIB OR ROOM AND AT HOLIDAY TIME THEY MAY BE USED AS TREE ORNAMENTS BY ATTACHING A LOOP OF RIBBON OR YARN AT THE TOP OF EACH CHARACTER.

"Huckleberry Pie

Strawberry Shortcake"

Lime Chiffon"

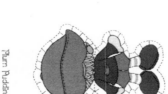

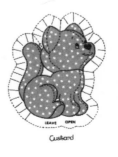

Plum Puddin"

Custard

"Welcome to the World of Strawberry Shortcake"

"Apple Dumplin'

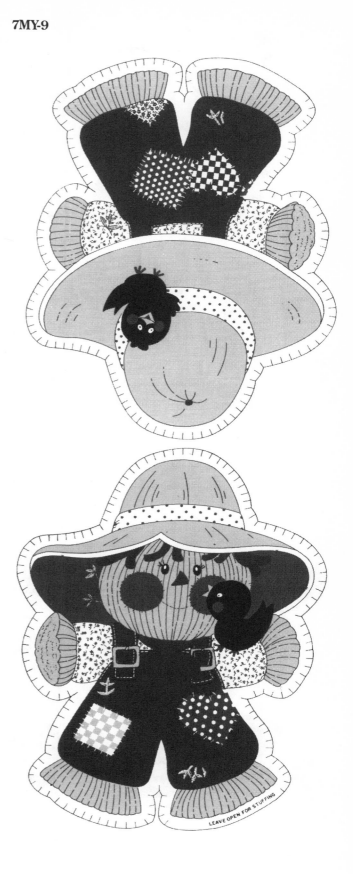

STITCH WITCH

LEAVE OPEN FOR STUFFING

LEAVE OPEN FOR STUFFING

Christmas Angels From Around The World

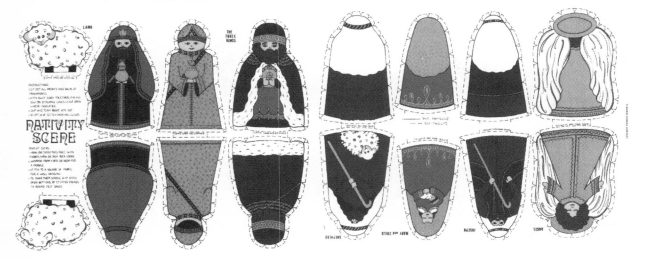

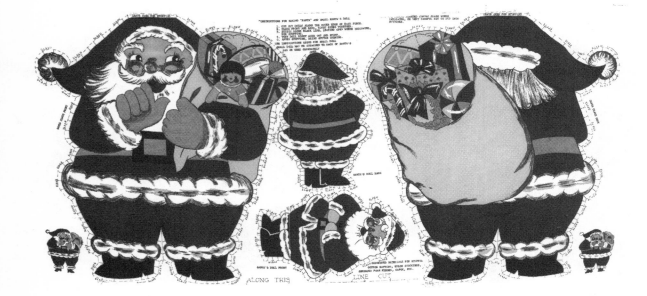

INSTRUCTIONS

Mr. & Mrs. Santa and Snowman

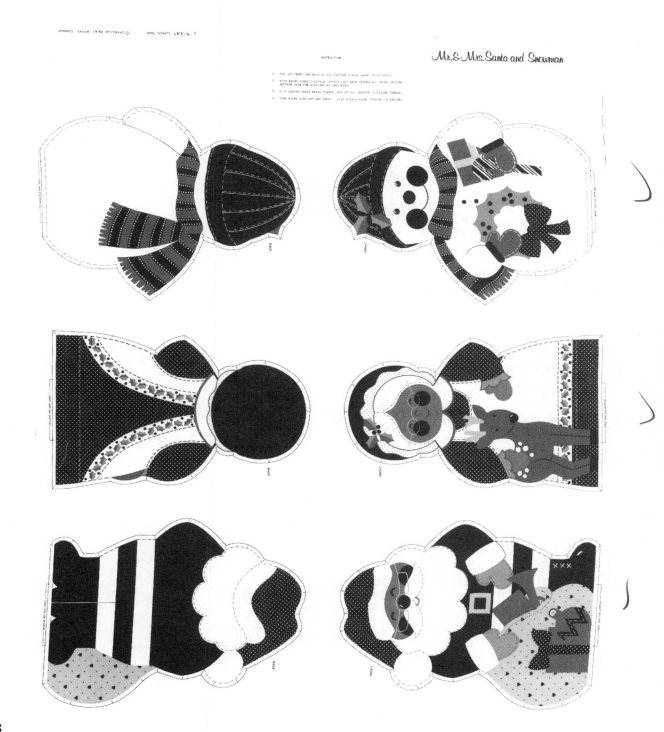

7MY-13

Miscellaneous Novelties

The Reely-Trooly Dollies

The Reely-Trooly Company of Boston, Massachusetts, has for its only known claim to fame the production of these most unusual dolls. Advertised in the April and August 1915 issues of *Playthings,* these dolls are a cross between a paper doll and a cloth doll. Here is the description from the advertisement:

> Something for Children to Make (Pat. Allowed) Made of Cloth. Fascinating, Entertaining, Educational, Durable. Heads, arms and legs in seven colors on gummed paper. Doll figures printed on six attractive patterns of cloth. Gummed parts are to be mounted on the cloth and then the doll is cut out, producing a set as shown in cut. Materials for six dolls in every package, making an incomparable 25-cent item.

The advertisement showed six dolls. By chance, I am presently the steward of two of these unusual dolls. Note that of the set of six, there are four that seem to match, while the remaining two, one on either end of the photograph, are more alike in style and rendering. One must wonder, then, whether two artists were involved in the design of this set.

In the August 1915 advertisement, claim is made that these are the "only cloth cut-out dolls ever produced and . . . are generally conceded to be the most attractive 25-cent item in the toy market. . . ." The twenty-five cents mentioned was the price for the full set of six dolls. The manufacturer not only sold wholesale to the trade through jobbers but also sold direct to the retailer.

7RT-1

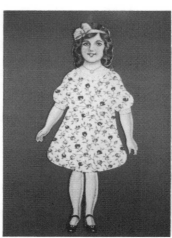

7RT-1   **The Reely-Trooly Dollies.** A set of six different dolls, each measuring 8¼", made of cloth and paper. Faces, arms, legs are glued onto doll's fabric shape. From an advertisement in the April 1915 *Playthings.* (Author's photograph. Courtesy the magazine)

7RT-2   **Reely-Trooly Dolly, 8¼".** Pink bow in red-brown hair, gold locket, black shoes with gold buckles. Dress is a print with lavender, red, tan, and green. Eyes are brown, head and limbs are glued to printed paper. Doll also shown in 7RT-1. (Author's collection)

7RT-3   **Reely-Trooly Dolly, 8¼".** Holds blue parasol and red purse. Her light brown hair is in longish curls. Her brown hat has dark pink roses for trim. Her stockings are long, and her shoes are high-buttoned. The dress form is white, printed with small rose-red flowers and trimmed with green ribbon. This doll is also shown in 7RT-1. (Author's collection)

7RT-2

 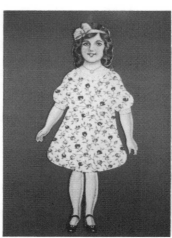

7RT-3

7C-1

7C-2

7C-3

Dolls from the Comics

7C-1 **Buttercup, 15″.** From the Jimmy Murphy cartoon strip, Toots and Casper (King Syndicate). Soft cotton construction, painted features, squawker voice. Also available as 18″, c. 1925, Modern Toy Company. (Courtesy Sears, Roebuck and Company)

7C-2 **Skippy and His Dog.** From the Gasoline Alley comic strip. Doll available in two sizes: 13½″ and 9¾″. Dog was 8¼″×6½″. Designs were printed on oilcloth-type material, sewn on the outside, and lightly stuffed for a fairly flat doll. Material is called imitation leather in advertising. (1927 catalog illustration courtesy Sears, Roebuck and Company)

7C-3 **Skeezix, 14½″.** Lithographed, stuffed oilcloth. Doll is flat with a three-dimensional effect. Arms are stitched on separately. Original blue chambray overall suit. (Author's collection)

7C-4, 5   **Wilma Flintstone and Barney Rubble, 20″ and 16½″.** From the cartoon series The Flintstones. With the other two characters, Fred Flintstone and Betty Rubble, the group has been made into many different doll sets in a variety of materials. Shown are two of a set of four purchased by the yard and sewn into pillow dolls, 1960s. (Wiseman collection)

Another cloth set of these characters is the 1973 Knickerbocker set, in 7″ to 8″ size, each boxed separately. Also included were the two children of these stone-age couples, Pebbles Flintstone and Bamm Bamm Rubble.

7C-6   **Little Orphan Annie and Her Dog, Sandy, 13⅝″ and 9″.** Stenciled on imitation leather (oilcloth). Both are made so they stand. Sewn on the outside, stuffed lightly for a flat effect. (1927 catalog illustration courtesy Sears, Roebuck and Company)

7C-7   **Little Orphan Annie, 18″.** Stiffened mask face, cotton body, mohair wig, original red dress and matching panties. Cloth tag on doll reads: **Saturday Evening Post.** One of a series of premiums offered by the magazine, possibly about 1938. (Author's photograph. Courtesy Ralph's Antique Dolls)

7C-4

7C-5

7C-6

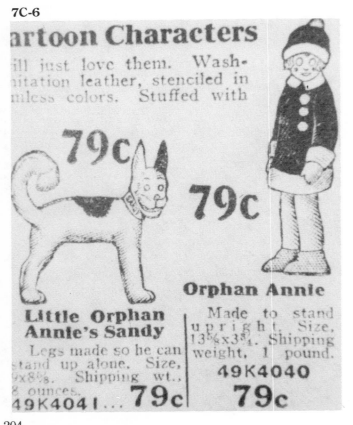

7C-7

204

7C-8

7C-9

7C-10

7C-11

7C-8   **Little Orphan Annie, 17″.** All-lithographed cloth, cotton-stuffed, red yarn hair, red dress, black belt. (1967 Remco catalog illustration)

7C-9   **Little Orphan Annie and Sandy.** Mid-1970s, doll is 24″, dog is 21″ × 15″. Probably one of the strangest renderings I have ever seen. Doll is stuffed, bright pink felt with mask face, painted features. She wears regulation red dress, white panties, black plastic shoes, has fuzzy red synthetic wig. Dog is of a tightly curled fabric, hard-stuffed, with felt and plastic features. A sewn-in cloth tag on both reads: **ALL NEW MATERIAL/ CELLULOSE FIBER/SYNTHETIC FOAM/ STERLING EVER PROD./BROOKLYN, N.Y./ PA. #23 MASS. T46 NY 7938/CALIF 28887 OHIO 3974.** (Author's collection)

7C-10, 11   **Gepetto and Jiminy Cricket, 15″ and 9″.** From a set of three dolls sold flat for home sewing about 1960. Set included a 13″ Pinocchio. (Courtesy Ralph's Antique Dolls)

7C-12 **Archie, 18½".** Lithographed cloth, orange hair, red shirt, orange and black bell-bottom trousers. A comic book came with each doll. Shirt has **Archie** imprinted on it. (Siehl collection)

7C-13 **Bugs Bunny, 10".** Felt and plush, stuffed, applied felt features, wire armature body, felt sombrero, cotton serape, felt hat, red pants, green shirt. (Author's collection)

7C-14 **Little Lulu, 15".** All cloth, molded-painted features, floss hair, red cotton dress, unmarked. From comic strip by Marjorie Henderson Buell. The 1958 Sears catalog shows a similar 14½" fabric doll. The 1959 catalog shows a similar 16½" doll in western outfit. (Zillner collection)

7C-12

7C-14

7C-13

7C-15

7C-16

7C-17

7C-15   **Nancy, 15″.** Black yarn hair, painted black eyes, stuffed cotton body, wears black, white, and red dress, yellow shoes. Made by Georgene Novelties, Inc., about 1961. There is also a Sluggo to match. (Thompson and Sheinwald collections)

7C-16   **Nancy, 20″.** Plush hair, lithographed cloth. Tag on front reads: **NANCY/©1972 UNITED/FEATURES SYNDICATE INC.** A sewn-in tag on hip reads: **CELLULOSE FIBER/SYNTHETIC FOAM/STACEY LEE ORIGINALS/ BROOKLYN N.Y./MASS T-10 PA (48 N.Y.).** There is also a matching Sluggo. (Gibbins and Sheinwald collections)

7C-17   **Betty Boop, 22″.** All cloth, reinforced face, designed and executed by Patti and Deet (PaDeet Productions). This is the first three-dimensional doll manufactured by Colorforms. Licensed by King Features Syndicate. The doll shown here is one of four sample dolls handmade by the designers. These identical samples were prepared for submission to manufacturers who then bid on the production of the item. The doll was only in production a very short time and is therefore somewhat difficult to locate. (Author's photograph. Courtesy the designers and Mr. Harry Kislevitz, President, Colorforms)

7C-18 **The Peanuts Gang, 7″.** From the 1976 Christmas gift catalog, Sears, Roebuck and Company. Characters were created by Charles Schultz and include Charlie Brown, Peppermint Patty, Lucy, and Linus. (Courtesy Sears, Roebuck and Company. Copyright United Features Syndicate)

7C-19-21 **Super Heroes.** Soft tricot material, screen-printed with costume detail. Figures can be posed alone or with each other. Each doll has Velcro pads on hands and feet. Characters are: Superman (7C-19), The Amazing Spider-Man (7C-20), and The Incredible Hulk (7C-21). Spider-Man and Hulk, © 1979 Marvel Comics Group. Superman is a trademark of, and copyrighted by, DC Comics Inc., 1978. Super Heroes is the trademark of DC Comics Inc. and Marvel Comics Group. (1979 catalog illustration courtesy Knickerbocker Toy Co., manufacturer of the dolls)

Personality Dolls

7P-1 **W. C. Fields, 17″.** Lithographed cloth, pull-string. Says eight different lines, such as "Ah, yes, I remember!" "Cash on the barrelhead," and "Beezlebub, I've been hoodwinked!" All in Fields' inimitable voice. (1972 Montgomery Ward Company catalog illustration)

7C-18

7P-1

7C-20

7C-19

7C-21

7P-3

7P-3

7P-4

7P-2

7P-2 **Tinker Bell, 19″.** Lithographed cloth pillow doll has separate wings, by Mattel. Tag includes two dates for copyright, 1962 and 1968. (Wiseman collection)

7P-3 **Flip Wilson/Geraldine Talking Doll, 16½″.** Lithographed cloth, pull-string. Doll says ten different sentences in two different voices. Copyright ©1970 Shindana Division of Mattel, Inc. (Wiseman collection)

7P-4 **Eloise.** Yellow yarn hair, painted black eyes, painted smile. Perfect little replica of the Kay Thompson fictional character who lived at the Plaza Hotel in New York City. Hillary Knight illustrated the book and also did a painting of Eloise for the cover of the 1955 Neiman-Marcus Christmas catalog in which the doll was featured. Neiman-Marcus also listed the Eloise doll in the 1958 catalog. The doll was created for American Character by designer Betty Gould. (Perry collection. Photograph courtesy the collector)

209

7P-5 **Talking Mrs. Beasley, 15½″.** Rooted yarn hair, lithographed features, stuffed cloth, removable polka dot dress. One of Mattel's Hold-Me-Tight dolls. (1973 Mattel catalog illustration)

7P-6 **Charlie Chaplin as The Tramp, 14″.** Lithographed features. Special mechanism allows Charlie to perform his famous waddle when the doll is walked. (1973 Kenner catalog illustration)

7P-7 **Beethoven and Lincoln, 16″.** Silk-screened faces in black ink on flesh-colored cloth. Clothes are integral part of body. Lincoln wears black. Beethoven wears green. Black fuzzy nylon is used for Lincoln's hair and beard. Sewn-in cloth tags read: **R Impulse Items Original/Copyright Made in U.S.A.** On the paper tag: **Impulse Items New York/Lincoln (Beethoven)/One of the Greatniks,** 1967. (Photograph courtesy Ruth Sheinwald)

7P-5

7P-6

7P-7

210

7P-10

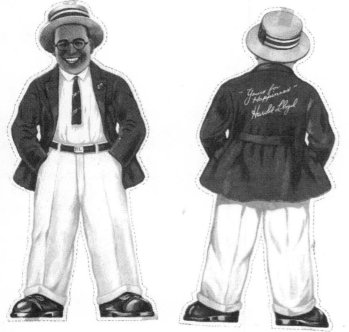

7P-9

7P-8   **Captain Kangaroo, 21″.** A Sears 1967 exclusive. Says eleven phrases when ring is pulled, by Mattel. (Catalog illustration courtesy Sears, Roebuck and Company)

7P-9   **Harold Lloyd, 12½″.** This doll has been carefully cut out but never sewn and stuffed. Or did these dolls come already cut out at the dash lines which delineate the seam allowance? I have seen several, all of which were cut in this manner. There is therefore no date or manufacturing information available on these dolls. This doll is slightly different from the example Walker and Whitton show, which has an extra width of dark fabric at the neck on either side, apparently intended as a reinforcement of that narrow section. This dark area is intended as a part of the doll since the dashes outline the area as they do the rest of the doll. Harold Lloyd was a popular performer in his day. He starred in the film *Safety Last* in 1923. The movie reportedly set new standards for screen comedy, which was still in its infancy. (Author's collection)

7P-10   **Harold Lloyd, 11½″.** A finished doll. Note the actor's initials on the belt buckle. The doll is apparently identical to 7P-9. Across the back is a replica of the star's autograph. Note the difference in appearance between the flat and the finished dolls. (Wiseman collection)

7P-11   **J. J. Evans, 23″.** A talking character doll based on the television show "Good Times." Doll has sewn-off jointed arms and legs, lithographed clothes and features. Pull ring to hear nine phrases in Jimmie Walker's own voice. Copyright ©1975 Tandem Productions, Inc., 1975 Shindana Toys. (Shindana catalog illustration)

7P-12   **Rodney Allen Rippy, 16¾″.** Four-color, silk-screened doll. Pull string and he says ten phrases in child actor's own voice. Copyright ©1974 Shindana Toys. (Shindana catalog illustration, 1975)

7P-12

7P-11

Souvenir and Commemorative Originals

In a class by themselves are these designs originated for very special purposes. Doll clubs that host conventions sometimes arrange to have a doll silk-screened on cloth to present as gift-souvenirs to conventioneers. Some such souvenirs have been given in pattern form. Others were printed with heat sensitive inks to be used as iron-ons. As one travels about the country, souvenir dolls printed on cloth squares may be found in museums and restorations, such as the Jennie doll available at Colonial Williamsburg. Three examples are shown here.

7SC-1

7SC-3

7SC-2

CASCADE DOLL CLUB of Seattle

PRESENTS ~ Molly and Ethan

The Bicentennial Twins

An Original Pattern by Elaine Chase

© 1975

7SC-1 **Cassy, 13½″.** An original design by Karen York. Two-faced doll, given by the Cascade Doll Club of Seattle, Washington, as a convention souvenir. Copyright ©1972 Karen York. Doll is silk-screened in four colors on white muslin. (Author's collection)

7SC-2 **Molly and Ethan, The Bicentennial Twins, 14″.** Original pattern by Elaine Chase. A souvenir from the Cascade Doll Club of Seattle, Washington, a UFDC affiliated club. Copyright ©1975 Elaine Chase. (Author's collection)

7SC-3 **Heritage Dolls.** A Limited Bicentennial Series of 2500. An original design by Kathleen Lyons. Book has heat transfer pages to make fronts and backs of four dolls measuring 15½″ and 15¾″. Included are George and Martha Washington plus a colonial man and woman. Copyright ©1976 Kathleen Lyons. Dolls are marked *K. Lyons 1975*. (Author's collection)

7SC-3

7SC-3

7SC-3

215

Potpourri

7MN-1 **Wide-Awake Two-Faced Doll.** From The Vivian Line of Rag Dolls. Three sizes: 13″, 15″, 17″. Patented March 17, 1908 by Lillian Sackman. These dolls had two faces hand-painted on a swivel head, with jointed hips and shoulders. Shoes, stockings, dress, and underwear were removable; assorted outfits. The doll was guaranteed to be stuffed with antiseptic cotton. Made by Bruin Manufacturing Company of New York. (Courtesy *Playthings*)

7MN-2 **The Multi-Faced Rag Doll.** A *Playthings* advertisement states this doll has "four different lithographed faces which can be changed by simply folding them into place. As shown in cut, the bonnet is removed and yoke unhooks at back. The face desired is placed on the doll and held in place by a bandeau. The other faces are concealed under the front of the dress when yoke is replaced. This doll is dressed in attractive gingham gown . . . has four faces, giving the little girl four dolls in one." Thus the author of this descriptive item in the July 1913 issue of *Playthings* provides us with a clear description as well as photographs of the doll in question, without even hinting at the manufacturer of the doll or giving its size. In 1940, the Reisman-Exposition Doll Corporation advertised a two-faced Goldilocks Rag Doll, 18″. "Flip up the bib and she goes to sleep," the copy read. The second face was apparently secured in position with the bonnet. The same principle has also been used in the design of the modern rag doll. (Author's photographs. Courtesy *Playthings*)

7MN-1

7MN-2

7MN-2

7MN-3

RAGGY-DOODLE

U.S. PARACHUTE TROOPER

"The Toy of the Time!"

Hello Boys and Girls:

My name is "RAGGY-DOODLE". I have come from the Land of "Shangri-La" where the American Fighting Planes live. My job is to help you to keep cheerful - because cheerful Americans are good Americans, and good Americans will win this war - I'm here to tell you! So keep cheerful and "KEEP 'EM FLYING"!

Yours for VICTORY --

RAGGY-DOODLE
U.S. Parachute Trooper

COPYRIGHT 1942 M. HOYLE

7MN-5

7MN-4

7MN-3   **Little Eva and Topsy, 14½″.** A topsy-turvy doll. All original; mohair wig on Topsy. Faces lithographed, hard-molded cloth. Doll was patented July 8, 1901, by Albert Bruckner and distributed by Horsman. (O'Rourke collection)

7MN-4   **Humpty Dumpty, 16″.** Unmarked. Doll is made of a silklike, very tightly woven fabric. Different colors are sewn-in, not lithographed. Face features are lithographed. Pants are blue, shirt is red, collar is light tan, bow is faded rose. Hands and head are of the same fabric, an orange-yellow. Doll has gusseted seat and the legs seem to have been designed to take a natural, seated position. (Author's collection)

7MN-5   **Raggy-Doodle, 6½″.** A U. S. parachute trooper. This doll wears brown duck-type material. Another in my collection is dressed in camouflage print green cotton. The parachutes of the two dolls are identical in design, fabric, and marking. Dolls have molded, painted mask faces. Clothing is integral part of body. Parachutes are silklike fabric, probably rayon. Doll was copyrighted in 1942 by M. Hoyle and produced by Prager & Rueben of New York City. Norah Wellings made a similar doll in 1940.

7MN-6 **Shirley Temple-Style Bed Doll, 26″.** Mask face, cloth body, blond mohair wig, painted features, composition forearms and hands. Doll is unmarked, probably late 1920s, mid-1930s. (Hoy collection)

7MN-7 **Lili Marlene, 7″.** Cloth over wire armature, dressed in red silk crepe dress, red embroidery floss shoes, net underskirt, 1920s. Hair is blond mohair, features are painted. Limbs are wound with black cloth over wire, body is lightly stuffed. She also wears red bow in hair and red underpants. Clothes are all hand-stitched. (Author's collection)

7MN-5

7MN-6

7MN-7

7MN-8

7MN-8

7MN-9   7MN-10

7MN-8   **French Dandy, 32″.** This bed doll has cloth mask
           face, silk floss hair with pigtail, cloth body, sawdust
           stuffing, blue velvet coat, silver lamé pants. From
           France, unmarked. (Courtesy Kimport Dolls)

7MN-9,10   **French Girls, 24″.** Cloth mask faces, embroi-
           dery floss hair, woven metallic cloth dresses,
           painted features. Hats are decorated with holly and
           flowers. These 1920s beauties are all cloth. The
           three dolls are of excellent design for the type.
           (Courtesy Kimport Dolls)

7MN-9

7MN-11

7MN-11 **Bed Doll Mask Face, 6″.** Painted, molded cloth. Shown here to illustrate how a mask is made. Note the buckram edges that will be turned back and carefully stitched down before the wig is applied. Marks: **7001 Patent Pending Wm. Glukin & Co., Inc., N.Y.C.** (Courtesy Camelot)

7MN-10

7MN-12

7MN-13

7MN-13

7MN-12   **Flapper Lady Bed Doll, 28″.** Floss hair, painted features, mask face, cloth body, swivel head. Note heavy eye makeup, 1920s, unmarked.

7MN-13   **Spanish Lady, 34″.** All cloth, mask face, caracul-type curled fabric wig, pink sateen body, dressed in red silk faille, real jet beads, tortoise hair comb, 1920s. (Rasberry collection)

7MN-14 **Spanish Dancer with Mandolin, 34″.** All cloth, mask face, caracul-curled fabric wig, pink sateen body, dressed in black satin suit trimmed with braid and bronze beads, red silk sash, white silk shirt, black velvet shoes, 1920s, maker unknown. (Rasberry collection)

7MN-15 **Miss Paris, 22″.** Blond silk floss curls, painted blue eyes with red, green, and white highlights, painted mouth, stuffed stockinette body and head, plaster composition arms and legs. Dress is red, white, and blue faille with screen-printed pictures and captions of historic Paris landmarks, 1920s. Red, white, and blue ribbon reads: **Miss Paris** and **Souvenir de Paris** in script. (Author's collection)

7MN-14

7MN-15

7MN-14

222

7MN-15

7MN-17

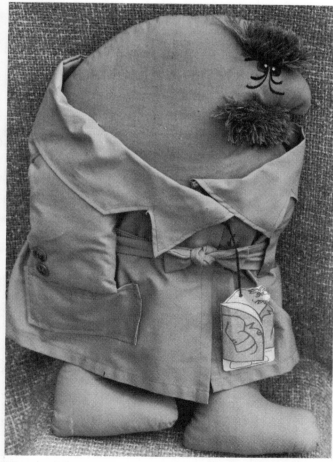

7MN-16

7MN-16   **Miss Liberty Belle, 15″.** A reproduction of a doll issued in 1926. Updated for the Bicentennial. Hand silk-screened in soft, antique-looking colors. Front of doll reads: **200 Years of American Independence/1776-1976/Bicentennial.** On back of doll is: **150 Years of/American Independence/1776-1926/Sesquicentennial/©THE TOY WORKS 1975 MIDDLE FALLS NY.** (A gift from Barbara Coker. Author's collection)

7MN-17   **Uncle Sherman, 19″.** A "dirty old man" who wears nothing but a raincoat that he opens at embarrassing moments. The character is from the television show "Soap," which at present is demised. Of yarn and cloth, pillowlike construction, the tailored tan raincoat is removable. (Uncle Sherman is anatomically correct, in a cartoonish sort of way.) Paper tag reads: **Uncle Sherman™/"The original flasher doll"/FLASHER FASHIONS-DIVISION OF FAVORITE THINGS INC.** (Meynen collection)

7MN-18 **Pregnant Doll.** Synthetic hair, all-cloth mother, felt features, vinyl baby zippered into her abdomen. Doll sold at Neiman-Marcus in 1971 for $18.95. Manufactured by Pintel of Paris, France. Compare the unnatural presentation of birth exhibited by this doll with the naturalistic approach taken in the design of 7MN-19. (Busch collection)

7MN-19 **Birthing Doll, 20″.** Cotton knit body, foam stuffing, yarn hair, embroidered features, 1974. Doll, which is unmarked, was purchased in Sweden and comes with a letter explaining in simple terms the development of a baby from conception to delivery. The baby is hidden in the mother's abdomen and is delivered head-first in the natural manner. The newborn baby is a boy. Both are well made, washable, soft, and cuddly — perfect for preparing a young child for a new brother or sister. Doll wears cotton robe and knit panties. Another birthing doll has been developed by Jan Alovus and is marketed through her company, Monkey Business (see Chapter 11). (Meynen collection)

7MN-20 **Four 19th Century Dolls to Press, Sew & Stuff.** Created by Johana Gast Anderton for Athena Publishing Company, copyright ©1975. Based on fashion plates from contemporary magazines, this iron-on book makes backs and fronts for four different pillow dolls. Issued in conjunction with the release of a book by Albina Bailey. (*Dressing Dolls in Nineteenth Century Fashions,* 1975).

7MN-18

7MN-19

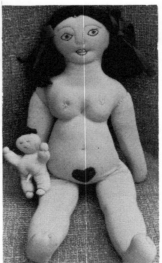

7MN-20

Fairfame

NOVELTY "SHIRLEY ANN" DOLL
No. 870

THREE PIECES—PART ONE, TWO and THREE

1st. Embroider doll face: Pupil in Steel Blue with China Blue in center. Black in center of China blue. Eyelashes, eyebrows and around outside of eyes in Black. Nostrils and lips in Turkey Red.

2nd. Cut out all parts on solid lines. Make darts in lower back of body. Seam front and back together. Stuff and close.

3rd. Stitch arms together, then legs. Stuff and attach in place on body. Be sure to have toes pointing forward.

4th. Hair: Cut strands of Yellow wool 9 inches long, fold to make long loops, stitch through loops. Make about 9 inches of this fringe. Sew stitched part along small dotted indications on head. Cut strands 21 inches, fold and make in the same manner as the other. After making 4 inches of this, sew stitched part on right side of her head pull across her forehead to left side and tie with Red ribbon. Make loops 2 inches long and stitch through center of these. Make enough of this to fit around bottom of head. Stitch in place and clip loops.

5th. Dress: Fold piece indicated into three pleats on each side of front of dress. Do the same with back, then stitch. Seam dress together at shoulders and sides. Use Blue binding to bind edge of sleeves and neck opening. Make a narrow hem at bottom of skirt. Bind outside edge of collar in Blue. Run two more rows of binding along small dotted indications on collar. Seam fast at neck of dress having raw edge come under collar. Attach a piece of binding on each side of neck opening.

6th. Shoes: Stitch shoes together and bind tops, leaving a piece of binding at each side to tie shoes on.

TO OBTAIN THE BEST RESULTS, USE SIX STRAND COTTON OR FOUR STRAND RAYON

Fairfame

NOVELTY "SAILOR BOY DOLL"
No. 867

THREE PIECES—PART ONE, TWO and THREE

1st. Embroider face. Pupil in Steel Blue, with Light Steel Blue in remaining sections. White in center of pupil. Black around eye, eyelashes, eyebrows and nostrils. Outline curve of cheeks in Indian Pink. Lips in Turkey Red.

2nd. Cut out all parts on solid lines. Make darts in back of body. Seam front and back of body together leaving open to stuff. After stuffing close body. Stitch arms together and also legs. Stuff and attach in place on body.

3rd. Hair is made by taking 6 strands of Yellow wool and catching it with two strands of embroidery cotton on small dots shown on head. After completing hair, clip wool in center between each catching.

4th. Seam front sides of Trousers together, then the same with backs. Now stitch front and back of trousers together. Make placket in back, then fold down raw edge at top of trousers and hem. Bind around bottom of trouser legs with Red binding.

5th. Stitch front and back of blouse together at shoulders and sides, leaving open for sleeves. Bind around bottom of blouse. Seam sides of sleeves together, then bind edge of sleeve. Stitch sleeve in place on blouse. Bind top of collar to underneath collar, making a double thickness. Make another row of binding ½ inch from binding edge. Seam collar on to blouse neck having raw edge come on under side of collar. Place trousers on doll and attach in place. Put on blouse, then make a small bow of red binding and in place at neck opening.

6th. Hat: Bind top of hat to underneath part of hat. Fold hat band double and stitch raw edges to hat where indicated. Then bind folded edge of hat band. Make a loop of binding and place in center of hat top. Place hat on right side of his head and tack in place.

TO OBTAIN THE BEST RESULTS, USE SIX STRAND COTTON OR FOUR STRAND RAYON

7MN-21 **Fairfame Novelty Sailor Boy and Shirley Ann.** Cut from printed sheets. Kits came complete with embroidery floss, wool yarn for hair, instructions. Clothes were printed on pieces of cloth. There may have been a complete line of these dolls, but my research has turned up only these two, which came to my attention by way of a collector-dealer from Alaska. Copyrighted 1935 to G. H. & E. Freydberg, Inc. (Courtesy Susan's Doll Shop, Fairbanks)

8 Handmade and Folk Art Dolls

The line between handmade folk art and commercial production is sometimes indistinct. As we have seen, handmade is often very commercial in that handmade items are always in demand. Many people, in addition to collectors, appreciate the appearance, the design, even the texture of what is handmade. To illustrate, one need only enter an arts and crafts shop to observe the reverence with which handmade items are handled and the respect for the obvious talents of the craftsperson.

One can imagine that the first person to make a mark on a cave wall must have been regarded with great awe. The first sculptor to fashion a recognizable object from a lump of clay must have been looked on as something of a god, too.

There is in the heart and mind something that cries out for expression. Many people succeed in sublimating that need, but there are few who do not possess it. Conversely, there are only a relative few who develop it to any degree. They are called craftspersons or artists and the rest of us hold great admiration for their works of art. How little we differ from the cave dweller in that respect.

Many of the dolls shown in this chapter reflect that desire for expression as well as the attempt to fill another, equally demanding need. In many cases, there seems to have been a plan to make a doll from available materials when other, more sophisticated playthings were unavailable. As a result, the naiveté of the needleworker, plus the degree of skill and imagination brought to the subject, have resulted in works that exude a special purity, an artlessness of form that becomes art form in its simplicity.

In other cases, the doll may be one of a vanishing group — a handmade object created especially for the tourist trade. In our present era of automated production and depersonalized marketing, handmade has given way to mass production. Many of the cloth handmade dolls of former years have their counterparts in the plastic and vinyl *mis*representations of national or regional costume to be found in the air terminals of the world.

Fortunate, indeed, is the traveler who is able to purchase a piece truly representative of the custom and costume of the area visited. In some areas, it is still possible to find such dolls, though the prospects become less likely each day. Such desirable examples must be sought in places off the tourist trail in most cases. The results are worth the trouble, however, when one is able to turn up a beautifully crafted, handmade example of the dollmaker's art.

Since these dolls have been regarded by some as secondary dolls in relation to collecting, they are still available at flea markets and the like. The interested collector would do well to make pilgrimage regularly to such gatherings of the folk who deal in "tired goods." Furthermore, the wise collector learns to *ask* about such items. (Who knows what may be packed in all those boxes under the table?)

In the category of handmade foreign dolls, one company stands out in terms of longevity in the field and in variety of sources covered. Kimport Dolls, Inc., of Independence, Missouri, has imported small, handmade dolls dressed in regional or national costume since the early 1930s. With their longstanding contacts abroad, they are still able to provide many handmade dolls for today's collector.

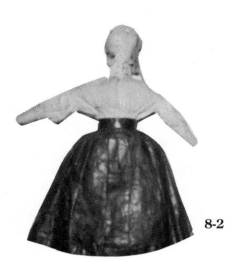

8-2

8-1

8-2

8-1

8-2

Mary, 9″. One of the oldest cloth dolls I have come across in a private collection. Construction is similar to the common linen doll shown in an article by Clara Hallard Fawcett in the September 1975 issue of *The Doll Reader.* Mary's head and arms are rolls of cloth. One foot has been mended with black cloth, or possibly the black fabric was intended to represent shoes. The dress is in surprisingly good condition, considering its age, c. 1775. The facial features have long ago worn away and the body is very crudely constructed. Clothing consists of cotton panties, two petticoats, and a tan silk dress gathered at the waist, all handmade, of course. This old doll belonged to the family of Mary Grimes, a registered nurse of Philadelphia, Pennsylvania. She has traced the doll through her family to colonial times. (Photograph and story courtesy Jane E. Sheetz, the present custodian of the doll)

Margo, 7½″. Another very old doll with a tale to tell, c. 1830-1840. Margo and her clothing are completely handmade. The body is of muslin stuffed with sawdust. She has no wig, only a net covering of some sort, pinned to her head. Her eyes are embroidered blue and her mouth is a straight pink embroidered line. Eyebrows are arched stitches and the nose is needle-sculptured. Margo wears sewn-on, brown chintz shoes and her feet are pointed "north and south," a designation used by doll collectors to indicate that the feet point left and right, rather than in a normal position. She wears a white, high-neck blouse-slip, a half-slip or petticoat, and a gathered, green chintz skirt. The doll was purchased by its present owner in Massachusetts in 1975. Pinned to the doll was an old slip of paper with the following: "Margo's great-grandmother's home-made doll, c. 1830-40." (Photograph and story courtesy Jane E. Sheetz)

227

8-3 **Lady Doll, 16½″.** This remarkable primitive, c. 1850, is completely handmade of muslin with features embroidered in a solemn expression. The hair is of black sateen, deftly fashioned to simulate waves, with small rolls of the same fabric coiled on the back of the head to make a bun. Double thread drawn from the back bun forward indicates the part. The feet are simple, pointed shapes covered with the same sort of black fabric used for the hair to indicate either shoes or stockings. The clothing is all original. The dress, of old printed wool challis, now has a few moth holes in back, or perhaps, as her present owner has said, her chair is uncomfortable and she has been squirming about a bit during her 132 years. (The chair and the rug came with the doll.) The apron and one of the petticoats are made of white lawn-type material with hand-crocheted lace across the bottom. The second petticoat is of hand-woven wool flannel with hand-crocheted red lace edging. Pantalettes are of the same material as the apron and first petticoat, trimmed with a commercially made lace. Her cap was fashioned from a piece of old lace net and her shawl is a square of fabric cut from an ancient shawl. The owner admits she is puzzled about the shoes. They are apparently commercially made and not as old as the rest of the doll. They are high-topped, laced, with a small heel, and appear to be made of a compressed-paper material, imitating leather. All the clothing is hand-stitched. The chair and rug are also handmade. A very old tag on one of the petticoats reads: *Made in San Bernardino, 1850.* The doll belonged to a woman who had lived in San Bernardino, California, most of her life. It had been made for her by her mother when she was a small child and had evidently been lovingly cared for. A collector in Pasadena either obtained the doll from the original owner late in her life or from her estate. The grandmother of the present owner bought the doll from the Pasadena collector and passed it along to her daughter who eventually gave it to her daughter, the present owner. It is not often that an old doll can be traced this closely, albeit the names of the first two owners are apparently not available. Even so, this wonderful old doll seems to have a fairly sound pedigree, and it may be of interest to note that there is another young collector coming along. The present owner's young daughter has shown a bit of interest in dolls and promises to continue the tradition. (Photographs and story courtesy Mrs. Russell Holdren and Mrs. Shelby Mongeon)

8-3

8-3

8-3

8-4

8-5

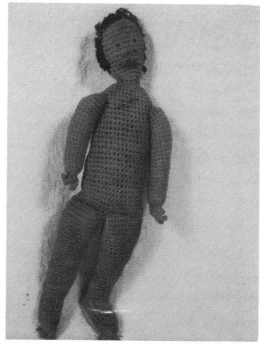

8-4   **Black Woman, 7½".** This small cloth doll has felt hands, fringed to simulate fingers. The features are embroidered and the hair is of black, curled yarn. She wears a gray dress, lace-trimmed apron, and a shawl. Her black shoes sport pink tassels. Nothing else is known about her history, c. 1900. (Mason collection)

8-5   **Crocheted Black Doll, 9½".** Made of single crochet stitch, stuffed with cotton, embroidered features. This old doll, c. 1900, gives mute testimony to the skills of her creator. The doll was dressed in a pair of homemade overalls with Lee trademark buttons when acquired by its present owner, so it must have played a male role at one time in its career. (Mason collection)

8-6   **Helga, 24″.** Helga is an enigma. Is she or isn't she pregnant? Perhaps she is just a little round in the tummy. Whether or not she is in the family way, Helga is definitely a character doll, one collectors dream of finding. Helga has curly brown mohair hair just on the edge of her bonnet. Her blue eyes are painted, as are the brows, in a rather strange shape. Her enigmatic smile is also painted and her cloth body is stuffed with straw or excelsior or some other similar material. She has long, skinny limbs and her fingers, which have pink nails, are wired. Helga was purchased in 1973 by her present owner at the Mary Merritt Doll Museum. The buyer was told the doll dated to 1927. The mark (Fig. 8-1) is somewhat dim. She is beautifully costumed. Her elegant undies consist of white cotton, kneelength drawers shaped to accommodate her delicate condition, whatever that might be, and a white cotton half-slip. On the top, she has a piece of lace, stuffed with cotton, sewn right to the body to give her a bosom. Her dress is burnt-orange, satin-back crepe with long, full sleeves, trimmed with fancy brown braid. There is a pale orange, ruffled ribbon at the neck, brown velvet bows at the neck and waist, brown buttons, white lace ruffle under the sleeves, and black lace half-mitts. The tan cloth shoes, with sharply pointed black toes and black side trim, are finished off with black rosettes. Her hat is brown straw with a high crown and fairly wide brim that turns up in front. A black veil and tan and brown feathers finish the effect. The short cape is trimmed with orange wool fringe, brown braid, and brown silk tassels. Altogether an enchanting ensemble and a highly desirable doll. (Sheetz collection. Photographs courtesy the collector)

8-6

8-6

Fig. 8-1

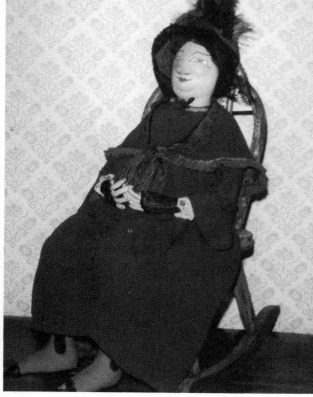

8-6

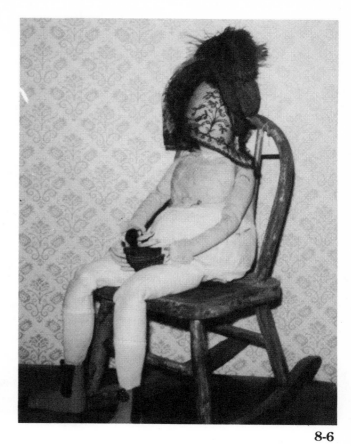

8-6

8-7

8-7   **Chain Gang, 10″.** This pre-1939 black man has
an all-cloth body, embroidered features, floss hair,
and original cotton clothing. Janet Johl shows one
of these dolls in her early work (*The Fascinating
Story of Dolls,* 1941), but lists no origin for the doll.
Her reference is an article, "Dolls from the Land of
Cotton," which appeared in the July 1939 issue of
The Lutheran Boys and Girls Magazine. The doll
shown in Johl's book was from her own collection.
(Gibbins collection)

8-8   **Ol' Cowhand, 15″.** This fellow has been carefully crafted with attention to detail in an effort to convey his character. Head is silk stocking with needle-sculptured features that are then painted. His body is of pink sateen, his hair is yellow yarn, and his fringed breeches are of felt. He also wears a cotton shirt and tie, but his ten-gallon hat, if he ever had one, is nowhere to be found. Note that his shirt has a shell pocket. This type of doll is often difficult to date. I hope someone will recognize this fellow and report his pedigree. (Mason collection)

8-9   **Colonial Lady, 20″.** Apparently constructed using one of the commercial patterns available in the 1940s, possibly one of the newspaper patterns (see chapter 12). She is all-cotton, as are her clothes, and completely handmade, except that the long seams were stitched on a sewing machine, of course. (Haag collection)

8-8

8-8

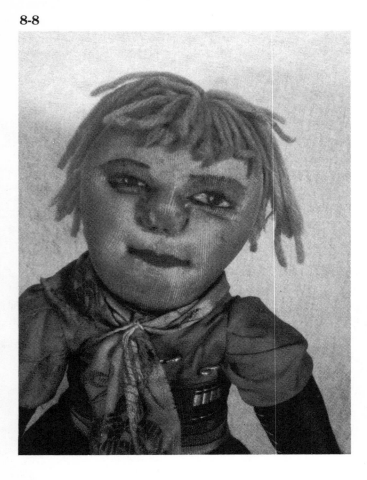

8-9

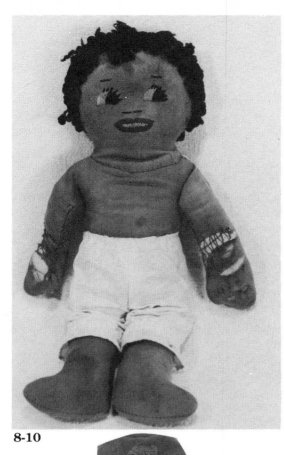

8-10

8-11

8-10 **Black Child, 19½″.** Dark brown cotton, embroidered features, floss hair. This child is of uncertain date. The mouth is embroidered with very bright red floss. The teeth and whites of the eyes are also stitched. Note that the head was constructed separately, then apparently applied to the body after both pieces were stuffed. The cotton pantalettes are all that remain of what may have been a Raggedy-type costume. (Author's collection)

8-11 **WAC, 20″.** This doll, c. World War II, is meticulously sewn from a commercial pattern, and beautifully representative of the military uniform dolls made during the period. Many young women became members of the Women's Army Corps and served honorably and well throughout the war. Too often, they did not receive the respect and honor they deserved. This doll has embroidered features, yellow yarn hair, an all-cloth body, and is unmarked. Her uniform is of army twill and the buttons are regulation GI. Gloves, shoulder bag, and shoes are all of leather. The temptation to speculate is too great for me to resist. Was this doll made by a returning service woman? Did she use parts of her uniform to create this doll as a memento of her service days? Or was it sewn for a younger girl by her service woman mother? Or was it made as a fund-raiser? There were many such events in those days, so it would be possible that one or more dolls may have been made for a charity bazaar. However, the workmanship speaks otherwise, for it seems that much care went into what was to be a very special doll. We can only wonder. (Gibbins collection)

8-12   **Navajo Woman, 12″.** This 1940 doll, purchased on a wedding trip somewhere between Albuquerque and Santa Fe, New Mexico, is an example of handmade dolls that are commercial. These beautifully made little dolls were available all over southwestern United States, at restaurants and train stations, souvenir shops and other locations. They were very popular as quality souvenirs of lovingly remembered journeys. The doll shown has an all-cloth body, hand-painted features, a mohair wig, and stitch-sculptured fingers. She wears a traditional red velvet shirt, "silver" belt and buttons, "turquoise" bead necklace and earrings, a wide, gathered skirt, and a faint, enigmatic smile. (Battagler collection)

8-13   **Mexican Man and Woman with Children.** The adults are 16″, c. 1941. These handmade, all-cloth dolls have deeply molded mask faces that have been hand painted. Eyes are inset glass beads with painted pupils. Fingers and toes are stitched. Bodies are stuffed cotton over wire armatures. The dolls were made completely by hand for the tourist trade. Detail is excellent. (Kirtley collection)

8-12

8-13

8-13

234

8-14

8-16

8-15

8-14   **Hula Girl, 13½″.** Brought from Honolulu, Hawaii, in 1945. A handmade doll sold commercially as a souvenir, this charming miss strangely has no mouth, although her nose is defined with painted dots as well as slight padding. Eyes are also painted. Fingers are stitch-indicated. She wears the typical Island outfit of brightly colored cotton topped off with a grass skirt. (Battagler collection)

8-15   **Black Mammy, 12″.** Purchased in New Orleans in 1946. Firmly stuffed black cloth, painted features, a cotton bole for hair, and appropriately dressed in bright colors. An eye-catching addition to any cloth doll collection. A fond remembrance of another vacation trip. (Battagler collection)

8-16   **Topsy and Her Dolly, 31″.** This 1950s all-cloth doll has felt features sewn on, is jointed at shoulders and hips, wears a cotton dress, and has her own little rag baby. Her yarn hair is done up in small pigtails all over her head. She just fits the child-size rocking chair in which she poses. Probably made from a commercial pattern such as those found in the newspapers. (Kirtley collection)

8-17 **Guatemalan Weaver Woman, 5″ (seated).**
Doll, 1970s, and setting are completely handmade by Guatemalan craftspersons using hand-woven cloth. Sticks wound with dyed yarns and swatches of cloth make an authentic display of the primitive methods employed by these weavers. The dolls are sold by a collector to help finance a medical mission in Guatemala. (Dr. J. E. Kendrick collection)

8-18 **Polly Heckewelder, the Moravian Doll, 16″.**
All handmade, created by the older Moravian Sisters, members of the Ladies' Sewing Society of Central Moravian Church, Bethlehem, Pennsylvania. The dolls are dressed as young girls of about 1872, which is the year these dolls were first made. Each doll carries a small handbag that has a copy of Polly Heckewelder's story. Polly is a member of that elite group, the fund-raiser dolls. A 1972 article by the Reverend E. Michel appearing in *The North American Moravian* periodical revealed this interesting history. Polly Heckewelder was the daughter of John Gottlieb Ernestus Heckewelder, born 1743, in Bedford, England. He came to this country as a young boy. In later years he was a missionary to the Delaware Indians along with David Zeisberger. Polly was born to John Heckewelder and his missionary wife in the Territory of Ohio in 1781. She is believed to be the first white girl born in that region. Polly's father became a noted historian of American Indians with several books on the subject to his credit. The Ladies' Sewing Society was formed in 1861 to do war work during the Civil War as the Soldier's Relief Society. After the war, work focused on former slaves and was renamed the Freedman's Aid Society. In 1869, it was again renamed and carries the same name today, the Ladies' Sewing Society. The first Polly Heckewelder dolls were made in 1872. Thousands have been made and sold since. Proceeds have gone to many worthy causes, especially to the assistance of Moravian ministers. Polly Heckewelder dolls are no longer made by the members of Central Church's Society. Many of the members find that the fine sewing is too much of a strain on their eyes. The finer fabrics that have always been used are becoming more difficult to obtain, and the number of Society members is too few to keep up with the demand. Thus, another lovely doll is no longer available. Conversely, those that were made over the years have attained an enhanced collector's value as a result of the discontinuation of the project. The Polly Heck e - welder dolls from Central Church were always dressed in pink and white or blue and white checked gingham. All the clothing has buttons and buttonholes so the doll could be dressed and undressed easily. Faces were handpainted and

8-17

8-18

when soiled could be replaced. (What a thought!) The dolls were made with great care and the tiniest, most even stitches were used in all the clothing. Fortunate is the collector who owns a Polly Heckewelder doll. Note: Other Polly dolls are made by other Moravian churches. It is only the Central Church's Polly that has been discontinued. (Story and photograph courtesy Marion Weaver)

8-19

8-20

8-21

8-19   **Pioneer Woman, Victoria, 20½″.** Purchased in Branson, Missouri. A sweet, embroidered smile and side-glancing eyes, gray yarn hair in a bun, calico print dress, starchy white apron, red felt boots — all beautifully crafted. This doll was made by Wilma Hamilton, whose tag is attached to the doll's wrist: **Ozark Made/From the Sewing Room/of/Wilma Hamilton/in Missouri.** The inside of the tag reads: **Hi, I'm Victoria/Oct. 1976/Branson, Mo.** This 1976 doll is another example of a highly desirable contemporary collectible that is also handmade and commercial. (Author's collection)

8-20   **Ozark Woman, 11″.** All cloth, painted and stitched features, stitched fingers and toes, wisp of gray mohair wig, removable clothes. Purchased in the Missouri Ozarks about 1947. (Author's collection. Courtesy Gwen Bower)

8-21   **Black Child, 18″.** Handmade of black cotton sateen, black yarn pigtails, painted features, original pink and white checked gingham sunsuit, c. 1930s. (Rogers collection)

8-22   **Mary and Laura, 15½″.** Little House on the Prairie dolls created by Judy Rankine for The Enchanted Doll House. Illustration from the catalog. All cloth, dressed in assorted calico clothes. (Courtesy The Enchanted Doll House)

8-22

9 Affiliated Cloth Doll Artists

Play Doll or Art Doll

How does one define an art doll as opposed to a play doll? Very simple, you say? Perhaps. And then, again, perhaps not so simple. Some of the most successful, most commercial of the cloth dolls we know are also among the most artistically conceived and executed examples of the genré.

A definition could be made that would place all commercially produced dolls in the play doll category, thus relegating handmade dolls to the art doll classification. But then, would the Kruse dolls, the Lencis, or the Sashas be correctly ordered? They were certainly intended as play dolls and were commercially produced. Yet few would argue the fact they are all ranked high artistically. Conversely, all handmade dolls are not of a quality easily defined as artistic.

The point of all this is: There is a line beyond which any effort to classify such dolls fails, where the lines blur. For purposes of definition in this book, I have arbitrarily chosen to define art dolls as those created by an individual dollmaker who makes either original one-of-a-kind dolls or original dolls in a limited series.

Furthermore, such working artists have again been divided into two subclasses. Those whose work has been recognized by any of the three major doll artists' associations (The International Dollmakers Association, the Original Doll Artists Council of America, the National Institute of American Doll Artists) have been included in one chapter. Other doll artists/dollmakers are grouped in a separate chapter. No doubt some of these latter eventually will be recognized by one of the organizations. However, for now, they are unaffiliated.

American Artists

Of all the doll artists at work today, relatively few have chosen fabric as their medium. The majority prefer high-fire porcelain, or bisque, as it is usually called in collector circles. Since most doll artists are creating limited editions in series rather than one-of-a-kind dolls, porcelain is the likely choice of medium.

Once created in clay, a head may be duplicated in porcelain as often as desired, or to an agreed-upon, limited-edition quantity. Such dolls, because of their lifelike coloring and form and scarcity, are extremely popular with collectors. There are many artists at work in the medium today.

Struggling to create character and detail in a one-of-a-kind doll for a very low profit margin often is impractical, particularly for those who seek to support themselves with their art. The prospect of profit, that naughty word of the art world, is often a major determinant in the choice of porcelain as medium.

A resurgence in consideration of the cloth doll as art form seems to have been generated in the early 1970s as preparations for the celebration of this country's 200th anniversary got under way. Time after time, during interviews with artists, dates in that period were given as a turning point in the career of an artist, a turning point that led to a deeper understanding and appreciation of the rag doll as art.

In the latter half of that decade, still other artists were drawn to the medium and began to express through their dolls their special vision. Further influence came from the handcraft revival that has been directly attributed to the Bicentennial celebration. Personally, I feel the continuing strength of the movement owes its momentum to those who are a part of it. The Bicentennial was a pebble dropped into a special pool. It is to be hoped the ever-widening ripples will be felt and seen in our society for many years to come.

The artists and designers mentioned in this book are representative of the larger number that time and space prohibit including. Whether or not an individual is listed here is in no way to be considered an evaluation of the comparative merit of that person's work. An author could never hope to review the work of every cloth doll artist in a single volume.

It is hoped that by reading about these artists and seeing photographs of their work, the reader will be inspired and encouraged to create his or her own original dolls.

There are several national organizations of dollmakers in the United States. On the rolls of these associations are many talented, hard-working, original doll artists. As indicated previously, only a small percentage of these artists work in cloth.

Among the membership of the National Institute of American Doll Artists (NIADA) are listed several artists who work in cloth. Prominent is the late Dorothy Heizer, as well as Gwen Flather, Betty "Wee" Paulson, Madeline Saucier, Bernard Ravca, Frances Ravca, France Rommel, and Jacques Rommel. While the handling of material and their styles of execution are different, all of these artists share a common medium—cloth of one sort or another.

Dorothy Heizer's dolls are known to most collectors as the epitome of excellence, artistically as well as structurally. Her forté was her portraits of famous people taken from paintings. Her figures are well balanced and believable representations of the human form — all in needle-sculptured cloth.

Her "Dolls That Are People" are illustrated here in black and white. An article from the November 1925 issue of *Woman's Home Companion,* written by Lucille Quarry, is repeated here in its entirety for its historical value as well as the interesting insights offered concerning the materials and techniques employed by the artist:

There were dolls to be dressed for the fair, and dolls one bought were stupidly alike.

"Why not make a rag doll, Mother?" said Dotty — and that was how it all began.

"Of course that first doll was very crude," said Mrs. Heizer, smiling. "It had a limp body, a big head and a flat painted face, but the children liked it and I made more, for my own children and for others. Then it occurred to me to apply my knowledge of anatomy to the making of the dolls and give them correctly shaped bodies — I use the Greek proportions — and to study the dress of different periods that their costumes might have added interest."

And the dolls that come from Mrs. Heizer's workshop to-day are slim, exquisite perfection. The little faces are modeled into delicate features — tip-tilted noses, rosebud mouths, softly shaded eyes. The small proud heads, the slender, softly rounded figures, the long, graceful legs and slim ankles, create a doll that, even before it is dressed, is a lovely thing.

How They Are Made

The frame for the body is of copper wire, many strands of it, doubled and redoubled, with proper joints made at elbow and wrist and knee and ankle, so that the doll can be stood in any position. This is padded with wadding and then covered with cotton. Over this goes flesh-colored Canton crepe, cut carefully to pattern, and then the face is "made up." Over the soft silk of the body goes the most frivolous of lingerie, usually net, because the graceful effect of the finished doll must not be marred by using more bulky materials than are absolutely necessary. Then out of boxes of silks and velvets and laces, of old-fashioned prints and sheer organdies, of bits of net and chiffon and crepe, the clothes themselves are made.

Some of the dolls are dressed in the vogue of to-day. They fairly swagger, so smart are their ensemble costumes, their tiny felt hats, their fringe-tongued pumps.

Then there are the costume dolls, of which the Spanish beauty on the opposite page is perhaps the loveliest. Her dress is of black satin, with godets of purple. Over this is fine black lace, and she wears a flame-colored shawl with long silken fringe. Her feet are encased in dainty high-heeled slippers, and from her black hair rises a comb which was cut out of paper, tinted and dipped in paraffin to give it the appearance of carved ivory.

The belle of a century ago, who stands beside the flapper of to-day, is dressed in lavender taffeta shot with silver. There is nothing new in fashion, Mrs. Heizer says, and sometime between 1830 and 1840 the young girls abandoned the skirts that swept the floor for shorter ones. It is a flapper of that day, whose costume is copied from an undated portrait, who poses demurely beside Miss 1925. It is really surprising how little we know of the dress of the very young girl of that day. From childhood she suddenly attained womanhood and adopted grown-up styles. There is little in old fashion prints for the *jeune fille*.

The woman in the picture below this one, in the quaint yellow gown, is a copy of an old Godey print of 1845, even to the little black horsehair bonnet with its wreath of flowers. The gentleman upon whose arm she leans is of a little later date, about 1860. He is not, as one might at first suppose, wearing frock coat and top hat for a Sunday call, but is wearing the correct riding habit of a horseman of that day. That is why one hand holds a riding crop.

Of the three children at the bottom of the page, the one in the center belongs to the period of 1840. Fashions for children of that time are also difficult to find, but the little green dress is a copy of one that belonged to a small ancestor of the doll's creator. The full scalloped dress and the pantalettes are of organdie. The modern child in the smart yellow costume carries one of the floppy clown dolls which is a miniature of the harlequins that are also made by Mrs. Heizer's clever fingers.

The slim-waisted French dolls at the left of the page are quaint characterizations of the beaux and belles of Louis XV's day. Their bodies are simply wire frames covered with silk tubing, and this type of doll was inspired partly by Kay Nielsen's exquisite illustrations for "The Twelve Dancing Princesses," and partly by Mrs. Heizer's youngest son's request for a valentine that would be "just a heart with arms and legs." The valentine had a heart-shaped face, and was dressed in crimson satin and lace ruffles, but there was something so expressive in the wasp-waisted figure with his long thin legs that the idea was developed into the amusing dolls shown here.

No photographs or description, however, can begin to convey an idea of the individuality, the personality, of these charming little figures. Mrs. Heizer is an artist, and she gives each one so much more than the ordinary doll face that they remain in the memory of those who see them as real people.

The dolls were made at first, as has been said, for fairs and bazaars. Some of them went to Philadelphia and attracted there the attention of the Arts and Crafts Society, who recognized the value of the dolls as exponents of by-gone and present-day fashions. The Arts and Crafts Society arranged an exhibition of the dolls last December and sixteen of them were shown and eagerly purchased. One, a modern flapper with a wardrobe trunk made to scale and filled with lingerie and frocks, brought the highest price ever paid for one of the dolls — one hundred and twenty-five dollars. People were eager to buy the dolls for Christmas presents to children and Mrs. Heizer was besieged with requests. She agreed to fill a few orders, but as it takes two or three days to make and dress a doll, and as the work is done by herself alone in the studio-workshop in her house, the number of children who could have a real

Fig. 9-1

Dolls That Are People
Created by DOROTHY W. HEIZER

PERFECTLY made in miniature, each one of these little character dolls is an exquisite work of art—the Spanish dancer in black lace with her gay shawl, the trio of elegant and frivolous courtiers out of a French history book, the old-fashioned lovers, the flappers of modern and Civil War times, the little girls of to-day and yesterday. Not only in costume but also in modeling, pose and expression they are remarkably true to life.

The whole story about them and their interesting originator will be found on the opposite page.

PHOTOGRAPHS IN
COLOR BY J. W. ALLISON

Heizer doll on their Christmas tree was decidedly limited. Others, long past the age of dolls, bought them for the decorative value they have in a room. And still a third use that the dolls found was in advertising, for a big lighting concern in the Middle West wanted a number of them for show windows.

The Dolls and the Stage

Last February the Art Alliance of Philadelphia realized the dramatic value of the dolls and asked Mrs. Heizer to create the dolls for a scene in a play. Accordingly she set to work on the characters in Cinderella, and dressed them for the scene in which the slipper is being tried on the two ugly sisters and Cinderella. The prince wore a satin costume made from brocade that was ivory with age, and Cinderella was in gray, with holes burned here and there in her shabby dress. When the little stage was set, a pompous footman was in the act of trying the slipper on Cinderella's foot.

Both Mr. and Mrs. Heizer believe that all children pass through an age when they love to create, to make things with their hands, and if the proper guidance is given them at this time natural gifts may be developed into real and charming ability. It is important, of course, to show just the right amount of interest in what the child attempts — too much will make him self-conscious and destroy his originality, and too little make him depreciate his own talents.

It is interesting in connection with this to know that the Art Alliance had also an exhibit of dolls made of wire and wool by Mrs. Heizer's sixteen-year-old daughter. These little "woolies," as she calls them, represented figures from fairy tales.

Gwen Flather, who like Heizer was a charter member of NIADA, also works in cloth to needle-sculpture marvelous portraits and original ideas, preferring the older faces that show a strong sense of humor. Madeline Saucier's dolls are of felt, hardened by a special process. Bernard and Frances Ravca both have worked in fabric, each in a unique style. Frances also needle-sculptures her remarkable dolls whose molded heads are based on fabric. Jacques and France Rommel work together on their sculptured fabric dolls built on armature bodies. Their dolls are unique for the lack of defined features, elegantly posed figures, and rich costuming.

Lewis Sorenson, although best known for his wax dolls, created a number of all-cloth dolls in the 1930s. There were little girls, fashionable ladies in both modern and period costumes, sailor boys, flappers, and college girls.

Carol Bowling, also a NIADA member, uses a molded cellulose mâché support for the silklike, knitted synthetic stretch fabric on which she paints her lifelike faces. The bodies of her child dolls are built of foam and fabric over armatures. Carol's earlier dolls were much less sophisticated, stuffed toddlers.

Only a few artists of the Original Doll Artists Council of America (ODACA) work in cloth. Many of them, however, have ventured into the field at one time or another. Phyllis Wright

created on commission a very special doll designed to be used as therapy by a stroke victim. Others admit to beginning their dollmaking careers by making soft dolls. A few have stayed in the medium with great success.

Elizabeth Fahr, an ODACA member, molds her Bettina dolls of felt over an original, sculptured clay model. Virginia Baldwin glazes her needle-sculptured faces with a special finish she invented, in an effort to add permanence to her needlework. Beverly Port's dolls have an old-fashioned look of individually crafted dolls.

The International Doll Makers Association (IDMA) also has several cloth doll artists in its ranks. Eleanor Todd specializes in dolls whose designs are flavored with the history of her hometown of New Orleans. Win Ann Winkler likes to try a variety of fabrics in the production of her dolls, including burlap. Cloth dolls and variety, the two terms seem to go hand in hand.

Virginia "Ginna" Baldwin

ODACA
Ginna Grannie's Nook and Cranny™

Ginna Baldwin made her first doll, a 6″ Chinaman, of sewing scraps found in her mother's workbasket. That was when she was only seven years old, and she has been making dolls ever since, using the sewing machine since she was eight. Why does she make dolls? Let her tell it in her own words:

> I was born with a compulsion to make dolls. They are fantasies and reflections of the mind. Dolls are enjoyable for everyone, all ages. Humans have a complex, mysterious process called imagination (that the dolls appeal to). Even though I studied art for fourteen years, loved painting portraits, and taught oil painting for five years, the making of the dolls is the best of all. To form the dolls in 3-D and design the clothes from fantasies and reflections of the mind is *it* for me.

Ginna began making her nylon knit dolls in 1975 while still teaching. She has now "retired" to an active dollmaking business. She conceives the idea, draws the patterns for dolls, clothing, and all accessories, including most of the leather shoes. Her husband helps her build the props and accessories.

Her needle-sculptured dolls are unique in that the faces are finished with a special glaze developed by Ginna especially for the purpose. Made of a blend of resins, petrol distillates, an original art medium, and a permanent nongloss finish, this treatment adds permanence to the finished needlework. Always she strives for realism.

Ginna uses a variety of techniques and materials to achieve the desired results with her dolls. Some have clay joints. The cloth dolls (she also works in polyform and porcelain) have padded wire armatures and the bodies are stuffed with polyurethane. She continually experiments with the jointing of the dolls, seeking to achieve more realistic stance and movement. Some heads turn in plastic sockets. Hair is mohair or fake fur, although she has used human hair on occasion. Ginna's dolls are copyrighted, numbered and labeled on the body, and have plastic trademark hangtags in full view.

When Ginna's children were small and in school, she decided what she really wanted was an art education. She studied with some of the best teachers in the country and lists Dan Toigo, Leslie B. DeMille, Darwin Duncan, and B. McGurin among her instructors. She has recently started working in clay and porcelain and plans to duplicate all her people figures including the soft ones, so they can be made in the hard mediums.

Her portrait training and painting experience show in the wide range of characters she has created with this three-dimensional medium. There are pirates, royalty, old grannies, an organ grinder, a jolly old fellow reminiscent of Santa, yet thoroughly believable as Grandpa Love, and a wonderful old black man, Ginna's rendition of Uncle Remus. Humor and understanding meld in the faces of Ginna Baldwin's dolls. It is as if they are saying to the viewer, "Well, here we are. We're just human, you know; not perfect, but we can laugh at our own condition, and enjoy life just the same."

Ginna's dolls have received many awards at UFDC conventions, doll shows, and fairs, with many first prize ribbons. Her dolls have also been shown on television several times. She is a member of ODACA and UFDC.

9VB-1

9VB-2

| 9VB-1 | **Grandpa Love, 23″ (17″ seated).** Seated on a milk stool, holding basket of vegetables. Typical of the realism Ginna Baldwin strives to achieve. Doll was made in 1979. (Photograph courtesy the artist) |
| 9VB-2 | **Queen Elizabeth I, 26″.** Shows Ginna's talent for detail. Some trims on this doll are c. 1870. Six stones used in the jewels are from the remains of a sunken galleon of the 1500s. This doll is dated 1980. (Photograph courtesy the artist) |

9VB-3 **Uncle Remus, 21″.** Wears a pinkish cotton shirt, dark green pants, gray felt hat, and brown leather shoes. His cane is hand-carved and his rocking chair was made just for him. A 1982 doll. (Photograph courtesy the artist)

9VB-4 **Grandma, 21″ (15″ seated).** Looks as though she is dressed up, ready for market. Dated 1977. (Photograph courtesy the artist)

9VB-4

9VB-3

Elizabeth Fahr

ODACA
Bettina's Doll Designs

Elizabeth Fahr has been creating cloth doll patterns since 1976 and now finds herself almost too busy to add any new designs to her line. Not only does she make her dolls for sale, she also teaches dollmaking classes at a local doll shop. Ultimately, she plans to phase out her pattern business and apply her talents only to dollmaking. She is also planning a book to help teach her methods, which she calls "home grown."

The heads of the felt Bettina dolls are molded over an original, sculpted clay head. No machinery or glue is used in the processing so the felt retains a soft texture and appearance. When the clay models are removed, the faces are hand painted, with particular attention to the eyes. Thus, each doll acquires its own unique expression and personality. No two ever look precisely the same.

Bodies are sturdily constructed and firmly stuffed. They have jointed limbs and swivel heads. The 15″ dolls have separate, articulated fingers, while fingers on the 12″ dolls are stitched, with separate thumb. Wigs are of human hair and the costumes are carefully sewn, often with touches of embroidery or hand painting. Each doll is marked on the sole of one foot with the Bettina logo (a doll in a square) and is numbered, dated, and signed. Fahr makes only ten of each model. The Collection I dolls are sold out, and she is currently working on her Collection II, which will include two boys.

Elizabeth does all the designing, molding, and other steps involved in the process, but admits to some help with the sewing. She has taken art classes in addition to her studies at the University of California, Los Angeles, but recommends practice as the best teacher. "I can never emphasize that enough," she says. Fahr is a member of ODACA and the Tucson Dollmaker Guild.

"All of these statistics seem so unfeeling," says Elizabeth. "The real truth is: I'm having a wonderful time!"

Many dollmakers have expressed similar feelings about their work and seem to be unusually happy in their chosen field. Fortunate, indeed, is the person who is doing something he or she likes. Dollmakers are lucky people, say many doll artists, because theirs is the rare situation of being able to create something new and different, something that is appreciated by collectors, and yet there is always the challenge of the next idea, the next project. So it is with Elizabeth Fahr and her peers.

9EF-1   **Theresa, 15″.** Molded felt, fully jointed with swivel head, painted features (brown eyes), human hair wig. Dressed in lavender print, full petticoat, white stockings, and handmade shoes. (Photograph courtesy the artist)

9EF-2   **Sally, 12″.** Same construction as Theresa, blue eyes, blue calico dress with hand-painted tulips on cotton organdy pinafore. Bear is Timmy, a 4″ fully jointed, handmade toy accessory. (Photograph courtesy the artist)

9EF-1

9EF-2

9EF-3 Kevin, 12″. Brown-eyed boy with red-brown hair. Has a sister named Kathleen who is dressed in coordinating outfit. Bettina dolls are produced in a series of ten each. (Photograph courtesy the artist)

9EF-4 The De Grazia Dolls, Flower Girl, Angel, and Flower Boy, 10½″. Based on the Indian children drawn and painted by internationally known Southwestern artist, Ted De Grazia. These characters have appeared on greeting cards, plates, jewelry, and many other collectibles. The exclusive Bettina patterns are authorized renditions of these famous children. (Photograph courtesy the artist)

9EF-3

Beverly Port

ODACA
Old-Fashioned Dolls

Ever since the Christmas she was eleven years old, Beverly Port has been making dolls. Her first dolls, made from old pillowcases, were under the tree that year, gifts from Santa Claus for Beverly's younger sisters. The features were drawn with crayons and the wigs were of yarn. "Those dolls were loved to pieces," remembers Beverly. She has been making dolls as an art form since 1969.

Beverly's dolls range in size from 3″ to 48″. She prefers cotton fabrics and acrylic paints, although she has employed wools in the costuming of some of her hard dolls. All her dolls are marked with the copyright circle, her name, and the date of completion. A hangtag bears the words: BEVERLY PORT ORIGINALS.

Port's cloth dolls are an attempt to retain the soft body and cuddly look and feel of the traditional rag doll in an art form. Separate thumbs, stitched fingers, reinforced necks, and hand-painted faces in permanent colors are all hallmarks of her work. No two dolls are exactly alike, of course, since each is an individually crafted work. All patterns for her dolls and their clothing are original and made by Beverly who admits she hopes to have help with the sewing in the future. Port works in other

9EF-4

mediums, including wax and bisque. However, the cloth dolls are "primary figures," since no molds are used.

Her subjects include Granny and Her Bible, needle-sculptured in stockinette; Jenny and Her Dolly, acrylic on cotton with hand-painted faces; La Fleur, acrylic on cotton with hand-painted face, felt body, and flower petals around the face; and Mandy, a black child with curly fur wig, acrylic on cotton with hand-painted face.

All of Port's dolls, regardless of the material used, are limited editions, ranging from ten to one hundred. Special-order dolls are produced as one-of-a-kind works. She dresses every doll sold because she feels the costume is an integral part of the design and character. She admits to spending hours shopping for the right fabric to complete her vision of a particular doll. Using fabric scraps, she constructs the costume, working to assure proper fit and proportion. Only when she is completely satisfied with the model costume does she cut the fabric from which the actual costume will be fashioned.

Art and design have been a lifelong interest and Port majored in art at Olympic College where she designed costumes for a college musical review. She is a member of ODACA, UFDC, and NAME. Her dolls are sold by special order only and since she has a long waiting list, she no longer takes deposits, preferring instead to work at her own pace without the stress of meeting deadlines.

9BP-1

9BP-1   **Jenny and Her Dolly, 18″.** By Beverly Port. This limited edition child took first place in the Cloth Section at the IDMA convention at Reno in 1974. It also won a third place ribbon at the UFDC Region 2 Meeting in 1975 and Best of Class and First Runner-up to the Gold Cup. (Photograph courtesy the artist)

9BP-2   **Meribeth and Her Teddy Bear, 22″.** A limited edition in Port's Old-Fashioned Series. Hand-painted face with slight smile. Doll was featured on the cover of *Bambini* doll magazine, April 1979. Won honorable mention award at UFDC National Convention in 1975. (Photograph courtesy the artist)

9BP-2

9BP-3 **Meribeth.** A closeup. Dress and bonnet have navy background with rose-colored flowers predominating. Black leather boots with rose-colored buttons; and tassels providing a matching note. (Photograph courtesy the artist)

9BP-4 **Merilee and Her Teddy Bear, 24″.** The older, taller sister of Meribeth. Made especially as a helper for the UFDC Region I Meeting in 1975. All dolls are copyrighted by Beverly Port. (Photograph courtesy the artist)

9BP-3

9BP-4

Phyllis Wright
ODACA

Phyllis Wright is represented in this work by only one cloth doll, since she ordinarily works in other mediums. The cloth doll shown was created for a convalescent stroke victim who needed to relearn the simple acts of dressing and undressing. The resultant doll is a work of art in its intricate seaming and exquisitely painted features as well as its carefully planned clothing.

Wright, a New Jersey born artist, studied art at Blackstone College in Virginia where she majored in fine arts and portraiture. This was followed by work in commercial art at Pratt Institute in Brooklyn. She has taught art at Harbour Country Day School in St. James, but now directs her energies to the House of Wright, a family-operated business that creates and markets original, limited edition dolls and a series of historical and military people figures. Also in the business are two sons.

Phyllis Wright is a member of the Lords and Ladies of New England Doll Club, UFDC, and a member and past-president of the Original Doll Artists Council of America. She has participated in shows and exhibitions throughout the United States.

248

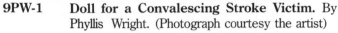

9PW-1 **Doll for a Convalescing Stroke Victim.** By Phyllis Wright. (Photograph courtesy the artist)

9EHT-1

Eleanor H. Todd

IDMA
Todd Dolls

Eleanor Todd's hometown lends special flavor to many of her dolls, for Eleanor lives and works in colorful New Orleans, Louisiana. It is almost to be expected that the history and people of that intriguing city should influence her work. Eleanor numbers among her dolls Mandy, a 10″ pickaninny, Marie Laveau, voodoo queen of New Orleans, Jean Lafitte, pirate hero of the city, an Ursiline nun, and a Casquette girl, plus many others.

Eleanor began making dolls shortly after World War II. She had been a member of the Women's Army Corps where she met the man who became her husband in 1946. She "caught the doll bug," as she says, in 1947 when she saw a display of Bernard Ravca's Real People at a department store. She says she simply "fell in love with them," but could not afford to buy one at the time. The next best thing, she decided, was to try to make a doll of her own. A trip to the public library yielded Edith Ackley's *Dolls to Make For Fun and Profit.*

9EHT-2

9EHT-1 **Casquette Girl, 10″.** By Eleanor Todd. Doll holds casquette or suitcase containing her dowry from King of France. (Photograph courtesy the artist)

9EHT-2 **Shirley Temple, 14″.** Face hand painted in acrylics. (Photograph courtesy the artist)

"A career was born," says Eleanor. "My first rag doll's body was made from my own discarded khaki army underwear. I still have her."

After a romantic honeymoon at the Mardi Gras, the couple decided to move from Connecticut to New Orleans. It was there that Eleanor became fascinated by the possibilities of creating her colorful southern-type dolls. Her earliest dolls were based on Ackley's patterns, but she soon began to design her own dolls and costumes. They are now sold in shops in New Orleans' French Quarter.

Todd says she taught herself — with books and experience, the best teacher of all. She is a member of the International Doll Makers Association (IDMA) and two UFDC clubs, Les Enfants d'Antan of New Orleans and Les Poupees d'Orleans.

9EHT-4

9EHT-3 **Mandy, 10″.** Round, childlike body. Wrist tag reads: **Mandy/A Todd-Doll/New Orleans, La.** Similar tags are used on all dolls by Eleanor Todd. (Photograph courtesy the artist)

9EHT-4 **A First Doll, 15″.** Using Edith Ackley's pattern. This doll has won ribbons in handmade categories at several doll shows. (Photograph courtesy the author)

9EHT-3

Win Ann Winkler

IDMA

The original fabric dolls of Win Ann Winkler are unique in that they may be ordered in a choice of three body fabrics — muslin, broadcloth, or burlap. Yes, burlap!

The artist, who has been making dolls for several years, works in the 18″ to 20″ size range. All her dolls represent little girls of from three to five years of age. Most have muslin bodies "antiqued" by a special process. Others are made of broadcloth. The ethnic dolls have bodies of dark, sueded cotton. In some cases, to achieve a natural fiber look, she has used burlap. Hair is of yarn, ranging in thickness from a thin crochet cotton to the heaviest of mohair yarns.

All the clothing is 100 percent cotton, mostly calico or Shaker-colored solids. Laces are usually all-cotton (Cluny, Val, Alencon), and ribbons are satins, the only synthetics used. Win Ann designs and sews all the dolls' clothing and no two costumes are ever the same. Shoes are of felt or sueded fabric.

Winkler marks her dolls in indelible black ink with name and date of completion on the outside of the left leg. In the case of dark fabrics (used for the ethnic dolls), the marking is done on a white ribbon that is then stitched to the leg.

The Winkler dolls are sold by word of mouth and custom orders are taken, based on photographs of children. Although the dolls are not intended as portraits, the photographs are used as a basis for matching coloring, hair style, and general appearance. Each doll is definitely a one-of-a-kind original.

Win Ann Winkler has an imposing list of professional credits including published books, feature magazine articles in such periodicals as *Harper's Bazaar* and *American Journal of Nursing,* radio and television appearances on both national and local programs, a regular weekly cooking column in a newspaper, and feature writing assignments. She has studied at the Fashion Institute of Technology, the School of Visual Arts, and Steven Stipelman's Fashion Workshop. She has worked as a photographer's stylist in catalog and high fashion work, as a designer of children's lingerie and sportswear, and as a fashion illustrator. Her black doll, Shaneeka, is a part of the permanent slide collection of Aunt Len's Toy and Doll Museum, New York City. Win Ann is a member of IDMA.

9WW-2

9WW-3

9WW-1

9WW-1   **Basic Doll, 18″.** Muslin with yarn hair, polyester fiberfill stuffing. All of Winkler's dolls have sanpaku eyes. (Photograph courtesy the artist)

9WW-2   **Winkler Girl, 18″.** Dressed in provincial print trimmed with ecru cotton lace and two shades of brown ribbon. All dolls have embroidered features. (Photograph courtesy the artist)

9WW-3   **Muslin and Burlap Children.** Dressed in print and plain cottons trimmed with white lace edging and black satin ribbon. All dolls are available in choice of three fabrics — muslin, broadcloth, or burlap. (Photograph courtesy the artist)

251

9WW-4

9BR-2

9WW-4   **Burlap Child.** By Winkler. Has yellow print dress trimmed with yellow edging and moss green ribbon. (All photographs by Martin Hechtman. Courtesy the artist)

Bernard and Frances Ravca

NIADA
The Real People Dolls

Bernard and Frances Ravca have been interviewed so often and at such length in so many publications that anything written here may seem redundant. Most doll collectors know the story of how the Parisian doll artist came to the United States on tour, and that while he was in this country, France fell to Germany and all at home was lost. The dollmaker continued his tour, met another doll artist named Frances Diecks and corresponded with her the remaining months of his tour. Eventually they were married and formed one of the most outstanding dollmaking partnerships known. He is now an American citizen.

9BR-1

9BR-1   **Lifesize Peasant Couple.** Created in needle-sculpture, this pair shows Ravca's realistic style. Also shown are smaller examples of the dollmaker's art. (Photograph courtesy the artist)

9BR-2   **Lifesize Dolls.** By Bernard Ravca. On display in a department store. Card reads: **LIFESIZE DOLLS/Won the last of Mr. Ravca's Gold Medals at PARIS WORLD'S FAIR, 1937.** On the right is a Basque woman. On the left, an old gentleman of Auvergne. (Photograph courtesy the artist)

9BR-3   **Parisian Beggars.** By Bernard Ravca. Done in the 1930s. Won eight first prizes and medals. Sold for $695 each, a fortune in those days. (Photograph courtesy the artist)

9BR-3

9FR-1 **A Burgundy Bride.** By Frances Diecks Ravca. From the early years. Priced at $535. (Photograph courtesy the artist)

9FR-1

Perhaps not all redundant — for talent, imagination, creativity, perseverance, and success are what this book is all about. Therefore the Ravca story is worth repeating endlessly so that others may learn and benefit from their experience.

Bernard and Frances Ravca have reached a period in their lives in which they wish to establish a plateau of privacy and peace. Such qualities were not always available in their professional lives as they worked to research and create the Real People dolls. When one elects to represent a specific province, tribe, religious sect, or individual, one does not dress the doll in question in anything but a well-defined, carefully researched costume representative of that group or person. Many hours, even a great deal of travel, may be required to achieve such a goal. Neither Ravca has ever been known to shirk such responsibility. Rather it was a part of the labor of love that has been such an important part of their lives.

Helen Bullard, in her book *The American Doll Artist,* has described Bernard Ravca as a "sculptor in cotton." The serious work of this fine artist is a testament to that appellation. Few doll artists have achieved the realism with fabric evident in the Ravca Real People dolls. Any mention of Bernard Ravca immediately brings to mind a picture of his French peasants. His wife's interests from the beginning seem to have been with portraiture of well-known stage and screen personalities. When their talents blended, the Real People dolls were the exquisite result.

Any illustration of the work of these two talented people must, of necessity, omit a huge body of work. At any one time, 2,000 or more dolls could be found in their studio, ready for travel to doll shows, department store appointments, lectures, or shipping to complete mail orders. The Ravcas are two prolific artists.

Retirement does not come easily to the Ravcas. The sometimes frenzied activity they knew throughout their careers was a way of life difficult to forget. The longed-for quiet time of retirement carries with it a sharp edge. The body of their work is there to remind them of other days. But more importantly, there is the question of stewardship. What will happen to their dolls? It is a question every collector, dealer, and dollmaker must face.

For Bernard and Frances, the consuming passion is their desire to find a place for their dolls. At one time, their small museum seemed the answer. Now they know the privacy and solitude, the opportunity to order their days to their own needs, is not possible in a museum situation. Long walks, enjoyment of the mountains they love, quiet evenings full of conversation — these are the things for which they yearn. A different life than they have known. But first, provision for the dolls must be made.

9FR-2 **Queen Elizabeth of England.** By Frances Diecks Ravca. Three feet tall and a remarkable likeness of the queen as a young woman. Note the rendition of the crown and jewels. (Photograph courtesy the artist)

9FR-3

9FR-2

9FR-3 **Easter Sunday, 11½″.** (White version.) Reflects the artist's great understanding of children. This child is of cloth over a wire armature, has blond mohair wig, brown painted eyes, molded stockinette face, and is all original. She is marked **ORIGINAL RAVCA/Paris-New York.** She has her very own rag doll to carry. (Author's photograph. Courtesy Kimport Dolls)

9FR-3

Ellen Turner
NIADA

Ellen Turner is one of those artists who, having found herself in a particular time and place and seeing the turning of an age, sought to express through her art that time before it was gone forever. Her marvelous representations of elderly mountain women, coupled with the fragments of poetic commentary she attaches to each, evoke a quality of time, place, spirit, and character rarely achieved by an artist.

The titles of some of her works fairly sing with the clear notes of the southern Appalachian country she knows so well. Who could not be attracted to a work entitled, "Sallie Bean — a little step to the right, a little skip to the left, and here comes that old Sallie Bean"? Or "Rosie Ashe — one day at a time"? (This latter depicting a wornout-looking young woman with a tote over her shoulder and patches on her clothes.) Or "Miss Callie Pace — waiting to remember, it comes and then is gone, sweet Miss Callie Pace"? This last old woman, gray-haired, with apron, shawl, and bag, wears a thoughtful, waiting, somewhat puzzled expression.

Ellen Turner is an observer of the human condition, a reporter of the facts she has observed, a communicator of the resourcefulness, courage, self-reliance, hardiness, resolution, and pathos of her subjects.

Turner has made dolls and sculptured figures most of her life. Her figures, though usually women of southern Appalachia, also include a comical Christmas angel, several children in a group, a boy named Ben (the boy on the corner), another boy, Charlie (from down the road), Papa McMullie (working so hard in the hot ol' sun, sure be glad when it goes down), and Amos McCloud (around the bend i came and right in the middle he stood, in the middle of the field, our Amos McCloud).

Turner tries to present a strong image, using body posture, finger articulation, facial expression, and style of clothing. The figures are developed from her imagination, drawing from many memories she has of the people who framed her life as a child and young adult. She is always working on some new character. Therefore, the dolls shown here are a mere representation of the total roster of her creations. Sometimes she makes new versions of characters already completed, expressing her subject from a different viewpoint.

All of her work is original and she employs a number of different techniques. Construction is on a wire frame (armature) built up with excelsior and cotton padding, then covered with cotton knit. Faces have stitched features, are sized, then painted with acrylics. Wigs are usually of human hair, although occasionally she uses mohair or some other interesting material. Hands are carefully constructed with wire and fabric.

Clothing is made from both new and old fabrics, designed, cut, and sewn individually for each doll. There are no patterns. Accessories are fashioned from common objects — dried flowers, baskets, walking sticks — or made from fabric. Stands are of mahogany or redwood, completely constructed and finished by the artist.

Each doll is given an individual name and a verse by way of introduction or explanation. Turner's dolls are in sizes ranging from 25″ to 32″ with the exception of one or two lifesize figures that she makes from time to time. All of her dolls are made to order. She has also developed a range of smaller dolls, 15″ to 18″. There are two designs in this line to date: Nellie, a young Asheville flower vendor, and Maude, an old woman from the hills. Bodies and faces are constructed using the same techniques as with the larger dolls. However, she has created her own set of patterns for the clothing of these smaller dolls. All of her dolls are signed, dated, and when appropriate, numbered.

Ellen Turner studied at the High Museum of Art, Atlanta, Georgia, the Gibbs Art Museum, Charleston, South Carolina, and with the Famous Artists School, Westport, Connecticut. She was elected to NIADA in May of 1982 and is also a member of the Southern Highland Handicraft Guild. Her work has been exhibited at the Renwick Gallery of the Smithsonian Institution in Washington, D.C.

9ET-1   **Minnie Moses.** "Down in the hollow she wanders at dawn." An Ellen Turner original, based on a memory. (Photograph courtesy the artist)

9ET-2   **Frady's Widow.** "Never forget me." Ellen Turner's insightful rendering evokes a widow's wistful sadness. (Photograph courtesy the artist)

9ET-1

9ET-2

9ET-3

9ET-4

9ET-3   **Nottie Becks.** "So busy like the squirrel as she hurries down the road." Turner's quiet humor is evident in this doll. (Photograph courtesy the artist)

9ET-4   **Farmer Allen's Daughter Jenny.** "From up Turkey Hill." One of Ellen Turner's young mountain women. (Photograph courtesy the artist)

R. John Wright
NIADA
On Becoming a Doll Artist

How does one become a doll artist? What series of events or circumstances leads a person into the pursuit of perfection? Many of us are curious. Perhaps there are even moments when some of us think we might like to become doll artists ourselves, but we lack the courage to take the first step, or don't even know what that first step ought to be.

Here is the story of how one artist wandered into something that changed his life. Here, in his own words, is the story of R. John Wright, who almost accidentally began making dolls:

I guess I should begin by saying that I was born in Michigan in 1947. All of my relatives still live in Michigan. However, in 1970 I set out to do some traveling across country. I intended originally to go to California, but my little car never would have made it that far, so I turned around and opted for New England. I did all this traveling with my cat; he's quite an old fella and he's been through everything with me, and I'm glad to say he's still around.

In the East I didn't know anyone, but being an artistic and creative person for as long as I can remember, it was just a matter of time before I fell in with some of the people involved in New Hampshire's League of Craftsmen. Now this was about the time of the crafts revival in this country and it was especially happening in New Hampshire, which already had a well-established craftsmen's organization that had built up since the Great Depression.

I met some really exciting and wonderful people who put up with me and my cat, and put me up. Although it was to be quite awhile before I would be a self-supporting artisan, they showed me how it was all a very possible and desirable alternative. Of course, one had to be willing to work and sacrifice and settle for a more modest standard of living, and it helped a lot if you had talent. One person of specific interest to me at this time was Gail Duggan, a craftsperson who made her living making porcelain dolls.

I think it was around this time that I started getting ideas about how maybe I could make dolls sometime. But a few years went by and I had several jobs in the "real" world. I was a professional fruit picker for a while. I picked apples in New Hampshire. I picked oranges and grapefruit down in Florida. I worked in a feedstore unloading 100-pound sacks of grain from boxcars. I sold men's clothing in a store. I worked seasonally on a farm, planting and harvesting field-grown pansies.

But the luxury of working for someone else was keeping me from using the talents that I knew I had and building something for myself. When I was working last, at a hardware store as a clerk, I was feeling like something had to give. I had thought off and on over the years of making a doll and when I was laid off abruptly in the fall of 1976, the opportunity simply presented itself. It was now or never. So I made a doll.

I must say it was one of the harder things I've ever had to do, and also one of the most exhilarating. In one afternoon, I made the first step in what I knew then was to be a long and exciting journey. This doll, by the way, was largely inspired by Steiff. I had had a lot of Steiff animals as a child and a lot of European toys, and recently I had seen some pictures of some early Steiff dolls which fascinated me.

I had given my wife that Christmas a little Singer Featherweight sewing machine, and I sewed a crude head and body of some rags. But when it came time to sew the rest, the bobbin ran out and I had no idea

what to do. I was pretty excited about finishing this, but didn't know what to do with the machine. So I sewed the rest by hand, and stuffed it with some sheep's wool which was around for spinning.

It seems now like an awfully small thing to get excited over. But, not only had I never made a doll before, I'd never sewn anything and was impressed by how easy it seemed to come, never having done these things before. And I kept thinking about how the second one could be, even while I was making the first. It all seemed to hold so much potential.

The very next day, I went up to Dartmouth College in Hanover, because I remembered a large selection of doll books and one picture, in particular, of some cloth hillbilly dolls by an early N.I.A.D.A. artist named Grace Lathrop. I was quite taken by those amusing characters that she made and I fashioned a similar type doll out of an old piece of yellow flannel with jointed arms, sewn knees, and button eyes. He looked like he might have lived under a rock.

It was obvious that I needed some flesh-colored material. My aunt, who worked at a big department store in Michigan, used to bring home lots of felt the window dressers would use for backdrops and throw away. So I was somewhat used to playing around with it, and I did have an idea that it would be cuddly and nice for a doll.

This time I made six men dolls out of flesh-colored felt with a seam down the center of the face. I made them some ill-fitting shirts and pants with suspenders, and they looked like a group of 49-ers with their bald heads and sheep's wool beards. I took these dolls, wrapped in a blanket, to the local crafts shop downtown and was very flattered when they took them on the spot. It was most exciting when these dolls sold almost immediately and a re-order came in the mail. All this was happening within a week of having been a clerk at a store.

During the next six months, I made and sold over 100 of these primitive cloth dolls, women as well as men characters. Some of the women had wooden rolling pins in their apron pockets and the men sported felt hats — the crowns of which were wet and stretched over custard cups and dried in the oven (my first felt molding).

As the dolls became more sophisticated, it was necessary to place a high priority on efficiency. It was easy enough to think of all sorts of ways to make the dolls take more time, but it was not as easy to think of ways to make it all more efficient. If five minutes was saved in one phase of the operation, I would take that time and lavish it on another aspect I'd been wanting to indulge in.

One of my production methods in making these early dolls was to silkscreen the patterns on the felt to avoid having to trace by hand around the increasingly complex shapes. Much later I was able to lower the cutting time as well by using a hydraulic press and custom-made dies.

Soon, I wanted the dolls to be self-standing and this required hip joints. To achieve this, I first used cardboard circles hammered out with a leather punch, then regular hardboard disks concealed within the doll, made with a drill press and "hole cutter." This joint problem was one of many involving research and innovation.

There was so much to learn: the stuffing methods, the turning procedures, the wig construction. Although most of these things had been worked out before (by others), the knowledge was not always readily available. Many of the more sophisticated production methods were closely guarded secrets which the manufacturers seemed to have carried to their graves.

Together, my wife and I worked day and night to keep up with production and learn all we could to make the dolls better. We wrote hundreds of letters, looked in books, called people on the phone (for awhile we got used to hundred-dollar phone bills). We took old dolls to the hospital and had them x-rayed. We knew that everything that we put into this was an investment in our futures . . . because I knew then that this would be going on for many, many years. Most people have an obsession, and it was becoming increasingly obvious that mine was dolls.

One of my accounts at this time was the Enchanted Doll House in Manchester, Vermont. Jean Schramm, then owner, had an extensive collection of old dolls tucked away in a back room and among these was a fabulous group of old Lencis. My eyes were really opened! Here I had been making dolls of felt and hadn't been at all aware of the full potential of the material. Alas, no one knew anything about how to mold felt. It was a "lost art."

We had used the oven in forming the hats and I used that as a starting point. We examined the waffle iron and talked with machinists, mold makers, and engineers. Finally, after much thought, invention, and time, we came up with a system that would work satisfactorily. I took these first molded dolls to a large wholesale trade show and was overwhelmed with the response. Within just a few hours we were booked up for a full year. It was just two years before that I had made that first doll.

I believe that part of the success of the dolls was a certain longing in people for a doll or toy made with a lot of personal care and ingenuity like they used to make things. Most of my early sales were not to doll collectors, but to ordinary people who, since they were children, hadn't seen a doll they wanted to own. This awakening in people is beautiful to behold, and it brings me a great deal of satisfaction. But first and foremost, I make dolls to make my own vision a reality and fulfill my own desire that something like this is being made nowadays and offered to people as an alternative.

Doll lovers who look for a certain quality and craftsmanship often turn to antiques, but the demand has skyrocketed over the past few years while the supply has dwindled. Prices reflect this very limited situation. I see it as a challenge to produce dolls in the same spirit as those sought-after older dolls. Especially the dolls made by the Kruse, Steiff, Schoenhut, and Lenci firms. Most collectors marvel at the artistic ability of the individuals whose names these companies bear, but to me the marvel is that they successfully produced their creations in quantity. Chances are that if these dolls had not been produced on a large scale, we would not know about them today.

Producing dolls in quantity calls for a completely different set of talents, not the least of which is the ability to keep "control" of the finished product. That is why I have no desire to sell designs to another company (for manufacture). I suppose that is where mass production gets its bad name — when it becomes so removed from the artist's initial vision that it ceases to have any soul.

At this point, we are producing some 600 dolls a year. Along with creativity and organization, I am always striving to maintain artistic control. Hopefully, each doll will continue to be even more artistic and structurally sound than the ones before. Whether they are ever played with or not, it is important to me that the dolls retain a certain "toy" quality as opposed to a figurine or purely representational aspect. Moveability plays a big part in this toy quality, as does sturdiness. I want the dolls to be like toys and appeal to the child in all of us — the child that wants to be able to "touch."

A few workers help us here at our home, where we still do most of the work. Some clothing and accessories are "farmed out" to people who work in their own homes. The wooden tools and baskets are made for me by craftsmen who normally make full-size versions of these same items. There is always so much that I feel only my wife and I can do: painting the features, styling the hair, molding the faces (the face molds are custom-made from my own patterns).

First, the face is sculpted in clay, then a plaster cast is made from that, and finally one in metal. These metal molds are lined with Teflon™ for easy release (of the felt part). The old doll makers had to use oiled paper, so sometimes new *is* better. Besides being bonded to very heavy buckram, the felt is treated with a special, clear sizing for added strength and to make a smoother surface upon which to paint the features.

The torsos and limbs are of felt which is completely lined with muslin to avoid distortion in stuffing and to provide additional strength. They are jointed at shoulders, neck, and hips, and stuffed with cotton and kapok. No synthetics are used at all in their creation. I even insist upon all-cotton thread and real pearl buttons.

I make the leather shoes myself on a little metal last and hammer tiny nails into the soles. The hair is all-natural fibers . . . karakul wool, yak hair, and mainly, finest quality mohair from England. This is custom-dyed in this country, and we make it into fringes which are sewn directly onto the dolls' heads, stitch by stitch, using a curved needle.

If the work seems endless, it is nothing compared to the great satisfaction when we see the dolls standing finished before us, knowing they could undergo the closest scrutiny. In addition to the signature on

the left foot, the dolls are signed, dated, and numbered. If the new owner desires, a doll may be registered with the National Institute of American Doll Artists, to which I was elected in 1979. I was introduced to N.I.A.D.A. and encouraged to apply by Elizabeth Andrews Fisher, one of my favorite doll people.

New designs are always developing, and a line of children dolls has been added to the character types which were first made. The dolls are sold in several exclusive shops across the country, even as far away as Hawaii, and also by individual mail-order.

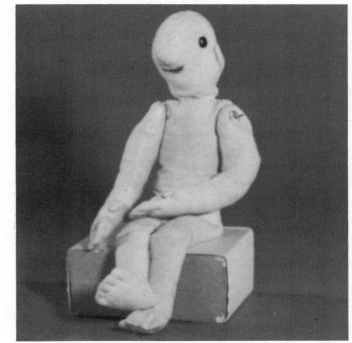

9JW-1

9JW-2

9JW-1   **The First Doll.** By R. John Wright. Yellow flannel, Steiff influence, November 1976. (Photograph courtesy the artist)

9JW-2   **The First Brochure.** None of these dolls had names. Only numbers were used in 1979. (Illustration courtesy the artist)

Fig. 9JW-1

9JW-3   **Becky, 17″.** From the Little Children Series I.
         Dolls are of felt with molded faces and hand-
         painted features, fully jointed. They have wigs of
         quality mohair. Clothes are completely removable.
         (Photograph courtesy the artist)

9JW-4   **Seth and Emma, 18″.** From the Character Doll
         Series 1981-1982. Dolls are wigged using all-
         natural fibers sewn directly to the scalp. Shoes and
         boots are handmade on scale-model lasts. All are
         limited editions. (Photograph courtesy the artist)

9JW-3

9JW-4

260

9JW-5

9JW-6

9JW-7

These handcrafted felt dolls by John Wright were pictured in his 1981-1982 catalog. All were described as being 18″ tall with swivel heads, jointed bodies, and removable clothing. Each doll was signed on the bottom of its left foot. Limited Edition certificates documenting registration with the National Institute of American Doll Artists were provided for each doll purchased (9JW-5-7).

9JW-5   **Erika, Gretchen, and Karl.** Erika's hair, braided in side buns, is topped with a brimmed, flower-bedecked felt hat. Dress and apron are felt with laced belt. Gretchen, a Swiss shepherdess, wears a felt bonnet, vest, and skirt and holds a bentwood crook. Karl carries a wooden staff, wears jacket, "lederhosen," and Alpine hat of felt, and leather shoes. (Courtesy the artist)

9JW-6   **St. Nicholas.** His red, hooded robe is worn over a felt tunic and sash and long underwear. Bishops' shoes, velveteen pack, and wooden cross-staff complete his ensemble. (Courtesy the artist)

9JW-7   **Bridget and Bernard.** Brunette Bridget has handcrafted straw hat, oak rake, tattersall dress with underskirt, and felt sabots. Bernard wears a flannel smock, felt knickers, and clogs of wood and leather. His pack basket is made of split oak. (Courtesy the artist)

British Artists

In Britain, a growing number of doll artists are becoming members of the British Doll Artists Association (BDA), an organization with somewhat the same aims as their American counterparts.

Valerie King needle-sculptures some very large dolls, sometimes 36″ or larger. (The British call it "quilting.") Thora Hughs creates beautiful cloth Victorian children that have proven to be popular with collectors. Sarah Jane Fisher makes big-eyed, all-cloth dolls with molded felt heads and soft, jointed bodies. These she dresses in contemporary styles and gives them wigs of human hair or mohair. The Fisher dolls have hand-painted features and often some hand-painted designs on the clothing. She works in the 24″ to 26″ sizes.

Another English cloth doll artist is Christine Adams, whose Tiny Tots have earned her an enviable reputation among collectors and artists alike. Her dolls have taken many ribbons at doll shows and conventions. Adams presently is making two styles, young children and sleeping babies, all with human hair wigs and hand-knitted clothing. She is planning another pair, a chubby-faced toddler and a wide-awake baby. The designing of these two new styles must be sandwiched between making dolls that have been ordered, a problem with which many doll artists are confronted. There is always the desire to keep customers happy by filling orders as promptly as possible. Always, too, there is the pull the artist feels toward the creative possibilities of developing new dolls.

9E-2

9E-1

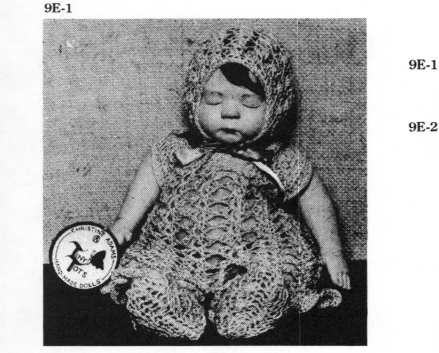

9E-1   **Tiny Tot Sleeping Baby.** Hand-knitted finery, displays the tag proclaiming its origin as a Christine Adams doll. (Photograph courtesy R. Lane Herron)

9E-2   **Tiny Tot Boy.** Looks a bit pensive and perhaps wonders if he needs to be all dressed up in fancy duds — especially that bow! One of Christine Adams' wistful little children, this boy exemplifies her understanding of her medium and subject. (Photograph courtesy R. Lane Herron)

9E-3

9E-5

9E-4

9E-3   **Tiny Tot Girl.** Hand-knitted coat, hat, and scarf, close-cropped curls and contemplative expression often seen in Christine Adams' children. (Photograph courtesy R. Lane Herron)

9E-4   **Country Folk, 36″.** Couple by Valerie King. These soft-sculptured old people exhibit a warmth and humor typical of King's work. The British call this method "quilting." (Photograph courtesy the artist)

9E-5   **All-Cloth Doll, 24″.** By Sarah Jane Fisher. Face is hand painted on felt, clothing is of contemporary styling. (Photograph courtesy the artist)

10 Unaffiliated Cloth Doll Artists

Many artists working in a wide variety of media have banded together in several different organizations for dollmakers. Such organizations provide the opportunity to exchange ideas and receive professional critiques of one's work in companionship with one's peers. For some, nothing is more lonely than working without such intercourse. The deep sense of being cut off from other creative people sometimes has definite negative effects on their work. They feel they are drying up, that their work suffers as a result of their isolation.

For many artists affiliated with dollmaker organizations, the opportunity to view the work of others is a prime reason for membership. These artists feel that their creative energies are buoyed by such contact. In addition, there is a market for their works not easily accessible to the unaffiliated. Most of the organizations participate in conventions, competitions, shows, and sales for their members.

Thus, the unaffiliated artist may be viewed as something of a maverick or even a lesser talent, moving outside the accepted circles. In fact, nothing could be farther from the truth. For every recognized, affiliated artist, there are perhaps dozens of unaffiliated dollmakers. This is not to say that unaffiliated and unrecognized are synonymous. Rather, many doll artists have managed to make names for themselves in the field while remaining outside the organizations. And it is from the ranks of these that organizations often draw their members.

What one must remember, therefore, is that affiliation is not the only criteria by which a dollmaker's work should be judged. Craftsmanship, originality, treatment of materials, believability of concept, the artist's understanding of anatomy — all these and more must be considered in judging a doll's worth and an artist's ability. Perhaps not coincidentally, these are some of the same criteria used by the organizations in making their choices of new members.

Another point: Not all artists wish to become affiliated, for reasons possibly as numerous as the artists involved. Organiza-tion membership is simply not everyone's cup of tea. Further-more, organization membership is not always available because of location, time, money, or even lack of awareness of existing associations. Some people admittedly are loners who find they work best without outside contact or influence.

For whatever reason, many doll artists remain unaffiliated, and their dolls range across the full scale of talent and ability, each bringing to the work his or her own particular concept and special vision. As a result, the dolls of these artists are as simple or complex, as innocent or sophisticated, as natural or stylized as one might wish to find.

The cross section of artists and their dolls shown here is only a small sampling of what one may find. The field continues to grow as more new dollmakers join the ranks of doll artists each year.

Virginia Black

The April 1963 issue of *McCall's* magazine featured a group of five dolls created by artist Virginia Black especially for the issue. The dolls were used to illustrate five of *McCall's* regular short features. A doctor doll, complete with stethoscope, headed "Medical News of the Month," written by Dr. Morris Fishbein. "Sight & Sound," a column dedicated to the burgeoning technology of television and stereo sound receivers and edited by Bart Sheridan, was represented by a reclining young lady doll. Propped on her pillows with book in hand, headphones in place, this doll looks for all the world as though she is settled in for an evening of easy listening.

Charles H. Goren, well-known author-expert, wrote a bridge column for many years. In this issue, a gentleman doll holds a regulation-size playing card with shoulder straps, signboard-style. His slightly perplexed though smiling expression is further underscored by the heading nearby: "Even Experts Can

Fumble," it chides. Another regular feature is "Pats & Pans," a letters-to-the-editor column, represented by a double image of the same doll holding the doll-size versions of joy and tragedy theatrical masks.

Finally, a very attractive blond lady, dressed *tres chic* with quill pen and scroll in hand, heads up "Without Portfolio," a monthy commentary by diplomat, playwright, politician, and generally busy woman, Clare Boothe Luce.

A brief paragraph in the issue stated that Mrs. Black had made over one thousand of what she called her adult dolls, some of which had been used on Hallmark greeting cards. (Research at Hallmark failed to turn up any of these cards.) Mrs. Black made all the clothing and accessories, including the doctor's stethoscope, the end of which was a salt-shaker top. The article emphasized that her dolls were all one-of-a-kind and ended with the comment that they had all been sent back to the artist in California.

In addition to the dolls presumably made for Hallmark's greeting cards, Virginia Black sold her dolls in gift shops. They were also used in advertising. However, further information about this gifted dollmaker-artist has not been found.

10VB-1

10VB-3

10VB-2

10VB-1   **Virginia Black's Sight & Sound Doll.** Relaxes with headphones and her favorite stereo music. From the pages of *McCall's,* April 1963.

10VB-2   **Black's Pats & Pans Doll.** Exotic-looking lady uses joy and tragedy masks. From *McCall's,* April 1963.

10VB-3   **Even Experts Can Fumble Doll.** A sentiment that seems to be reflected in the face of this Virginia Black doll. From *McCall's,* April 1963.

10VB-4   **Medical News of the Month Doll.** This good-looking fellow created by Virginia Black headed up "Medical News of the Month" in *McCall's,* April 1963 issue.

10VB-5   **Without Portfolio Doll.** Virginia Black created this very "with it" lady to head a commentary by Clare Boothe Luce. Luce is remembered as a playwright, political worker, and diplomat. Her column, "Without Portfolio," appeared regularly in the pages of *McCall's.*

10VB-4

MEDICAL
NEWS
OF THE
MONTH

10VB-5

Karen Butcher
Out of My Hands™

Karen Butcher has been a dollmaker for the past fifteen years. Her first dolls were balsa wood carvings of Rhett Butler, Scarlett O'Hara, and other characters from *Gone With the Wind*. She has been especially interested in portraits and has done a John Kennedy, Jr., which is now in the Kennedy Library.

Three years ago she began making soft dolls, starting with an Emily pattern from *McCall's Needlework* magazine, and a Lucy by Rainie Crawford. Later, she redesigned a commercial pattern, McCall's Button-Eyed Baby, and renamed it Amy Lynn. The 20″ doll has been a big seller for the dollmaker, with its big, wide face, painted smile, and ruffled bonnet made as part of the head. She has also created a boy version with a billed cap. Since the body is in one piece, Karen comments, the legs cross just like a baby's legs. A drawstring smock and bloomers, along with hand-crocheted booties, complete the cuddly doll effect.

With this much experience, Karen gained confidence and designed from scratch a Shirley-type doll with crocheted curls, jeans, a fisherman-style sweater, and Nikes (running shoes). From the Shirley doll and several other prototypes, Butcher developed her Sweet Bonnie Bluegrass. Bonnie has a gingham dress, white pinafore, and handmade shoes. Her Dynel™ wig is brunette. Her panties and socks are from Dollspart. She is 24″ tall and her iron-on face, developed from an original drawing, is hand-colored.

The artist's next effort was to create a soft doll that would resemble as much as possible a real baby. Bonnie Babe, 22″, with a Dynel™ Dollspart wig trimmed for a better fit, was the result. This doll wears a real baby gown and real Pamper disposable diaper to give her a nice "pat-pat" feel, says Karen. The artist has also added a built-in voice box that emits a real-baby cry.

All the dolls are constructed of peach-colored poly-cotton fabric and stuffed with polyester fiberfill. Clothes are of a variety of ginghams and calicos. All have sewn-in cloth labels marked with the copyright symbol, the correct date, the name of Butcher's operation (Out of My Hands™), and the address.

Karen Butcher studied figure drawing and pottery-making at Morehead State University and has had a home pottery studio for six years. She is a native Kentuckian and is employed at WLEX-TV in Lexington, Kentucky. She recently became interested in creating porcelain dolls and plans to release a new series.

10KB-1

10KB-2

10KB-1 **Sweet Bonnie Bluegrass, 24″.** Crocheted hair and painted face. This is first prototype of Karen Butcher's original design. (Photograph courtesy the artist)

10KB-2 **Sweet Bonnie Bluegrass.** The current version with hand-painted, iron-on features and brunette Dynel™ wig. Shoes, dress, and pinafore are all handmade by the artist. (Photograph courtesy the artist)

Dianne Dengel

10KB-3 **Bonnie Babe, 22″.** Dynel™ wig, real-baby gown and Pamper disposable diaper. Has a built-in cry voice "that will break the stoniest heart." (Photograph courtesy the artist)

10KB-4 **Amy Lynn, 20″.** One of the dollmaker's first dolls. Based on a redesigned commercial pattern. (Photograph courtesy the artist)

Dianne Dengel is a self-taught artist with a very special vision. Widely known for her oil paintings, Dianne has created her dolls in the image of the children she paints, capturing even more, in her three-dimensional works, the special looks of childhood. She has traveled to many cities for exhibits of her paintings and dolls, and her designs are patented because of her unusual method of stitch-sculpturing. All her work is hand-signed, usually on the back, with a laundry marking pen.

Dengel has been making dolls since she was eight years old. She works in all sizes from 2″ to lifesize and has created, in addition to her babies and children, a variety of adult figures. These include old women, an old fisherman, and clowns, in a variety of situations.

Her large figures are more correctly termed cloth sculptures, and many of them are arranged in situation groups. There is the white-haired gramps trimming the hair of a sheet-draped boy while two other young fellows look on with trepidation, awaiting their turns. Meanwhile, a young girl admires the effects of the barber's work on another little fellow who has quite obviously just finished his turn in the barber chair and wears a somewhat shocked expression as he touches his shorn head.

In another group, a plump, lifesize housewife and mother holds a beaming baby on one hip and a washcloth in the other hand. Before her are two more babies, happily at play in a wooden tub of sudsy bath water. (This group has taken prizes.) Each of her groups has a story to tell in the tradition of that dean of American storytellers, Norman Rockwell. Warmth, sympathy, humor, and understanding are evident in these Dengel groups.

Dianne makes each doll from cloth, preferring the stretch qualities of jersey, and hardens them with modeling paste. She then sands them to a fine finish and paints the surfaces with oils. The result is a true work of art. No two dolls are ever alike. Even when viewing a display of fifty or more Dengel dolls, one has the feeling of looking at a group of children who have been told to sit nicely for just a minute or two, and who are just barely able to contain their youthful exuberance long enough to avoid a bit of discipline.

Each is different, and yet with all the differences handmodeling and painting make, these children must be sisters, brothers, perhaps cousins, because there is a definite style apparent in all Dengel's work.

Many of Dianne Dengel's dolls and paintings are on display in museums and galleries across the country. She is a member of the Lords and Ladies of New England, UFDC.

10KB-3

10KB-4

10DD-1

10DD-2

10DD-3

10DD-1   **A group of Dianne Dengel's Children.** Looking for all the world like a group of kindergartners waiting their turn at show and tell. (Photograph courtesy the artist)

10DD-2   **Granny and the Baby.** A favorite subject for Dengel — depicting the interplay of young and old in groups. (Photograph courtesy the artist)

10DD-3   **Gramps and the Littlest One.** Here again we see Dengel at her best, portraying the very young and not-so-young in special relationships. (Photograph courtesy the artist)

269

10DD-4 **Dianne Dengel's Original Painting.** The artist draws special inspiration for her dolls from her paintings. (Photograph courtesy the artist)

10DD-4

Rebecca Iverson Needlesmith

Rebecca Iverson says she has always made dolls, and goes on to say she refers to herself as a needlesmith. Beginning when she was four or five, she learned to cut and sew, but only began selling her creations in 1974.

Each doll is unique, cut from her original patterns, of unbleached muslin, usually with yarn hair, and hand-painted face. Rebecca does all her own costuming, creating her own designs, preferring cottons and old laces.

Her dolls are usually 19″, although occasionally she makes a 10″ doll, some odd in-between sizes, or adults. Her raggedy dolls are also 19″. Iverson's dolls are signed © **R. Iverson** and the appropriate year. Earlier dolls have the embroidered signature, **Becky** on their bottoms. A little later she marked them **R. Iverson** on the back of the neck. Her card is attached to each doll (Fig. 10-1); label with **Rebecca Iverson•Needlesmith** is sewn into each costume.

Iverson usually sells her dolls through the mail and reports that her list is endless because each doll is different, names and costumes vary, and there are no series or editions. She goes on to say that although she has created several hundred dolls, lately the dolls have become so detailed that she makes far fewer each year.

Rebecca Iverson's training includes a B.S. degree from Wisconsin State University, River Falls. She is an associate member of the St. Croix Valley Doll Club, UFDC.

Fig. 10-1

270

10RI-1

10RI-2

10RI-3

10RI-1   **Seated Ballerina, 10″ (standing).** In pink and white with kid slippers. An early Iverson. (Photograph by W. Barry Iverson. Courtesy the artist)

10RI-2   **Alice.** The 1980 version. Compare this doll with Rebecca Iverson's later version. (Photograph by W. Barry Iverson. Courtesy the artist)

10RI-3   **Lady in White and Children.** Small child, 10″, dressed in blue calico and chambray, black stockings, lace-up leather boots. Lady in White, 22″. Child, 19″, in brown with black stockings, lace-up leather boots. All three dolls created 1979. (Photograph by W. Barry Iverson. Courtesy the artist)

10RI-4   **My Own Special Raggedies.** Iverson's interpretation of a classic type, 19″, with hand-painted faces, brown and auburn rug yarn hair, various faded calico and denim outfits. (Photograph by W. Barry Iverson. Courtesy the artist)

10RI-5   **Kajsa, 20″.** All cloth, hand-painted face, yarn hair. Note the detailing. Costumes are extensively researched for authenticity.

Here is an unusual opportunity to study the development of an artist's skills over a period of several years. The first four dolls are examples of Rebecca Iverson's earlier work, from the 1978 through 1980 period. The remaining dolls are representative of her more recent work and evince a certain developing style. (Photographs by W. Barry Iverson. Courtesy the artist)

10RI-4

10RI-5

10RI-5

10RI-6

10RI-7

10RI-7

10RI-6 **Astrid, 20″.** All cloth, hand-painted face, yarn hair, dressed in blue cotton prints. Each Iverson doll reveals its character in the flawlessly painted, individualized features, which at the same time convey the artist's unique style. (Photograph by W. Barry Iverson. Courtesy the artist)

10RI-7 **Karin, 20″.** All cloth, hand-painted face, yarn hair, hat, dress, apron in shades of brown. Iverson completes the ensemble with her almost-signature black stockings and lace-up leather boots. With the doll undressed, one can see the anatomical accuracy achieved by the artist. Karin stands alone, has correctly proportioned hands and feet, shapely and believable legs, gusseted thumbs. (Photograph of dressed doll courtesy Betty Rossi, Kutztown Gallery. Photographs of undressed doll courtesy the artist and Betty Rossi)

10RI-8   **Amy, 13″.** Hand-painted face, Caracul hair, dressed in blue cotton print with embroidered white apron, white shoes. (Photograph by W. Barry Iverson. Courtesy the artist)

10RI-8

Miriam Lust Handmade Dolls

Miriam Lust has been making her dolls on a family hobby basis for about ten years. Miriam designs and sews all the dolls and their clothing. Daughter Marsha Wakely hand paints the faces and stuffs the bodies very firmly with polyester fill. (Miriam thus differentiates her cloth dolls from the soft, floppy, less firmly stuffed rag dolls.) Husband Howard hand-crafts the real leather shoes used on some of the dolls.

Lust uses flesh-colored fabrics and mostly human hair wigs that can be combed and styled. All her dolls have hand-painted facial features and are jointed at shoulders and hips. The dolls are made to order. Miriam takes no deposits, preferring instead to work at her own pace for the fun of it. She does try to make up a stock of dolls each year to show at the Bratwurst Festival in Bucyrus, Ohio, her hometown. (Bucyrus, she says, is the bratwurst capital of the world!)

The Lust dolls are carefully and thoroughly marked. Miriam handsigns and dates them in addition to sewing printed cloth labels into the clothing and onto the backs of the dolls. Some of the labels, such as those for the Little House on the Prairie dolls, have the doll's name printed on them. Other labels simply read: **Hand Made by Miriam Lust.**

While Lust admits to no formal training in dollmaking (all trial and error, she says), her credits are impressive. Her Laura won first in class at the 1980 Dayton convention of the Guild of Ohio Dollmakers (GOOD). Her Dolly Dingles was a cover doll for the April 1977 issue of *Bambini* and was also featured as the cover story for the September-October 1976 issue of *Doll Castle News.*

In addition, she recently sold the rights for plate decoration and figurines using her copyrighted and trademarked Dolly Dingles design to the Goebel Company of West Germany, who will produce the items in Massachusetts. Miriam has retained the cloth doll rights for producing up to one hundred dolls per year — something she says she never does, since her family dollmaking team works only part-time and there are the other designs to complete as well.

Miriam Lust is one of the trusting souls who shipped her dolls to me in order that they might be photographed. She is a member of the Indian Trail Doll Club of Ohio, Region 12, UFDC.

10ML-1

10ML-2

10ML-3

10ML-1   **Mary Poppins, 16″.** From a 1966 McCall's pattern, one of the first cloth dolls made by Miriam Lust. Carpetbag, which holds new penny, was cut from a deteriorating handwoven throw made by a W. A. Wolfe in 1847. (Author's photograph. Courtesy the artist)

10ML-2   **Betsy Ross, 13″.** This one-of-a-kind original by Miriam Lust is a special Bicentennial doll. Completed doll was painted in oil colors (a lot of work, says Lust), wears layers of clothing (pantalettes, slip, blouse, striped bodice with attached petticoat, mob cap) all in red, white, and blue. Features were painted by Marsha Wakely, the artist's daughter. (Author's photograph. Courtesy the artist)

10ML-3   **Laura and Albert, 15″.** Original dolls inspired by the television program, "Little House on the Prairie." Laura has human hair pigtails. Albert wears a synthetic wig. Pale, flesh-colored cotton is used for bodies. Real leather, high-topped boots are handmade by Howard Lust, the artist's husband. (Author's photograph. Courtesy the artist)

10ML-4   **Dolly Dingles™, 14″.** This doll by Miriam Lust is copyrighted and registered in the U.S. Patent Office and will appear on various porcelain items made by the Goebel Company. All Lust dolls are well marked with cloth tags sewn into clothes and on bodies, as well as hand signed and dated. (Author's photograph. Courtesy the artist)

10ML-4

Will R. Parker
Good Little Indian Boys
Fabric Dolls by Win

Will Parker has been making his Good Little Indian Boys for several years. He says they came about almost by accident after he saw a cloth baby doll at an arts and crafts show and decided to try making one himself.

Fortunately, he says, he could find no suitable pink fabric, although he was able to buy a bolt of appropriate (for dollmaking) tan material. The color of the fabric set off a reaction in his mind. Parker remembered the little Indian boys he had seen while growing up in the center of the Creek Nation in Oklahoma and decided to make an Indian doll. After several attempts, he completed Talasi, which means "the runner" in the Creek language, and admits he loved the little boy doll.

Other people liked Talasi, so Parker made another, then another and another. Soon, he was getting all the orders he could keep up with and found himself in the dollmaking business.

The unique tradename devised by Will Parker was arrived at by lopping off the tops of the last two letters of his signature. Thus "Will" became "Win." All his dolls are marked on the right hip with the doll's name, its number, and Will's professional signature.

Each doll has its own personality and name. Will emphasizes that no two dolls are ever alike. Naming the dolls has led to some fascinating research, he notes. He has learned a great deal about Indian languages and customs while researching the names or seeking new names for his latest dolls. Every new owner who writes to Parker receives a certificate giving the doll's name and its meaning, the tribe represented, and the doll's number.

The Win dolls are 18″, made of tan-colored jersey, stuffed with fiberfill. Their faces are painted with acrylics and lightly needle-sculptured. Black "fur" is used for hair. Some of the boys have straight arms; others have bent arms. Some have divided fingers; others have needle-sculptured mitten hands. The clothing is all faded denim and calico, print or checked. Overalls and shirts are reminiscent of the outfits worn by the little Indian boys Will saw when they came to town those Saturdays long ago.

The Sequoyah boys are dressed somewhat differently. Their shirts are plain cotton trimmed in a band of colorful ribbon-work around the shirttail. The designs are all original and each doll and its clothing is made completely by the artist.

Parker has a B.A. degree in art from Harding University, Searcy, Arkansas. He did additional work at Oklahoma State University, Syracuse University, the University of Arkansas at Little Rock, and Southern Arkansas University. He is a graduate of Wetumka High School, Wetumka, Oklahoma.

The artist is art director of Magnolia Public Schools, Magnolia, Arkansas, and is also a professional watercolorist. He is a member of the Doll Collectors of Central and Southern Arkansas and the United Federation of Doll Clubs, Inc. He was UFDC's first regional director elected from Region 7.

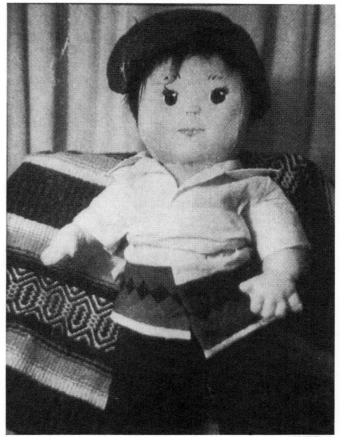

10WRP-3

10WRP-1

10WRP-2

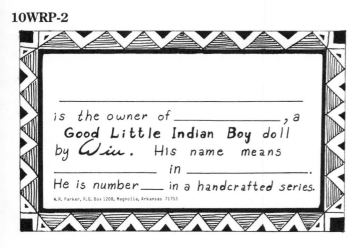

10WRP-1 V'lv, 18″. Soft-sculptured Good Little Indian Boy by Will R. Parker. V'lv means "buckeye" in the language of the Muskogee Indians. (Courtesy the artist)

10WRP-2 Certificate of Registration. Sent to new owners of the Good Little Indian Boys. (Courtesy the artist)

10WRP-3 Sequoyah, 18″. Good Little Indian Boy. Sequoyah was responsible for the invention of the Cherokee alphabet, or syllabary, which enabled many Cherokees to read and write their own language. (Courtesy the artist)

10WRP-4 Talasi. Means "the runner" in the Creek language. Parker uses this photograph on his Christmas cards. (Courtesy the artist)

10WRP-5 Good Little Indian Boys Hangtag. Fastened to each doll as it is completed. Gives the doll's name and the address to which the new owner can write for a registration certificate. (Courtesy the artist)

10WRP-6 Replica of the Cherokee Syllabary. Invented by Sequoyah. This syllabary allowed his people to read and write their own language.

10WRP-4

10WRP-5

GOOD LITTLE INDIAN BOYS

fabric dolls by *Win*

Each doll is individually needle-sculpted and finished by the artist. Each has his own individual Indian name, and each is numbered and signed.

Send the name and number of your doll to:

W. R. PARKER
P. O. Box 1208
Magnolia, Arkansas 71753

and you will receive a certificate of authentification.

10WRP-6

Xavier Roberts
The Little People™
Original Appalachian
Art Works, Inc.

Xavier Roberts and his fantasy, the "adoption" of his Little People, are a facet of doll collecting that provides amusement and amazement, depending on one's point of view. The feeling many collectors enjoy, that their dolls are truly real little personalities, is magnified in Roberts's approach to the marketing of his dolls. Playing on sentiment and whimsy, Roberts never *sells* his dolls. He places his Little People for adoption.

Roberts's dolls are not manufactured. They are born, not in a factory, but in the Cabbage Patch, and then cared for at Babyland General Hospital in Cleveland, Georgia. The building was actually constructed, in 1919, as a doctor's clinic and was renovated for its present purpose by Roberts in 1978. Employees at the "hospital" are "doctors, nurses, surgeons, adoption agents, orthopedic specialists, and fashion consultants" and are "all trained to deliver and care for the Little People."

The fantasy is extended to the completion of a birth certificate and official adoption papers. Furthermore, each Little Person has an individually selected name suited to his or her disposition and personality. Shops carrying these dolls are designated as adoption centers and an adoptive parent must take the Oath of Adoption as prescribed by Babyland General. Each baby receives a birthday card from the hospital on its first birthday.

The range of characters in this fantasy of fun is cleverly worked out. There is Otis Lee, Xavier's very own Little Person, who seems to be the guru of all the babies. Parents write letters to him reporting on the progress of the babies in their new homes. Then there are the Preemies, the tiniest ones, so very delicate and rare. The big babies are dressed in a variety of outfits, from just a diaper and blanket to the nattiest blazer and pants. Finally, there are the Grand Edition Little People who resemble nothing so much as the babies dressed up in finds from grandma's attic or the parents' closets. They are dressed in real mink and satin or in tuxedos.

The Little People arrive with seven different shades of hair and seven different hairstyles, resulting in many combinations. There are also extra outfits such as christening gowns for the Preemies and professional uniforms for the serious-minded Little People. These are scrub suits, doctor and nurse uniforms, and a candy striper uniform.

The babies are made of four-way stretch polyester. Each is hand stitched, eyes are hand painted and glazed, and the hair is of yarn. They average about 23″ long and weigh about two pounds. Some have birthmarks, freckles, or even diaper rash. If a baby is signed by Xavier, it is considered to be a more important collector item than an unsigned one.

Xavier Roberts, the designer who first imagined the babies, is a native of the small town in which his "hospital" is located. He is quite talented, but describes himself as a junior college dropout. He and his babies have been written up in the *Wall Street Journal, Venture Magazine, Newsweek, Time,* and the *Chicago Tribune,* among other publications. They have also appeared on television.

As a result of such coverage, the Little People came to the attention of promoters who perceived the marketing possibilities of Xavier Roberts's little personalities. There was, however, some doubt at Babyland General about sending the babies out into the world without the tender, loving care of Xavier and his staff.

After much thought and many meetings, Xavier Roberts and Coleco reached an agreement. The Little People, with certain changes owing to the requirements of the production line, would be manufactured in quantities never before imagined by their creator. But they would remain unique little individuals thanks to the wonders of computerized selection of details and features. For the first time, children all over the world would be able to adopt their own Cabbage Patch™ Dolls. These new editions, it should be noted, do *not* have cloth heads. They are mentioned here only to point out what can happen in the doll world today.

Few people in the industry were prepared for the impact with which the Cabbage Patch™ Dolls hit the Christmas market of 1983. Perhaps not since the introduction of the first Chatty Cathy by Mattel had there been such a widespread demand for a particular doll. The groundwork had been laid carefully: television "spots," news releases, and shopping center "incidents" all helped create a mild hysteria for Cabbage Patch™ Dolls. References to the dolls appeared in political cartoons and editorials as well as in regular-running cartoon strips.

Disc jockeys mentioned them and a few set up the sort of silly situation events for which DJs are famous, involving Cabbage Patch™ Dolls. One DJ reportedly caused a mild panic when he announced, late in the gift-buying season when shelves were empty of the dolls, that several would be dropped from an airplane onto a shopping center parking lot. Half a dozen were either flown in from England or flown to England, by charter plane or on reserved seat commercial flights, depending on which story was being told. Otherwise sedate, mature, sane people were seen and photographed in heated conflict as hundreds of customers descended on toy departments across the nation. Store owners were greeted by waiting crowds when they unlocked their shop doors each morning. The "Cabbage Patch Phenomenon" it was called — a unique happening.

Doll collectors, however, are able to take the historical view and know there have been other such crazes. There was the Kewpie doll, the Bye-lo Baby, the Shirley Temple doll, and of course, there is Barbie.

What *is* unique about the Cabbage Patch Phenomenon is the high-tech approach used both in the manufacture and selling of the dolls. Computerized selection of features that allows for thousands of combinations, highly organized multimedia promotion that concentrated demand in a very short selling period, and modern transportation methods that allowed huge inventories of the dolls to be moved quickly halfway around the world all contributed to the Cabbage Patch Phenomenon of Christmas, 1983.

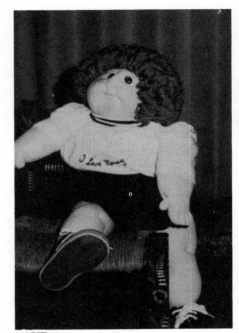

10XR-1

10XR-1   **Hartwell Sean.** Born at Babyland General Hospital, Cleveland, Georgia. Delivered by Xavier Roberts. Adopted by Alice Wardell. (Photograph by Mr. Wardell)

10XR-2   **Hartwell Sean's Birth Certificate.** Duly signed, witnessed, and notarized. (Courtesy Alice Wardell)

10XR-2

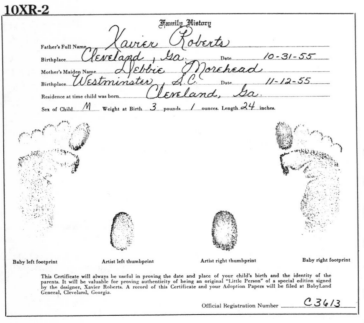

10XR-2

we will NOT sell our babies!

(you have to adopt them!)

These totally original, one-of-a-kind soft sculptured babies live only at Harzfelds in Kansas City. (Well, you KNOW we're suckers for anything sweet, new and different!)

Some are mischievous, some have fussy tempers, a few even have diaper rash—but most just love to be held. Like most children they play, need lots of gentle love and a little discipline too.

They're our Little People.™ No two are alike. Yes, they have birthmarks. They even have birth certificates and official adoption papers (if these babies prove to be the collector's items we think they're going to be, these papers authenticate baby's exact age!)

On your baby's first birthday, you'll get a nice birthday card—'cause Harzfelds misses its kids when they're adopted. Should your baby skin an

elbow or stub a toe, we'll send it right to the Dr. in emergency ("Dr." Xavier Roberts, the designer of these soft sculptured treasures).

We think this is a very special present for a child (and we have a hunch that people who are known for having everything might well end up with a set of adoption papers!)

Our adorable collection of babies can be seen and held in Harzfelds Kids, Downstairs at the Plaza.

Come by Today & Tomorrow to meet our guest nurses who will administer the oath of adoption and make your new baby official.

Adoption fee for Dawn Nicole (left) and Crosby York (right), 125.00. Christmas and signature series babies, 200.00.

Of course, if you want a real baby, we can't blame you!

HARZFELDS

10XR-4

10XR-3

10XR-3   **Blond Pig-Tailed Baby Girl.** One of Xavier Roberts' Little People waiting to be adopted. (From the Babyland General catalog)

10XR-4   **Advertisement by Harzfelds.** Example of the type of marketing approach used by Xavier Roberts to retail his Little People™. This ad was placed in the *Kansas City Star* by Harzfelds, a prominent, old-line, women's fashion store. (Author's collection)

Nerissa Shaub
Nerissa™

Nerissa Shaub is a maker of uniquely styled dolls — her Opulent Older Persons, as she calls them. Nerissa is a fiber artist with a printmaking background. Her images have gradually grown from flat drawings of older people to three-dimensional pillows and the needle-sculptured dolls she presently creates.

Nerissa considers her dolls to represent people who have matured to a point in life where they are most beautiful. She tries to capture a bit of poignant reality in each of her dolls with exacting stitchery that sculptures the face and form. The bright, expressive eyes are touched with eyeshadow, the lips are painted in two shades of color, the cheeks are blushed, and each doll has a navel and a suggestion of sexuality. Arms and hands can be arranged in countless positions and the mohair or fur wigs also have a certain reality about them.

The Opulent Older Persons are copyrighted, one-of-a-kind dolls of cotton or silk in several shades. They are 20″ tall and each is signed by the artist on the left thigh next to the copyright symbol. The doll's individual name is placed on the right thigh and the dolls are dated.

Nerissa's dolls have won awards in regional doll and art shows and were included in the traveling show, Needle Expressions 1980, which toured the United States and Canada. In May 1982, Nerissa completed her one-thousandth doll in this needle-sculptured series.

Shaub, a fulltime fiber artist earning her living from her art, has been making and selling her dolls since 1979. The designs and patterns for the dolls and costumes were developed and copyrighted by Nerissa. A kit is also planned for those who would like to create their own older persons. All parts and accessories are made in the artist's studio by Nerissa and her partner, Roger Armstrong. About thirty art shops and galleries carry the dolls, and they have also proven popular at art shows in the Eastern states and California.

Nerissa's background includes a B.F.A. in printmaking and fiber from Edinboro State College, Edinboro, Pennsylvania. She is a member of Kanawha Valley Doll and Miniature Club, UFDC.

10N-1

10N-2

10N-1   **Vesta, Flordia, and Wendeline, 20″.** In street dress. Nerissa Opulent Older Persons. Note the different skin tones of these three dolls. (Photograph courtesy the artist)

10N-2   **Deerdre in a Negligee, 20″.** A Nerissa Older Person with a Mona Lisa smile. (Photograph courtesy the artist)

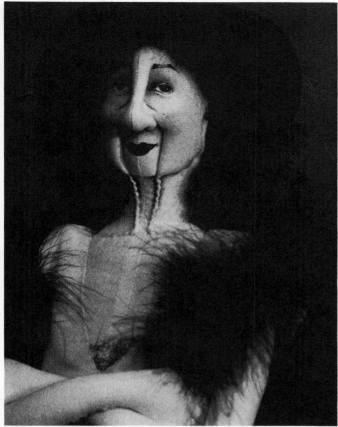

10N-3

10N-4

10N-3   **Hamilton, 20″.** Another Nerissa Older Person. Closeup of this doll shows the unique design and stitching used to achieve a lifelike form. (Photograph courtesy the artist)

10N-4   **Scarlett in a Gown, 20″.** A Nerissa Older Person. Shows the realistic anatomy of the dolls. (Photograph courtesy the artist)

Cynthia Harvey
"Goose" Winston
Goose Kingdom Dolls

Goose Winston (no one ever calls her Cynthia) is a third-generation dollmaker, although she has been selling her dolls for only a few years. In that brief time, with the assistance of one helper, she has registered over seven hundred dolls, every one stitched on an old 1925 Singer treadle sewing machine, which says something about the stamina of artist and sewing machine alike.

The Goose Kingdom dolls are produced on an extremely limited basis. Production for 1983 was limited to 182 dolls sold on a first-come basis. Since many of the dolls are sold in quantity to retail shops, there is always the danger of an artist growing stale when repeating designs. By keeping her total production relatively low, Goose feels she can avoid this problem.

Many of her designs are sold to single dealers who buy the entire year's production of a favorite doll. Goose also likes her retailers to have total production figures on each design because she knows their collector customers are interested in the information as a reference for future values of the dolls. Since the types of dolls vary from year to year, an annual production of fewer than two hundred dolls assures all designs are actually limited editions.

Each doll has a registration number entered on both cards tied to the wrist. One of these cards is a stamped postcard that the retailer removes and mails back to Goose Kingdom after entering the name and address of the purchaser. There, the information is entered into a permanent record. The other card, a folded hangtag, is personally signed by Goose Winston and contains the following information (this taken from a tag attached to a clown doll):

> The head and hands of this clown doll are a cotton canvas which must be washed and tinted before cutting and stitching. Each piece is then hand-stuffed with a forceps tool, holding only a tiny amount of nonallergenic poly-fiber at a time in order to achieve the strength, springy texture for painting, and ability of a doll to pose. Small wire loops are added to curve the hands, with fingers gingerly topstitched. The legs of the clown were especially designed to assume a variety of sitting and kneeling poses, and he is quite fond of perching on a mantle or shelf.
>
> Next, a "cap" of yarn or rayon fringe is stitched directly to the head, the face is needle-sculpted, hand-tinted for rosy accents, painted with acrylics, and finished with trimmed human hair eyelashes. Various trims and accesories are added until at last Clown is assembled with 100-lb-test jewelers twine.
>
> As you can imagine, his creation takes several days of coordinated effort by several patient and skilled people, and each clown finds his own joke along the way . . . And then, if the clown makes ME smile . . . he is named, numbered, signed and registered in my book that day. Look for his identifying marks at the back of the head just beneath the hairline.

The name and address of the purchaser of this clown doll will be sent to Goose Kingdom on the attached card by the store, and will be put into my record to insure that you are registered as the original owner of this precious heirloom.

Winston also signs her dolls "by Goose" directly on the doll. She uses a great variety of materials for the hair, the most common being yarn or fringe. Dolls are button-jointed, limbs are movable at hip and shoulder, and costuming is designed into the construction of the doll rather than added. Heads of dolls are made of artist's canvas, a fabric she uses for the entire doll in her separate gallery line.

From the age of ten years, Winston studied art with private teachers. Later she received a university degree in Fine Arts. Drawing and stitchery are other main interests.

10GW-1

10GW-1 Ada Lee, A Calico Lady, 17″. An original by Goose Winston. Hand-painted features, yarn hair, button joints at hips and shoulders are standard on all of Winston's dolls. (Photograph courtesy the artist)

10GW-2

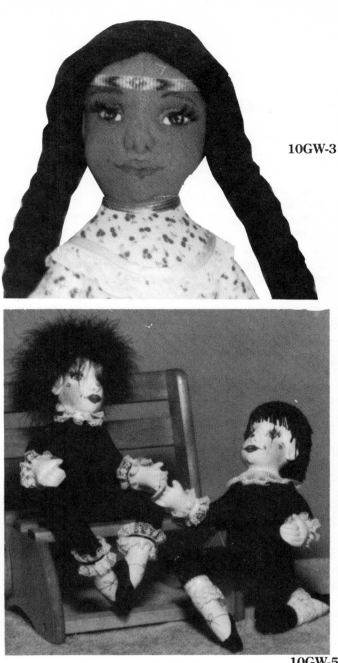

10GW-3

10GW-4

10GW-5

10GW-2 **Calico Lady, 17".** Another in the series shows the distinctive logo and hangtag employed by Winston. This is Loma Lee. (Photograph courtesy the artist)

10GW-3 **Prairie Flower (Daughter of Cynthia Ann Parker), 17".** An Indian Maiden Calico Lady by Goose Winston. (Photograph courtesy the artist)

10GW-4 **Baby Doll.** So new she is not listed on Winston's catalog sheet. Beautifully painted bent-leg baby. (Photograph courtesy the artist)

10GW-5 **Mimes, 17".** These dolls feature one leg with a special knee joint that enables them to assume various positions. A very popular doll with Winston collectors. (Photograph courtesy the artist)

Marilyn Potter's Mini-Collection

From Hawaii came a letter one day written by cloth doll artist and collector, Marilyn Potter, generously offering photographs and information about four charming handmade cloth dolls. Three are original dolls designed and executed by the artists. The fourth was created by a dollmaker who used the Judi's Dolls Shirley Temple pattern shown elsewhere in this book.

These four dolls are representative of the variety to be found in cloth artists' dolls. All share the basic medium, yet each is completely different from the other. Each exhibits the skill and artistry of its creator in very special ways.

10MP-1 **Hawaiian Keiki, 15″.** Original doll by Marilyn W. Q. Potter. Tan, tightly woven fabric, stuffed with polyfill. Hair is brown yarn, features are embroidered. She wears a puka shell necklace. This doll was given to Dorothy Hamill in 1980. Keiki is Hawaiian for child, little one, or baby. (Photograph courtesy the artist)

10MP-2 **Shirley Temple, 18″.** Made by Kathy Mears from a Judi's pattern. Peach-colored knit, stuffed with polyfill. Features are hand painted, curls are of fake fur, shoes and socks are commercially made. Remainder of costume is handmade. (Artist's collection. Photograph courtesy Marilyn Potter)

10MP-1

10MP-2

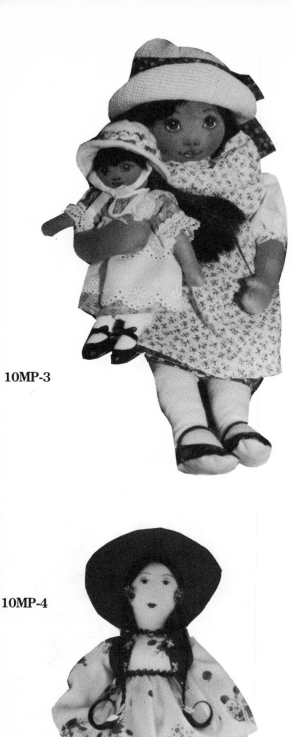

10MP-3

10MP-4

10MP-3 Annabelle and Her Doll. Original dolls by Lorna McGee. Large doll is 14″. Tan stockinette stuffed with kapok. Features are hand painted in artist's inks, wigs are human hair. Annabelle's wired arms hold the smaller doll, which measures 5″. Knees are stitched so doll assumes sitting position. (Artist's collection. Photograph courtesy Marilyn Potter)

10MP-4 Strawberry Damsel, 16″. Original by Charlene Bashlor. From white, tightly woven fabric, stuffed with polyester fiberfill, embroidered features, human hair, dated 1980. Wig is made from a lock of Marilyn Potter's daughter's hair. (Potter collection. Photograph courtesy Marilyn Potter)

Miscellaneous Artists

10AW-1

10AW-1 A Trio of Babies. From the skilled needles of Alice White. Pima cotton stuffed with polyester fill, embroidered faces. All of Alice's patterns are developed by her mother, Elizabeth Buckler. (Author's Photograph. Courtesy the artist)

10AW-2 **Crawling Baby.** By Alice White. Seen at the Melbourne, Florida, Space Coast Doll Club show. (Author's photograph. Courtesy the artist)

10NR-1 **Uncle Remus.** By Noel Richards of Florida. Photographed at the Space Coast Doll Club show by author. (Courtesy the artist)

10EDH-1 **Mary and Laura Ingalls.** From the book *Little House on the Prairie* by Laura Ingalls Wilder. Judy Rankine created these dolls for The Enchanted Doll House from the early 1970s through 1979. Judy made all types of dolls for the shop and her costume work was regarded as outstanding by the owners. As far as is known, Rankine no longer makes dolls. (Photograph from The Enchanted Doll House catalog)

10MD-1 **Dolly Dingle Quartet.** Created by Matt Dillon, staff artist for Hobby House Press, Inc., publishers of the dolls between December 1979 and May 1982. (Photograph courtesy Hobby House)

10AW-2

10NR-1

10MD-1

10EDH-1

11 Kits and Patterns Today — A Modern Cottage Industry

The topic of rag dolls seems a simple one. After all, just how much could one write about such a prosaic thing as a doll made of scraps? There are only a few different types of bodies, only a limited number of things one might do with cloth to create a doll. Right? Wrong!

A survey of this chapter should prove the following point: Rag dolls, cloth dolls, fabric dolls, art dolls — whatever the nomenclature applied — are as varied in conception and design as the imaginations and skills of their creators.

What may be even more surprising to the uninitiated is the underground support system of pattern designers doing business in nearly every corner of the land. These people not only publish large catalogs of patterns for rag dolls, but also create the originals from which their patterns are developed. The character of choice determines body shape and styling as well as costuming, which is often elaborate and always well researched and complete.

As a result, many persons who otherwise might never have ventured into dollmaking, for lack of the skills required to develop their own patterns (or a certain lack of confidence in attempting to do so), have been able to establish themselves in small dollmaking businesses or, simply, to sew dolls as gifts or for church bazaars.

Even the daily newspapers of this country periodically include rag dolls in their pattern offerings. As a result of all this activity, one could spend a lifetime sewing cloth dolls without ever repeating a single design.

Many of these small and not-so-small pattern companies also offer their designs in kit form, a boon to the dollmaker who is isolated or housebound. The women's magazines historically have offered kits, as we have seen in previous chapters. They were created by artists of talent and skill, some of whom, as in the case of Dorothy Heizer, went on to make names for themselves in the collectible doll market. Another more recent example is the Cuddly Doll pattern designed by Madame Alexander for *Woman's Day* magazine, which appeared in the November 1966 issue of that periodical.

Some of the designers offer their dolls not only in pattern and kit form, but also as finished dolls, although the latter are in the minority. As more than one artist has stated, the finished dolls take time away from the creative part of the business. A designer often would rather be engaged in creating new dolls, thus new patterns, than in repeating an already published pattern in finished doll form.

Most of the designers I have talked to indicated they had sold finished dolls at first, but as their businesses grew, they found the only way to reserve needed time for creating new dolls was to discontinue selling finished dolls. Consequently, a collector who owns an early doll made by one of these designers has a nearly one-of-a-kind doll and a true collector's item.

Many of the pattern and kit dolls employ needle-sculpture as a means of creating more naturalistic anatomy. In some there is a definite effort to encourage users of the patterns to take that extra step toward art form. Others merely contain simple instructions for making play dolls. Whatever the approach, all the designers display real concern for giving explicit, easily understood instructions that will implement creation of a soundly constructed doll with great play or collector appeal, or both.

Jan Alovus
Monkey Business

When Jan Alovus redesigned a sock monkey in 1976 as a gift for a friend's child, she did not realize she stood at a crossroads in her life. In that year, a small friend of hers was about to become a brother, and Jan thought about the adjustments ahead for the child. The sock monkey was overhauled so that she could "give birth" from a pocket between her legs. The "baby" had a detachable cord and placenta, and after the birth, the mama monkey could hold the baby.

The response from all who saw the doll encouraged Jan to send samples to several magazines and she received favorable reviews in *Birth and Family Journal* as well as *CoEvolution Quarterly,* the ongoing publication of *The Whole Earth Catalog.*

She soon discovered that what she had felt intuitively about her little friend was being dealt with on a professional level by birth educators and was coming to be known as sibling birth education. Children were being prepared in some cases to attend births. In other cases, they were being informed of the process that would so dramatically change their lives.

The monkey, called Bertha, proved a useful tool and the design was improved and modified, including a caesarean option. In 1979, after numerous requests, Natalie, the human birthing doll, was created.

Jan never advertised the dolls, but various articles about them kept her busy. Then Natalie was recommended in *MS Magazine,* and the *Tallahassee Democrat* ran a feature story that was picked up by UPI, API, and Knight-Ridder News Services. She taped about twenty radio interviews, and the dolls were subsequently mentioned on French and Italian television as well as the Johnny Carson show. An avalanche of orders arrived, accompanied by some fulfillment problems.

Jan turned to friends and members of her cooperative for help in filling the orders. Monkey Business, she says, is developing into a decentralized, nonauthoritarian way to produce and market alternative goods, and the company's structure promises to be as creative and educational as the products it promotes.

"We're going through a lot of changes here to meet the growing interest in our birthing doll," she adds. And her biggest problem right now is finding seamsters.

Natalie is available in kit form and as a finished doll. She has Velcro to help hold her baby, and there is a pattern for her dressing gown included in the kits. There is also a leaflet for duplicating the original Bertha birthing monkey sock doll.

Jan Alovus, if one may judge from the response to her idea, has found a way to support herself through her craft, but also has created a unique kind of rag doll that is not only beautiful but fills a very special need. Birth education groups, hospital auxiliaries, and other health-related groups are successfully using Natalie and Bertha kits for fund-raising projects. Jan Alovus is a woman of purpose. She has a Masters Degree in Art Education from Teachers College, Columbia University. With such a background she was able to see the needs of a little boy and do something about it. She has changed her own life in the process.

11JA-1

11JA-1   **Natalie, 22″.** The human birthing doll. Printed on high-quality fabric, available as a finished doll or in kit form. Velcro closures allow the doll to "hold and nurse her baby." All dolls are marked with a silk-screen tattoo: © **Monkey Business 1977.** (Photograph courtesy the artist)

Alice Ann Beecham
The Kurly Kuddly Kids
The Astro-Knots
Corporation

When a beloved granddaughter asked Alice Beecham in 1977 for a doll that didn't *do* anything, Alice designed the dolls that eventually evolved into the Kurly Kuddly Kids. When the dolls were shown to toy, hobby, and craft shop buyers, a landslide of orders resulted, and the Astro-Knots Corporation was formed to wholesale the dolls in kit form. All of the first dolls were 18", but public demand soon brought about the creation of a 9" model. Many customers, however, wanted only the patterns.

"Kits are fine," says Alice Beecham, "but those (customers) who are bogged down with cartons of fabric, yarn, and trims do not need kits."

Alice and her husband operate their business out of their home. There they have arranged several pleasant work areas for themselves. Alice's favorite is a screenhouse overlooking her rose garden where many dolls have been created. Alice has studied several art courses, but has no degree. A friend, who is a professional artist, discouraged her from going back to art school, saying she might spoil her natural gift for what she does.

And what she does is keep very busy. With a pattern and kit business, a regular newsletter, and a catalog to keep up-to-date, her dolls have succeeded beyond her wildest dreams. The business also keeps her husband busy with bank deposits, paperwork, assembling kits and patterns, and trips to the post office.

Alice has been sewing since she was about six years old, dressing dolls in her own creations. Today she cuts all the parts from pellon and reworks them until she is competely satisfied with the shape and fit. She works with size and measurement charts from pattern magazines and her dolls are realistically proportioned. They range in size from 7½" to 22". She uses fine woven blends of fabric, but prefers soft, brushed knits, especially for baby dolls. There are dolls of children, babies, Orientals, blacks, a clown, a little old lady, and many others shown in her catalog.

An outstanding feature of an Alice Beecham doll is the wig. Each of her dolls has a head full of washable, stay-in curls. A simple twist on an old crochet stitch results in a string of charming curls. A wig may be crocheted in an evening or two and patterns are available in individual styles suited to the particular dolls.

When Alice Beecham first began making dolls, she marked each one on the sole of a foot with ASTRO-KNOTS/KURLY KUDDLY KIDS/(date). Later dolls have a label sewn in. She no longer sells dolls, however, but has a long list of dollmakers who use her patterns and sell regularly at shows and sales. In addition, she no longer sells wholesale, preferring to pass the savings along to her customers.

Alice has taken a reverse course to that of many of the other patternmakers. She began with a wholesale business that quickly evolved into a retail business. One suspects from discussing the matter with her that she enjoys the direct customer contact of her mail-order business more than dealing with shop owners or buyers who are not the actual consumers of her wares.

"What I am striving for," she remarks, "is to bring happiness to my customers with and through my dolls." One can only believe that the Kurly Kuddly Kids are doing just that for the many customers of Alice Beecham.

11AB-1

11AB-1 **Polly and Little Alice, 18" and 9".** Made from the first kits produced by Alice Beecham. (Photograph courtesy the artist)

11AB-2 **Kelly, 13″.** Dimples, auburn washable stay-in curls, wears bright green pinafore and slippers. (Photograph courtesy the artist)

11AB-3 **Baby Janet.** This baby has a Bye-lo type, carefully shaped body and permanently curled wig. (Photograph courtesy the artist)

11AB-4 **Mary Jo, 14″.** A country girl. Designed as the cover doll for an issue of *Crafts Magazine*. This doll now appears in the Beecham catalog in various outfits. Other Beecham designs will be seen in *Crafts* in the future. (Photograph courtesy the artist)

11AB-2

11AB-3

11AB-4

11AB-5

11AB-5 **Six of the First Dolls.** Woven fabric bodies, embroidered faces, crisp fabric dresses, vinyl shoes. All by Alice Beecham. (Photograph courtesy the artist)

Colleen Bergman
Colleen's Cottage
Ethnic Dolls

Each of the designers mentioned in this book seems to have seen a need and tried to fill it through their particular talents and skills. Colleen Bergman is no exception. There are forty different ethnic dolls in the Colleen's Cottage collection. Patterns and kits are offered via a carefully illustrated catalog.

All the costumes and patterns are designed by Colleen after many hours of research. Every detail of every costume must be absolutely authentic. There are Japanese, African, Mexican, Norwegian, and Scottish misses. There is a Corfu Greek, a Korean bride, a Krakow Pole, a Lowicz Pole, and a Southern Belle. The range is ever widening as Colleen continues to add to her line when requests for specific ethnic dolls come from her customers. She also hopes to add several more boy dolls in the future.

The doll kits are in the 19″ size and completed dolls are finished in 14″ and 19″ heights. All of Colleen's finished dolls are signed, dated, and numbered in indelible ink. She has miniaturized her patterns so the home sewer can make 10″ dolls. However, Colleen emphasizes that no one should choose the 10″ size thinking to save time since the smaller dolls require as much work as the larger ones.

Colleen has been making dolls since 1979, although she has worked in the costume design and craft design fields for ten years. She has been drawing and doing needlework for twenty years and is currently enrolled in the correspondence course of the Art Instruction School. She is now editor and publisher of a new quarterly devoted to promotion of quality cloth dolls. The first issue of *The Cloth Doll Quarterly,* released in July 1982, included articles about making and marketing cloth dolls, where to find and buy supplies, copyright laws, history of cloth dolls, and doll repairing and cleaning. The quarterly will also feature specialty cloth dolls from the collections of the finest quality cloth doll designers in America. Each issue includes a full-size pattern for a quality cloth doll, with the first issue being a fully jointed version of the *Godey's Lady's Book* doll.

11CB-1

11CB-1 **A Knight and Maiden of the 1400s.** By Colleen Bergman. Available in kit, pattern, or finished doll form. (Photograph courtesy the artist)

11CB-2   **Eskimo.** By Colleen Bergman. Wears real fur parka. (Photograph courtesy the artist)

11CB-3   **Colleen's Cottage Ethnic Dolls.** Indicates the wide range of subjects in the collection. Standing (l to r): Dutch, American Pioneer, Seminole Indian Maiden. Seated: Italian, Swiss German. (Photograph courtesy the artist)

11CB-4   **Drawings from Colleen's Cottage Pattern Catalog.** (Courtesy the artist)

11CB-2

11CB-3

11CB-4

La Raine Crawford
pattern*plus

Rainie Crawford started pattern*plus, a mail-order company, in 1976, by offering cloth doll kits, patterns, and hard-to-find dollmaking supplies. She had noticed that most of the cloth doll patterns being offered made use of the traditional materials and decided to try to update the cloth doll for the home sewer. She liked the convenience and workability of some of the contemporary fabrics and developed brushable two-seam wigs from fake furs, faces created with fabric crayons, and iron-on face transfers in full color.

She found that her customers loved the time-saving features of her patterns as well as the "plus" she put into each design — Jed's overalls with worn knees created by sandpapering the denim; big, bold hats; pert little faces with wistful pouts or playful grins or surprised expressions; and the accessories designed especially for each doll. There are teddy bears and tiny bunnies, a clown and a goose, a felt sailboat and suitcase, and even felt musical instruments.

Jenny and Jed were featured in the October 1978 issue of *Woman's Day* magazine as "The Farmer Dolls," with a slight change here and there for the special presentation. Kits for each doll were offered through the magazine's craft department. The following year, Rainie designed Lucy for *Family Circle* magazine, and Lucy was featured on the cover of the February 20, 1979, issue with her teddy bear in tow.

Rainie's dolls range in size from 11" to 16". She does her own designing, costuming, and patternmaking. She has had no formal training in art, but says she is enjoying a "happy marriage of past skills in sewing, portrait painting, and understanding dolls through the old bisques and chinas." She is a founding member of the Carousel Doll Club of Region 14, UFDC, which has forty-two members from three states on its rolls.

Rainie does not sell completed dolls and does not consider herself a doll artist, but rather a designer. Whether artist or designer, La Raine Crawford's skill and talent are evident in her dolls. Her humor comes through in everything she does.

11RC-1

11RC-1 **Jenny, 15½".** The daydreamer of Rainie Crawford's pattern*plus dolls. Hair is fake fur, features are an iron-on transfer. (Photograph courtesy the artist)

11RC-2 **Jed, 15½".** Jenny's kissin' cousin, tousled carrot-colored hair, freckles galore, and worn-at-the-knees jeans. The designer has tucked a roadside weed into Jed's hat. (Photograph courtesy the artist)

11RC-3 **Lucy, 15½".** The cover girl from *Woman's Day,* February 20, 1979 issue. (Photograph courtesy the artist)

11RC-4 **Amelia, 15½".** Carries a brown felt suitcase covered with stickers that are included with her pattern. Her face is made from an iron-on transfer. All of these designs are copyrighted by Rainie Crawford. (Photograph courtesy the artist)

11RC-2

11RC-4

11RC-3

Dorothy Nell Foster
The Scrapbox Dolls

Dorothy Nell Foster, with her daughters Sharon Kaye and Karen Sue, create, draft, and sew all dolls at The Scrapbox. Since 1972, these three women have created a multitude of cleverly designed and named dolls, then made the patterns available to others for home sewing. With Dorothy's commercial art training at the Federal Art School and her experience as a commercial artist before her marriage, the two daughters grew up in an environment of artistic endeavor and have drawn and painted "all their lives," as Sharon expresses it.

Their dolls range in size from 7½" to 28" and are made of unbleached muslin, stuffed with polyester filling. Heads and necks are painted with flesh-colored gesso, then faces and shoes are painted with acrylic artist's colors. The entire production is a group effort. Mother does the hair and makes the clothing, while the daughters stuff dolls and paint features and shoes.

Dolls are marked on the lower back of the neck: **The Scrapbox Dolls, (date).** The number of dolls made for sale is limited annually in order that the women may devote more time to creating new dolls and patterns. Much good humor is evident in the selection of names for the dolls. Names are chosen also to match each doll's character.

Dottie and Priscilla and Zeb and Jenny are Yesterday's Children dressed in appropriately nostalgic costume. Becky of Runnybrook Farm is a tousle-curled tot. Billy the Kidder is a cowboy with boots, hat, and lariat. Peggy wears a sailor dress, real shoes, and carries her own toy boat. Penny is a bright-faced child in gingham pinafore. All of these dolls are 21".

Dewey and Daisy are the 18" Ittle Bitty Hillbillys. Herbie is a 20¼" clown in suspenders. Cindy and Sandy, the Tiny Tow Head Twins, are also 18", as are Mr. and Mrs. Santa. (Their helper is 13" Elfis, a merry gnome of red and white striped fabric with felt clothing.)

In the 24" size are Melinda, a very beautifully dressed young city miss, and her country cousin, Molly, dressed in checked gingham and white apron. Baby Sue is a 19" charmer, and another baby, just 16", is billed as the Happy New Year Baby — Baby Patty Cake. This infant wears a long christening dress and has a unique body design. Her legs look like a very young infant's legs. There is also a 16" Angela, the Littlest Angel, with fuzzy house slippers and white fur hair topped with a pipe cleaner halo.

The Little Women dolls are 28" and designed to recreate the characters that are favorites of dollmakers and movie buffs alike. Thus far only the four girls, Jo, Meg, Beth, and Amy have been made. However, it is most likely they will be joined in the future by Marme and perhaps even Laurie. Such is the way with dollmakers. A collection, be it of patterns or dolls, is never complete. There are always one or two more that need making.

11FS-1

11FS-2

11FS-1   **Jenny, 21".** Red-haired charmer with green eyes and a print dress to match. In her white apron she carries colorful felt flowers. Her pantaloons are lace-trimmed to match her dress. (Photograph courtesy the artist)

11FS-2   **Zeb, 21".** Jenny's friend. His coloring matches hers. He is ready for a fishing expedition with his own twig fishing pole and can of worms. (Photograph courtesy the artist)

11FS-3 **Melinda (left) and Molly (right), 24″.** Dressed appropriately for the city and country, respectively. All Scrapbox dolls are of unbleached muslin, stuffed with polyester, with hand-painted features and fluffy yarn hair. (Photograph courtesy the artist)

11FS-3

Carolee Alt Luppino
Carolee Creations
The SewSweet Dolls

Carolee Luppino learned to sew on her grandmother's treadle machine while still quite small. She spent a great deal of her time as a child sewing clothes for her dolls. Years later, she made her first cloth doll for her one-year-old daughter and claims she was forever after "hooked" on cloth doll making. The skills she gained in childhood serve her well in her present pursuits.

"Back in 1975," she relates, "I developed a simple, four-piece head construction that many designers are now using. I also made a cloth doll with four faces and a rotating head, which was unique in 1975. The idea has since been used by other designers."

Leafing through Carolee's all-color pattern and kit catalog is a delightful experience. Her dolls are displayed against sets that show off their charms to best advantage. Her SewSweet Dolls include a long-limbed basketball player named Stretch plus two Little Dudes, baby cowpersons (a boy and a girl) who wear cowboy boots and hats, ride padded stick horses, and sport twin holsters loaded with, of all things, baby bottles complete with nipples. These babies, as do many of the others, have navels, a feature normally covered on most dolls, but quite evident on this diapered pair. There are twin babies with applied noses and ears, dressed in identical sailor-suit diaper sets and wearing identical yellow yarn mops of hair, known as the Sunshine Twins.

There is Trixie-Turn-Me, the baby with four expressions on one head. There is a group of oriental children, a flock of angels, a den of elves, and a whole kindergarten of other charming moppets. There are also a number of characters, including the 22″ Calvin Clown and 20″ Lulu, the Classy Flapper. And last, but not least, there is the Tooth Fairy, a 16″ maiden with pink angel hair and a huge toothbrush.

Most of Carolee's dolls are made of peach broadcloth, although some of the babies are of pink fleece that has just a bit of stretch to it. Yarn and craft fur are used for hair. Sizes range from dollhouse scale to lifesize babies and toddlers. The dolls are three-dimensional and many have delineated fingers and toes, plus round little applied noses. Carolee signs all her sample dolls on the back and adds the date she finished each doll. Many of her designs come in kit form as well as patterns.

Carolee's only art training was in high school, but she has developed her innate skills to a degree that has enabled her to create a large body of work and build a successful business in a relatively short time.

11CL-1

11CL-2

11CL-3

11CL-1   **Amy, 16½″.** This doll is featured on the cover of the SewSweet Dolls catalog, has complete wardrobe, and is available in kit or pattern form. (Photograph courtesy the artist)

11CL-2   **Katie, 18½″.** This toddler by Carolee Luppino is available in kit or pattern form. Eyes are ready-cut felt pieces available from the artist. (Photograph courtesy the artist)

11CL-3   **Tootie (left), Corky (right), and Stretch (center).** These dolls can be made up in your favorite team colors. Stretch also stars in track and tennis. Girls are 18″. Stretch is 22½″. (Photograph courtesy the artist)

11CL-4 **The Sunshine Twins, 23″.** By Carolee Alt Luppino. Applied noses and ears, delineated fingers and toes. The smaller doll is Baby Squeeze-Me. (Photograph courtesy the artist)

11CL-4

Tressa E. Mabry
The Nettie Dolls

Tressa Mabry began by making simple, flat rag dolls with yarn hair and embroidered features in 1974. Within months, she realized she would never be able to keep up with orders, and her pattern business was born. With her husband, George, Tressa owns and operates NETTIE™ Doll Patterns and has registered her trademark for both dolls and patterns. Their corporation is T.E.M. of California, from Tressa's three initials.

Both Mabrys have degrees in electrical engineering from the University of Illinois and no art background. They seem, however, eminently suited to running a business that began as a hobby and has now become a very successful venture.

Tressa designs the dolls and clothing and sews the complete doll and wardrobe. When she is satisfied with the design, she pencils the layout and George inks the final pattern. In addition, he photographs the model and helps Tressa write the pattern instructions. George is also in charge of the computerized mailing list, inventory, and order-filling system.

The catalog of NETTIE™ patterns features Tressa Mabry's Fashion Dolls on the cover. The stance of the dolls and the authenticity of the costuming is such that at first glance one might think these dolls were expensive antique French bisques. A closer look reveals they are beautifully executed cloth dolls dressed in styles ranging from a nineteenth century bride to a lady in 1920s street dress. Their coiffures are correct and chic, their chapeaux elegant. And the dolls are only 11½″ tall.

300

The NETTIE™ dolls include three series of Childhood Dolls (8″ to 9″ children dressed in period fashions); Dollhouse Dolls (scaled 1″ to 1′); Keepsake Dolls (11″ dolls dressed in four different sets of period fashions); the Slim Dolls (9″ school children); the Baby Dolls (9″ Pram set and Cradle Roll set); and the Toddler Dolls (9″ chubby Romper set and Play Pals set). There are also the NETTIE™ Escort Dolls, the 12″ men whose fashions correspond to those of the Fashion Dolls.

Tressa continues to offer the pattern for her original NETTIE™ Doll, a 9″ flat-body play doll. Her Nugget Patterns line features tiny Christmas tree ornament dolls, Victorian lingerie for the 11½″ Fashion Dolls, a layette for the Doll House Baby, more clothes for the 11½″ Fashions, plus five beautiful 12″ children that any collector or child would treasure.

All the patterns are professionally printed, a point made by many of the patternmakers. The NETTIE™ patterns are unique in that they are printed on high-quality paper punched to fit a standard three-ring binder, a feature that makes them easy to use and store. Each pattern set has sixteen pages (eight sheets printed both sides), plus a cover page. (The Nugget patterns are on two sheets only.) There are patterns for a wide assortment of wardrobe items in each set, including hats, caps, shoes, and underwear.

Tressa Mabry does not sell her dolls. They remain in her home, a part of her collection, a reference for her patternmaking projects. She has marked all her dolls with hangtags on their wrists and urges that dollmakers sign their work from the beginning. There seems to be a consensus among dollmakers: Many who did not sign early dolls regret the omission. Collectors would heartily agree that all dolls should be signed and dated.

11TM-2

11TM-1

11TM-1 **Fashion Doll, 11½″.** This doll by Tressa Mabry evokes the essence, the *elan* of the antique bisque French fashion dolls. This doll is from her 1880s Carriage Patterns. (Photograph courtesy the artist)

11TM-2 **Baby, 9″.** From the Pram Patterns. This baby is dressed in a 1900s layette, trimmed in ruffles and lace. The Cradle Roll Baby wears contemporary fashions. (Photograph courtesy the artist)

11TM-3	**Toddler Girl, 12″.** The Nugget Patterns include this as well as a Toddler Boy, a Baby, and a pair of 12″ Childhood Dolls representing a slightly older boy and girl. (Photograph courtesy the artist)

11TM-4	**Little Charmers, 8″.** From the Childhood Dolls Series III. In clothing styled from 1920s fashions. Each pattern has four changes of clothing for both dolls. (Photograph courtesy the artist)

11TM-3

11TM-4

Sheila Peters
Sheila's Kids

Sheila Peters uses her four children as models for her dolls. She has been making and selling dolls since 1977, but only began offering patterns for her designs in December 1979. She is presently developing three new series of dolls, each based on a single basic body pattern, with several sets of clothing, hairstyles, and features.

Sheila's dolls are made of flesh-colored broadcloth, although she has experimented occasionally with felt. All the clothing, wigs, and accessories are handmade by Sheila, who says she has had no art training. She just likes to sew, and cloth dolls were a special interest. She especially dislikes some of the commercial cloth dolls and wanted to make a very special doll for touching and hugging. She always places a sign on her display tables at shows that reads, "Please Touch."

Brenda is her first doll, made from a photograph of her daughter at nine months. Patricia was made to enter in a fair where she won first prize in the doll category as well as Best of Show in the Textile Division. The hair for Patricia was made from a full-size adult wig and the eyelashes are of single-strand embroidery floss, sewn in.

Sheila also has designed a bespectacled Grandma doll with matronly figure, the pattern for which includes a grandmotherly hairdo and instructions for the wire eyeglasses.

Sheila's Kids are play dolls, the dollmaker stresses, but she is amazed at the collector interest she has encountered in both the dolls and patterns.

11SP-1

11SP-1   **Brenda, 17".** The first doll created by Sheila Peters. A baby-type complete with disposable diapers. (Photograph courtesy the artist)

11SP-2   **Patricia, 14″.** Made especially to enter in a fair, this doll brought home a first prize in doll category and Best of Show in the Textile Division. (Photograph courtesy the artist)

11SP-3   **A New Series, 14″.** These babies are the Brenda doll in 14″ size. They are so new, at this writing, that they have not yet been named. (Photograph courtesy the artist)

11SP-2

11SP-3

Dorothy Avey Sanders
The Dorida Dolls

Dorothy Sanders believes she may have been the first American designer of realistic, detailed fabric play dolls also intended for collectors. Her first dolls were made by Dorothy and her mother, Ida Avey, in 1945, after a year of experimentation, although her patterns were not marketed until December of 1978. The dolls were named Dorida, using the names of both women.

With a B.S. and M.A. in art education, Dorothy taught art and crafts for twenty-five years, all the while working to perfect her designs and techniques and producing many dolls for collectors in the Van Nuys, California, area where she lived. Dorothy says her designs were probably influenced by a night school class she took in the late 1930s taught by a Walt Disney artist. She remembers the Disney studio was in production on

"Snow White" at the time.

All of the Dorida dolls are signed on the left hip **DORIDA** © **(year),** with an entwined **DS,** and the proclamation **none authentic without this signature.** Sizes are from 7″ to the lifesize 18-month-old babies. All-cotton muslin is used exclusively for the dolls and Dorothy dyes the material to the exact flesh shades she requires. She also does all her own designing, cutting, fitting, and sewing of the costumes.

Without prompting, Dorothy brought up the matter of what to call the sort of doll she makes, unconsciously repeating the litany of many of the cloth doll artists:

> Doll artists who work in fabrics sometimes rebel at having their creations referred to as "rag" dolls. It somehow seems a little bit of a "put down." They prefer to call their creations "cloth" dolls or "fabric" dolls. The dolls of today are a far cry from the true rag dolls which I understand were actually made from discarded clothes and stuffed with rags. This was from necessity — cloth being dear in those days.
>
> Today cloth doll makers buy the best of materials and spend many, many hours creating their dolls, so the term "rag" hardly applies, do you think?

However they are designated, it is true that Dorothy Sanders's dolls, as those of the other doll artists featured in this book, are clearly not of the "ol' rag doll" school. The imagination and creativity that go into the making of these dolls is eloquently illustrated in the winsome expressions, the cleverly designed bodies, and the carefully worked-out costuming of these charming cloth dolls.

11DS-1

11DS-2

11DS-3

11DS-1   **The First Doll.** Made in 1945. Dorothy Sanders had never examined a doll pattern in her life when she set about making the pattern for this doll. As a consequence of what she calls her ignorance, the doll had a completely different appearance and construction from other cloth dolls of the period. (Photograph courtesy the artist)

11DS-2   **The First Dorida Dolls.** Made in 1947. These were made from the original pattern and have set-in eyes and lashes that Dorothy made herself, since there were none on the market at that time. The first Dorida dolls were a dumpy 18″, stuffed with wool combings from a blanket mill, and had curled woolen yarn hair. (Photograph courtesy the artist)

11DS-3   **Tommy and Tammy, 19″.** These toddlers have embroidered features and wigs of wool yarn. The girls' wigs are permanently curled. Dolls are stuffed with polyester. All clothing has finished seams and the shoes are handmade. These two dolls are the first published in patterns. (Photograph courtesy the artist)

11DS-4 **Baby Joy, 14″.** Baby Joy also has a brother, Little Buddy. Both babies illustrate the refinement of her style from the almost caricatured babies of the 1940s to the naturalistic human infant of today. These babies are the latest patterns to be released by Dorothy Sanders. (Photograph courtesy the artist)

11DS-4

Judi K. Ward
Judi's Dolls

Every collector knows just how difficult it can be to find a 27″ composition Shirley Temple doll. Judi Ward's customers have no problem, however. They can sew their own 27″ cloth version of that elusive collectible. Judi does cloth reproductions of old porcelain and composition dolls. Shirley Temple is just one of the familiar faces in Judi's extensive catalog.

There is a set of 18″ Dionnes, a pair of Sasha look-alikes, a 22″ Patsy Ruth, a 16″ Kewpie-type, and a 13″ Troll, plus Terri Lee and Jerri Lee. What more could a collector want? Perhaps a cloth Buddy Lee? Judi has one, plus a bevy of other desirable collectible dolls reproduced in cloth.

Judi's patterns are created for the dollmaker market. She seldom sells finished dolls except an occasional special order. She prefers instead devoting her time to the development of new designs. When she is able to make up a small inventory, she sells at doll, craft, and hobby shows.

Ward has been making and selling dolls since about 1973 and first marketed her patterns in 1978. Her dolls are marked JUDI and the date on the buttock. She uses velours, polyester knits, and felt to make dolls ranging in size from 13″ to 30″. Faces are painted with acrylic colors, although most of her dollmaking customers embroider the faces on the dolls made from Judi's patterns. She designs and makes each item of clothing and says

her only training was a high school commercial art course.

In addition to the cloth repros, the Judi's Dolls catalog includes patterns for making lifesize marionettes of cloth, a real innovation. These 24″ to 26″ marionettes are operational and may be dressed in babies' clothes. Conversely, the clothing patterns Judi has designed for the marionettes will fit real babies.

Judi's Four Stages of Infancy dolls are also unique. There is a newborn designed to represent an infant up to three months old. The second doll is a three to six-month baby, the third, a six to nine-month baby, and the fourth is a nine to twelve-month toddler. There is also a lifesize boy who is the big brother to the infants. David is an eighteen- to twenty-four-month-old boy with "fur" hair and delineated fingers, toes, and ears. All of Judi's dolls are three-dimensional as opposed to the flat rag doll type.

Ward has developed special beginner's patterns that she recommends since they include many teaching hints and instructions for the inexperienced dollmaker. Her basic beginner pattern makes three different dolls and teaches three different arm, leg, and foot styles, three different faces, and three different hair styles. This doll is 24″ and little-girl proportioned.

Judi's patterns are designed to be made and sold by the dollmaker, and her copyrights cover the dolls in pattern form only. She says many of her customers have very successful dollmaking businesses based on the dolls made from her patterns.

11JW-1
11JW-3

11JW-2

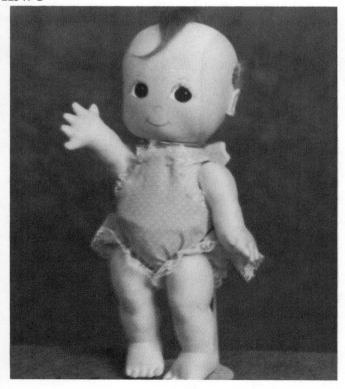

11JW-1	**The Bi-Lo Baby, 20″.** Judi Ward's cloth version of the Bye-lo Baby. Face and hair are done in ordinary crayon. (Photograph courtesy the artist)
11JW-2	**Mary (left), Bed Doll (center), and Beth (right).** Mary, 22″, is a cloth reproduction of a bisque-head, shoulderplate antique. The Bed Doll, 30″, is also a shoulderplate construction with non-removable, high-heeled shoes. Beth, 24″, is a shoulderplate reproduction of a composition and cloth collectible doll. (Photograph courtesy the artist)
11JW-3	**Cupie, 16″.** Judi Ward's version of a VFF (Very Familiar Face). Three-dimensional, jointed doll. (Photograph courtesy the artist)

11JW-4   **Shirley Temple, 27″ and 18″.** One of the most popular of Judi Ward's patterns. Wardrobe patterns are based on Shirley's movie clothes. (Photograph courtesy the artist)

11JW-4

Sandy Williams Crafted Heirlooms

Sandy Williams is the eldest daughter of Paul Ruddell who founded Hobby House Press and published doll-related materials for many years. Sandy grew up in the rarified atmosphere of doll book publishing. One summer she was an associate of Clara Hallard Fawcett, noted doll author and illustrator, at a summer camp in Maine. She worked as a layout artist for Hobby House, and since 1976 has worked on many freelance projects for the publisher.

Sandy contributes dollmaking and doll-dressing patterns on a regular basis to *Doll Reader,* also published by Hobby House. When she approached the publisher with her idea for the Crafted Heirlooms series, beginning with the First Ladies, the idea was welcomed warmly and a tradition was born. The uncut First Ladies kits were quickly followed by Little Linens and Little Lingerie, hand-screened fabric sheets ready to cut out

and complete. Victorian Little Linens and Twentieth Century Little Linens were also added to the line, as well as unique doll-related tote bags and other items. Collectors hope that additional First Ladies will be forthcoming.

11SW-1

11SW-2

11SW-3

11SW-1   **Martha Washington.** By Sandy Williams. Published by Hobby House in their Crafted Heirlooms Series. Kit includes doll and complete costume. (Photograph courtesy Hobby House)

11SW-2   **Martha Jefferson Randolph.** By Sandy Williams. Another kit in the Crafted Heirlooms Series. (Photograph courtesy Hobby House)

11SW-3   **Abigail Adams.** By Sandy Williams. Third in the Crafted Heirlooms Series. (Photograph courtesy Hobby House)

12 Kits and Patterns from Newspapers, Magazines, and Pattern Companies

Women's magazines have long been a guide to fashion, a handbook of housekeeping methods and equipment, and a source of patterns for clothing, soft toys, dolls' clothing, and rag dolls.

McCall patterns were featured in *McCall's* magazine and Butterick patterns were advertised in a number of periodicals. Crowell Publishing Company, publishers of *Woman's Home Companion* and *Farm and Fireside* magazines, advertised a complete line of patterns, including rag dolls. The *Ladies' Home Journal* touted its own line of patterns. *Modern Priscilla Magazine* regularly featured patterns and kits for rag dolls, as did many other women's magazines.

One of the earliest commercial rag doll patterns known to me is Butterick No. 81, published by Butterick in 1882. Two tracings for faces were given so the doll could be made up as a caucasian or a black. This doll seems to be the forerunner of a variety of later designs offered by several different companies.

No. 81.

Length of Doll, ... **18 inches.**

Quantity of Material, 27 inches wide, ... ⅝ *yard.*
Or, Quantity of Material, 36 inches wide, ... ⅜ *yard.*

PRICE, 15 CENTS.

CAUTION:—FOLLOW THE DIRECTIONS CAREFULLY.

PATTERN FOR A RAG DOLL.
(ISSUED DECEMBER, 1882.)

This pattern, suitable for flannel, muslin, linen, jean or any material from which it is desirable to make the doll, is in ten pieces: Arm, and Half of the Body. The parts are notched to prevent mistakes in putting together. Fold the material *lengthwise* through the middle. Lay the pattern on the goods: placing the *longest straight edge* of the body on the fold, and the arm *lengthwise*. Pin them smoothly, mark all the notches and perforations, cut the parts out, and take off the patterns. Take up the darts, placing the perforations *exactly opposite* each other. Close the seams according to the notches, leaving an opening between the single notches in the center-back seam. Also close the seams of the arm according to the notches, terminating the outside seam in dart style, at the perforation. Sew in the arm according to the notches. Now stuff the doll with cotton, bran, saw-dust or rags, packing it closely, and stuffing the arms and legs first. Then shape fingers and toes by rows of stitching. Close the opening at the back with over-and-over stitches. With indelible ink or cotton, outline the mouth between the lowest perforations in the head, the nose between the middle perforations, and the eyes at the remaining perforations. The back of the head may be covered with ravelled stocking yarn, jute, lamb's-wool or curled hair, and the eyes may be formed of beads and outlined with cotton or thread.

Allowance for ¼ inch seams is made in the pattern.

Address: THE BUTTERICK PUBLISHING CO. [Limited], 171 to 177 Regent St., London, W.; or 535 Broadway, New York.

At least as early as 1910, *Woman's Home Companion* offered their Pattern No. 1667 for a rag doll in 14″, 18″, and 22″ sizes with a middy suit and sailor hat. A lovely gift for a child, and some "nice, sensible clothes," the description read. These dolls were to be finished with hand-painted or embroidered faces, the success of which depended entirely upon the skill of the mother who was sewing the doll. Price per set was just ten cents.

This same cloth doll pattern, or a very similar one, was advertised in the December 1912 issue of *Woman's Home Companion* as Pattern No. 1913. The same sizes were given for the dolls, dressed that year in the very popular Russian dress, still with hand-painted or embroidered faces and only ten cents.

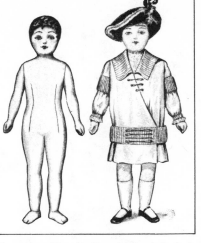

No. 2426—Rag Doll and Dress, including Transfer Pattern for Face

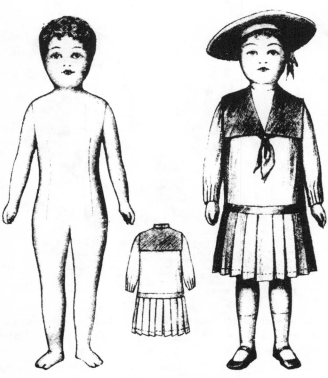

No. 1667—Rag Doll and Middy Suit

Patterns cut for dolls 14, 18 and 22 inches high.   Quantity of material required for the rag doll, in medium size, or 18 inches tall, three fourths of a yard of thirty-six-inch material.   For the middy suit, one yard of thirty-six-inch material, with one fourth of a yard of contrasting material for trimming.   The price of each set of patterns illustrated on this page is ten cents.   Order from Pattern Department

No. 2669

The December 1914 issue of *Woman's Home Companion* featured Pattern No. 2426, again a pattern similar to previous ones, only this time in one size only (size not given). A heat transfer pattern for the face was included. Price was ten cents. In the same issue was Pattern No. 2669, a very human-looking stuffed bug, cut in one size (again size not stated). Only ten cents for this unusual pattern.

Also illustrated in the December 1914 issue is another ten-cent pattern, No. 2672, for a clown doll and costume cut in one unspecified size. The offer indicates the dolls may be stuffed with sawdust, bran, or small pieces of rag. One can only wonder at the condition of a well-loved doll stuffed with either of the first two materials. Such stuffing materials would certainly not have made for a washable rag doll, a fact that should make the modern cloth dollmaker most thankful for polyester fiberfill.

By 1917, the magazine was offering Pattern No. 2928, an 18″ "old-fashioned" rag doll with an iron-on transfer face, for fourteen cents. Also illustrated was a Yankee Doodle Gollywog with a big smile, furry hair, rakish feather, and American flag. The last doll was designed to be made of old stockings. The pattern cost ten cents.

No. 2672

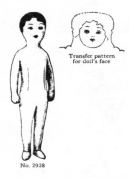

Transfer pattern for doll's face

No. 2928

In the November 25, 1908, issue of *Farm and Fireside*, Pattern No. 1241 for a 22″ doll, dress, and sunbonnet was offered. The doll is probably the same as those offered in *Woman's Home Companion* in 1910. This issue of *Farm and Fireside* also listed Pattern No. 1050 for a 22″ doll and dress of a different style, also priced at ten cents for the set. These patterns were to be ordered from Madison Square Patterns and were copyrighted by Crowell Publishing Company, the same publishers who claimed copyright for the patterns offered in *Woman's Home Companion.*

No. 1241—Rag Doll, Dress and Sunbonnet

Pattern cut in one size, for doll *22* inches high. Quantity of material required for this doll, three fourths of a yard of thirty-six-inch material.. Quantity of material required for dress, one yard of thirty-six-inch material, one fourth of a yard of velvet and one eighth of a yard of lace. Quantity of material required for sunbonnet, one fourth of a yard of material.

A rag doll pattern was shown in the *Quarterly Style Book — Winter Number* (approximately 1910), the catalog for *Ladies' Home Journal* patterns. Pattern No. 4126, a 15″ doll complete with chemise, kimono, and bonnet, was priced at fifteen cents. The doll appears to be a very simply styled, classic rag doll with large eyes and big, watermelon grin.

The following year, the old-fashioned doll had become a Salvation Army Lassie in complete uniform. The same pattern number was used on this edition as in the previous year.

This year the rag dolls have a new costume — the red and blue of the Salvation Army Lassie

Transfer for rag doll's face

No. 2928
No. 3644

The brave Red Cross dog will take good care of all the dollies. No. 3645.

No 2928

It is pleasant to be a rag doll, because dropping on the hard floor doesn't hurt you a bit.

4126

Modern Priscilla
Patterns and Kits

Favorites with many needleworkers were dolls based on popular subjects of the day. Designers for *Modern Priscilla* magazine often chose topical subjects. At least two of the Dorothy Heizer kits offered by this magazine represented the modern woman.

Another kit with this theme is Dulcie Daring by Eveline Johnson. Dulcie is a striking young aviatrix. In 1929, the lure of flight had touched the women of the day in a very special way. (What good were freedom, equality, short hair, short skirts, and labor-saving devices unless one struck out to find excitement and fulfillment in new fields?)

Dulcie's only wardrobe was her flying costume. Pattern No. 29-11-1 was actually a kit furnished with stamped gingham, mohair, brown leather, embroidery floss, and complete directions for finishing Dulcie. Although the size is not given in the illustrated offer, the ordering information lists Dulcie as 19″.

In contrast, Dulcie's young contemporary, Felicity, offered in the December 1928 issue of *Modern Priscilla,* had a wardrobe of several pieces, including a pair of very practical jodhpurs. Felicity was also quite different in that she had a cloth body and flesh-colored felt head and limbs. Felicity, being the younger of the two, was also given to frilly drawers and sleepwear, in contrast to Dulcie, who wore athletic underwear.

November, 1929

Dulcie Daring. The Flying Doll
By Eveline Johnson

Since Santa Claus now comes by aeroplane, the Thread and Needle fairies are now outfitting modern dollies for airway travel. Dulcie Daring, a young "rag" doll of smart toy Society, has consented to pose for us in her flying togs

No. 29-11-1

DULCIE DARING is made of a fine gingham cloth. Her body is like a little mattress pincushion, her arms and legs are long and slender, and a knitting needle comes in handy to poke in the stuffing. She has a short curly bob of auburn hair made of crewel wools. She wears "athletic" undies, shorts and shirt of white, with green bands. Her suit is tan palm beach cloth with soft brown leather buttons, belt, and sleeve straps. Her sports shirt is of fine beige colored shirting with a brown tie made of bias fold. Helmet, goggles, gloves, and high boots are all of brown leather and distractingly cunning. She is really easily made by any Thread and Needle fairy in a holiday mood — it's fun to do all the "little fixings," and she is such a realistic little person when she is done that you can't resist perching her on the topmost bough of the Christmas Tree. Little girls will love her because she has "truly" clothes that can be taken off and put on — big girls would love her as a collegiate mascot.

The perennial baby doll and child doll were also included in the kits and patterns offered by *Modern Priscilla*. In the December 1928 issue was another Dulcie, this time a little girl who brought along her pet kitten, Dizzy. The kit contained unbleached muslin stamped with the doll pattern, plus fabric and patterns for a rose-pink gown with bonnet and panties to match. Outing flannel was included to make the kitten.

12-3

12-2

The December issues of many periodicals traditionally include instructions for Christmas decorations and gifts. *Modern Priscilla* was no exception. The December 1926 issue offered patterns for charming dolls and toys. (One wonders how a busy mother or grandmother could have had time to order the patterns and kits, receive them in the mail, then sew them — all before the holiday.)

Many references to dolls and toys being made from discarded silk underwear have been noted. The frugality of the pioneers, and before them, the earliest settlers of our country, is well known. Today, we still salvage old nylon stockings for use in stuffing dolls, pillows, and whatnot.

Catherine Vogus designed four dolls offered in *Modern Priscilla*, as well as six tiny animals. Yarn was suggested for the hair, the features were embroidered, and one supposes the dolls were stuffed with scraps of silk fabric, thus rendering them completely washable. They are quite obviously intended as crib toys. Pink or white underwear and dyed fabric for the clothing was recommended.

12-4

Hans and His Goose No. 26-12-36.   *Mistress Pussy-Cat* No. 26-12-37.

Made from Old Silk Underwear

By Catherine Vogus

FROM your old silk underwear and stockings you can make the most cuddlesome toys for the wee ones to love. White or flesh colored silks are the most useful for making the bodies, and as for the apparel, you can dye the underwear any colors you choose. Use yarn for the hair and one or two threads of stranded cotton to embroider the features. Cut out the toys, using the paper pattern as your guide. Hem all the cut edges before sewing the seams as this prevents runs in the silk. Leave openings at the top of the head for stuffing the doll people for their hair covers the whipped opening. Dolls are about 9 inches tall, the carriage toys are but 3 or 4 inches.

Hans' nice goose has a yellow bill satin stitched through the head after stuffing. Mistress Pussy-Cat brings her lunch — a wee gray mousie! She wears a one-piece frock, knickers, and a scarf. Humpty Dumpty has satin stitched hair and a skull cap. Tom, the Piper's Son, wears a jumper and overalls. Mary has two braids of yellow wool. Wee Pussy and Wee Bunny are carriage toys.

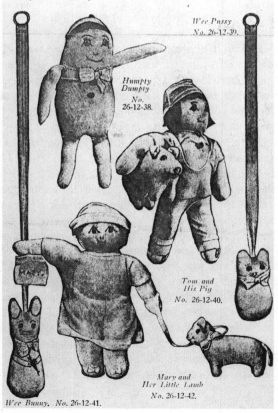

Wee Pussy No. 26-12-39.

Humpty Dumpty No. 26-12-38.

Tom and His Pig No. 26-12-40.

Mary and Her Little Lamb No. 26-12-42.

Wee Bunny. No. 26-12-41.

In the May 1929 issue of *Modern Priscilla*, at least two very interesting characters were shown. Whoopee is an Indian Chief, "a really red Indian" the copy read, "made out of pebble finish oilcloth with gorgeous yellow oilcloth for feathers and fringes and black for long hair and battle axe. He is stuffed very little and a few stitches work wonders in shaping his anatomy and trimming his clothes."

12-5

Oleander Oilcloth was touted as "the original jazz water-baby! She'll be right in the swim with her Hollywood red bathing suit and cap." Apparently both Whoopee and Oleander were available in kit form, since such specific descriptions were given of the materials involved. Furthermore, they were stitched on the outside and stuffed very lightly, thus adding to their individuality of style.

315

Design credit was given in the magazine for these last two characters. However, somehow over the years, this copy became separated from the rest of the page. Perhaps another copy of the magazine will come to light and this designer's name may be added in future editions.

Calico Sal and Gingham Bill, designed by Georgia M. Hanley, were offered in pattern form in the November 1926 issue of *Modern Priscilla*. These dolls were 13″ and featured as the barefoot Kountry Kids. Also available at the time were the Gingham Dog and Calico Cat, intended as pets of the dolls, also designed by Hanley.

12-6

Anatomy of a Rag Doll

One evening in the summer of 1973, I was visiting a doll collector friend in Nebraska. We had settled ourselves in her doll room to browse through a collection of old magazines, unaware that the evening would bring one of those rare discoveries that keep life interesting. By chance I picked up a copy of the November 1928 *Modern Priscilla* and began leafing through its pages. The magazine was never finished that evening, for there on the fourth page was an illustration of a doll — and what a doll it was!

Flossie, the All-American flapper, gazed out at me from the page. This sweet-faced doll had been designed especially for the magazine by a doll artist named Dorothy Heizer. In 1928, Mrs. Heizer had not yet attained the renown she was to enjoy in later years. However, her skills were already developed to a high degree as was evidenced by the illustration of the college flapper and her wardrobe in the pages of that old magazine.

How I longed to find an example of that doll. I mused that somewhere, perhaps, there might be a collector who treasured such a doll and might not even know of its origin. I glanced again at the magazine.

The doll was offered in kit form for a mere $2.98. She was 16″ tall, and her form was stamped on a piece of fine, firm cotton. A hand-colored face (by Mrs. Heizer?) on a separate piece of fabric was to be sewn over the head, which was part of the body. There was pink crepe-de-chine for brassiere and knickers; figured cotton crepe for pajamas; black sateen for

mules; green, blue, or red jersey and tan trim for a dress and coat, plus its tan lining; brown suede leather for hat, shoes, and bag; as well as patterns and explicit instructions for cutting and finishing. All for $2.98!

My hostess and I were delighted with the find. She had never taken the time to examine her magazines closely and had not been aware of this gem waiting to be discovered. I immediately asked to borrow the magazine for a column I was writing for my regular spot in *The Antique Reporter*. The entire page was later reproduced in the *Reporter*, along with the story of how I found her, and a request that any collector who might have such a doll write me.

Three years later I received a letter from a reader who had seen the article in a reprint of my columns and articles. She wrote that she believed she owned an example of the Heizer doll in question and enclosed several photographs.

Although the photographs were excellent, it was difficult to be sure if the two dolls were the same. Besides, I longed to get my hands on that doll, to examine its construction, to photograph its parts. After some correspondence, Bee Davis of Bee's Doll Hospital agreed to ship the doll and her wardrobe for my examination. When the doll arrived, I photographed, examined, and handled it extensively, meanwhile instructing my staff that no one else was to even touch the doll. If anything happened to it, I wanted to know that it was of my own doing.

In one afternoon I measured, poked, and prodded gently at that wonderful doll and her marvelous costumes, all the while speaking into my tape recorder, giving a complete description of what I found. Then Miss Flossie, or whoever she was, was packed in tissue and returned to her owner. I must admit that at the time I was convinced I had found the 1928 doll. Now I am not so sure. In fact, I believe we are dealing with two entirely different dolls.

Helen Bullard mentions Heizer's Fashion Doll of 1930, and I am more inclined to believe the doll I have examined is of that or some other unknown origin. First, the clothing is so dissimilar. Second, the fabric described for the 1928 doll is a "fine and firm cotton," whereas Bee Davis's doll is made of some sort of silk knit or textured fabric. (It is sometimes difficult to identify older fabrics, since fabric fashions come and go.)

There is even a possibility that the doll is from the hand of Dorothy Heizer and not from a kit at all. Others may concur with this premise, especially after reading the detailed description of the doll and its clothing, coupled with the knowledge that this doll came to me from New Jersey where Mrs. Heizer had lived since 1914.

On the other hand, Bee Davis tells me she bought the doll at a garage sale from a young couple who told her the doll had belonged to an aunt who was an art teacher. A seamstress with art training, and therefore a probable knowledge of costume construction, would certainly have been capable of achieving the degree of expertise evident in the execution of the doll and wardrobe. It is even possible, depending upon where the art teacher received her training, that the doll and costumes could have been created in partial fulfillment of the requirements for a degree in art, particularly one with a focus on fashion and costume.

No—I'm only   a Doll !

Designed by
Dorothy Heizer

Doll
No. 28-11-12

ELLO everybody! How's every little thing? This is me, Flossie, the all-American flapper, ready to date all comers. Invite me out—I'll go anywhere, any time. I never have to walk home. I stay for keeps.

Want references? Aren't my looks enough? Well, I'll spill all there is to know about me that the Editors will give me space to tell. I got myself psyched and X-rayed so as to give you all the "inside stuff." The chief operator gave me this line.

Says the Doc—"Miss Flossie, you haven't a single complex to worry about—I could put you together quite easily myself! You are of a highly individual make-up, however; so much so, in fact, that you look almost human! Your skin is a fine and firm cotton, a nice healthy creamy tint. (It *does* take the rouge well.) You are delicately built, but strong, with a complete quota of arms and legs so cleverly seamed to your body that you should be the best little jazz lady in town. (You said it, Doc!) Those flexible joints are contrived for you by stitching across your wrists, knees, and elbows. Your limbs are slender, made of two pieces of material, seamed, turned, and stuffed smoothly with cotton—a knitting needle is a fine instrument to use in operating on you! Your body is compact, and knotted like a little pincushion, which preserves your boyish form perfectly. Your head is a fascinating study—you really have two heads (one inside the other); a practical head piece for brains which is cut right on your body—and a pretty head piece for looks, with your rosy lips and pink cheeks painted on it, which goes on over the 'brains'. (What a cinch for the beauty doctors when *my* face needs lifting!) That sleek wool bob of yours covers all the head seams."

He didn't tell you the half of it, girls! I wear it black, or brown, or yellow, or auburn, according to what "gentlemen prefer".—But why tune in on this "inside information". I'm loads more keen on my clothes. Isn't my ensemble the darling? Three-piece jersey coat with patch pockets and scarf collar — two-piece dress, same color with tan bands on the blouse, and a pleated skirt. My jersey's green, but some of the crowd will cry for those Wellesley blues or Radcliffe reds. Like my swanky hat? It's brown suede and the shoes and the collegiate brief case match it—sportsy, what! I've some marvelous pink silk undies that don't show in these pictures—but they are the last word—knickers and a brassière all in one piece. Yes, the stockings are silk all the way up.

Aren't my pajamas a wow! Prints make the positively perfect dormitory duds—mine have plain gingham trims. I made the mules out of black sateen and trimmed them with the gingham leftovers.

Ask me home for the holidays. I'm easy to like and easy to look at—and I've a lot more "It" than those snaky boudoir beauties some people pet. Give me a ring—or say it with postage stamps!

EDITOR'S NOTE: We apologize for Flossie's diction— but we completely capitulate to Flossie's slim little graceful self. She *is a dear!* Dolls of this type are much more inspiring to make than the average stuffed toy. And little girls like dollies that are "real." College girls get the thrill of a lifetime out of such swagger mascots.

Price List of Patterns Obtainable from the Modern Priscilla Co. Will Be Found on Pages 64 and 65

So there is the enigma: Whence came this charming creature, product of a skilled and imaginative needleworker-artist? Perhaps we shall never know. What we can know is what this doll and her clothes look like, how they were trimmed, lined, color-coordinated. Such a description, though admittedly long and perhaps a bit tedious, will nevertheless serve to illustrate several points.

First, to achieve the goal of creating a work of doll art, one must plan carefully all aspects of the project. Design, color, cutting, fabric and trim selection, stitching by hand or machine, application of linings, trims, and finishing stitches — each step in the process is just as important as any other step. The final overall picture must be considered in an effort to achieve the desired effect.

Second, one can learn by observation, by studying the works of others. This is one of the reasons why workshops, from watercolor to wigmaking, are so popular. One learns by watching an expert at work, by observing skilled hands in the act of creation. One also learns by close inspection of the products of skilled hands. Thus the function of galleries, shows, fairs. One can also learn much from books.

For these reasons, it seems a good and proper thing to describe in detail for my readers the doll sent to me by Bee Davis.

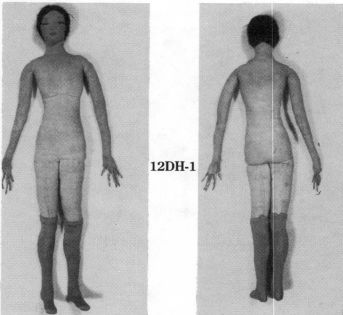

12DH-1

The fashionable young miss (see 12DH-1), of silk textured knit, measures approximately 15″. The fabric is not quite a lingerie type, but is a very light crepe. The face has been hand painted by the artist, and tiny stitches delineate the chin and corners of the eyes and mouth. There is a small seam about one-half inch long just under the chin, but not visible from the front. This seam helps to define the chin line. The body is built on a wire armature and is needle-molded all over to attain proper anatomical contours. It is very evident that the doll-maker had a working knowledge of anatomy as well as of the armature method. The hair is of black embroidery floss, parted in the center, stitched to the head to represent a flapper bob complete with spit curls on each cheek.

The wardrobe, as mentioned earlier, is gorgeous and shows the same care and attention to detail as does the doll. There is a long sheath of East Indian printed silk fastened with minute snaps covered by tiny beads along a front closing. The fabric is beige printed with a design of dark brown, light brown, gold, red, and light red. The beads are red and the collar is finished with embroidery floss that has been rolled around a nail or pin to form a trim that was then stitched to the collar. Very short cap sleeves are formed by bias bands sewn into the armholes (see 12DH-2a).

12DH-2a   **12DH-2b**

Another sheath is of black velvet with a shaped hemline and shoulder straps of minuscule iridescent black beads that glint blue, green, and red. On the right hip is attached a piece of bright orange ostrich feather. On the left hip is a rosette of long strips of ribbon backed by the same orange as the dress facing and centered with a large (for the doll) rhinestone. This ribbon has a black edge, then a band of iridescent blue that picks up the color in the beads. From the rosette hang three narrow silk ribbons, one each of dark blue, orange, and lavender. The color scheme has been carefully carried through on all parts of this flapper-style dress. (See 12DH-2b.)

A coat and dress ensemble (see 12DH-3) of very fine velour in a soft magenta-purple shade is accessorized with shoes and two hats. The straight sheath dress has a standup Empire collar of ecru lace. The front is bound in soft red silk. Down the front, between the two bands of red silk, is a strip of woven trim with a black background and bright royal blue woven flower design. The cuffs, which were probably white at one time, as was the collar, are now an ecru shade. They are pleated with six tiny red beads matching those on the dress. The end of the ecru fabric forms a ruffle edged with the same lace as the collar. Around the neckline is the additional touch of blue thread picking up the blue in the woven front panel. The hem of the skirt is finished with black ostrich feathers. The coat is very narrow and straight with a front opening faced with the same soft red crepe that trims the front of the dress. It is trimmed with the blue silk embroidery floss and the hem is faced with the red crepe. Sleeves and collar are finished with black ostrich.

12DH-3

Two hats match this ensemble. The first (12DH-4) is of the magenta velvet with a round circle crown gathered to a small brim to form a cloche. The wired brim is pulled to a peak in front and crimped. The edge of the brim is worked in bright royal blue thread over black ribbon and rolled to form a solid edge. The hat is topped with an ostrich plume.

12DH-5

A third hat (12DH-6) is a large picture hat, created on a black horsehair foundation topped with pieces of artfully arranged black lace. A long train of lace trails down the back to be draped around the shoulders. The lace has a large, flowered pattern, and the hat is beautifully designed and shaped.

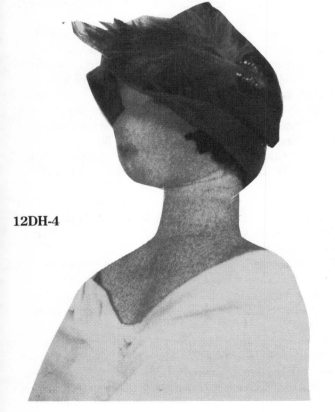

12DH-4

The second hat (12DH-5), also a cloche, has a small, flat, circular crown with a bias-cut side, faced in magenta satin turned up narrowly over the side of the hat to form a trim or almost a very narrow brim. This hat is trimmed with a bit of very soft gray and orange-brown pheasant feather put through a small buckle formed of extremely tiny gunmetal-colored beads.

12DH-6

A fourth headpiece (12DH-7) is another cloche, of very fine soft red wool draped with a long scarf of very fine silk crepe of a matching color. One end of the scarf is gathered to a point with a black bead, red bead, and a black floss tassel. The other end of the scarf is arranged across the front of the hat. The edge of the brim has a very fine beading effect of silk crepe attached with an overhand stitch of beige-gold thread. The crown is in four sections, like a beany, but one section is cut shorter and the other three are shaped in the fashionable cloche of the twenties. This hat seems to have been intended to be worn with the India-print dress, as it picks up the red color in that print.

12DH-8

12DH-7

The silk items in the wardrobe (see 12DH-8) are in very poor condition, almost to the point of disintegration. A pajama set of pink silk trimmed with turquoise thread and binding has a painted Chinese design on the front of the jacket.

An evening dress, in silken tatters now, is of iridescent rose with a silvery cast. The tight-fitting bodice is centered with tiny knotted embroidery floss flowers. Four very narrow ribbons hang from the waist. The skirt is quite full, gathered to the bodice, and lined with fine net. There are snap fasteners at the back.

A layered ballgown has a very full outer skirt over a fine silk gauze underskirt, which is over a fine silk crepe sheath. Tiny silk flowers and leaves trim the underskirt. A larger, matching rosette backed by lace trim, centers the bodice front. The fitted bodice is made of woven ribbon, over which, to form the draped shoulder effect, is stitched a piece of the same ribbon with

320

bands of beige-gold alternating with deep gold. The outer edge of the ribbon is of a different texture, almost a ruffle effect. It is very clear that a great deal of thought went into the selection of these trims.

The underwear consists of a peach silk slip plus two other garments known as combinations. The first is of pale peach silk. Both have matching lace hems and ribbon crotches sewn in. They are tied halter-style with lavender embroidery floss. The second combination, or teddy as it was also called, is of lavender silk organdy with lace at the top and bottom. The doll was wearing another teddy that was somewhat shorter, made of lace, including the crotch, and tied with gold floss.

There are two pairs of shoes and a pair of slippers in the collection. The shoes show the skill of the maker — high heels, soles, inner soles, covered heels — all part of the shoemaker's art. One pair is of printed watersilk, carefully lined, cut low on the vamp, and trimmed with light aqua tassels and deep aqua beads. The shoes are embroidered all around with the same thread as used in the tassels.

The second pair of shoes is of black silk, cut much the same as the first, although somewhat higher on the vamp. The trim is black floss, finished with flat black beads set with rhinestones. The slippers are flat-soled, padded with pink silk, and have aqua silk vamps.

The remaining accessories include a leather-lined brocade bag of eggshell color (possibly originally white), with green leaves, dark red flowers, and blue birds. A handkerchief case of grosgrain ribbon contains two hankies that measure a mere 1½" square and are finished with a delicate overhand stitch. One hanky has a lace edge. The case has ties of red embroidery floss with lavender tassels. Finally, there is a wreath of tiny pink, yellow, lavender, and blue silk flowers and delicate green leaves, apparently intended to be worn on the head, perhaps as an evening adornment.

These clothes and accessories are definitely of the fashion lady type, whereas the 1928 *Modern Priscilla* doll is billed as a college girl. Perhaps Flossie, the All-American Flapper, will yet cross my path.

Pretty Miss Penelope Comes for Christmas

By DOROTHY W. HEIZER

WE have all bought dolls, dozens of them, for our own children, or our neighbors' children, or those children to whom we are fortunate enough to be related. Some of them were good dolls, some of them not so good. Some of them cost a few cents, some of them many dollars. The world is full of dolls. Anybody can buy one.

The world is so full of dolls that it is hard to believe that there can be a really new one. But here she is, stepping daintily out of this very page, with her bandbox on her arm, and a demure little look upon her face, as if to say, "Try me, and see if I am not the least little bit nicer than all the others." And any one can make her, — can fashion with their own hands this doll of their dreams. For who has not dreamed of a doll that shall be beautiful to look upon, with real dresses that put on and take off, a doll that can begin by being a little girl with her wee mistress, and grow up as she grows, and still be beautiful for other little girls to come.

It is because one mother wanted such a doll for her small daughter that this one is here. She was making some rag dolls for a bazaar, and as she worked she dreamed, and the little girl stood at her knee and helped her, both with the work and the dream. So it happened that she made another doll, a doll that was like a real little girl, with curls, and a quaint dress and wee shoes and stockings, and dainty underthings. And because the little girl helped, it was simple and easy to make — a soft body stuffed with cotton, and all the tiny garments cut on straight lines. They started in the morning and the doll was quite finished by supper-time.

Other little girls saw the doll, and came to learn how

Doll No. 23-9-2

The instruction sheet tells you just how to coil her curls deftly about a pencil and fasten them in place.

As this small person is but thirteen inches tall, you will understand that she is very slightly built. The body is made in sections and put together as the pattern indicates, the neck cover and face are so cleverly done that the little lady can wear her low-neck frocks without a qualm.

PENELOPE'S WARDROBE

For outer apparel this fastidious young person wears a smart little cape of tan duvetyn which you can bind with ribbon or blanket stitch. Her piquant poke is made to match her gray calico frock and is faced with orange crêpe and piped with a bit of the same around the crown. You must have a piece of narrow black velvet ribbon in the scrap-bag which you can use for ties — and also a tiny bit of black lace or net from which you can cut two straight little pieces and seam them up for her mits.

Her every-day frock is of demure figured calico, dove gray in color, but the scalloped skirt is faced up with gay orange crêpe and a tiny piping of the same is used at the top of the bodice where the white chemisette and sleeve ruffles are attached. For parties Penelope has a ruffled rose organdy piped at the bodice with lavender. Call on the scrap-bag again for bits of organdy to make flowers for the nosegay and hair posy, for the bit of Val., too, to make the bouquet frill, and for the tiny black velvet streamers.

For her intimate apparel the young lady chooses a soft, checked voile, and for trimming you might use very fine tatting or pieces of the narrowest lace edging. Her nightie is of snow-white nainsook, made with modest long sleeves as all smart "night rails" were when Granny was a girl. Penelope's nightcap is a fetching thing with its little gathered crown and lace-trimmed face band caught back with a bow of pink ribbon.

(Continued on page 59)

Penelope in calico tarries for tea.

she was made. A group of bigger girls of thirteen and fourteen volunteered to help, and until the day of the bazaar, worked busily at making more dolls. Meanwhile the patterns and proportions and costumes kept improving, until finally this charming little person stepped demurely forth, with her bandbox on her arm, and announced she had come to stay.

ABOUT MAKING PENELOPE

The doll's body is stamped on flesh-color fabric, and has only to be sewn up and stuffed. Best of all, the sweet face with its rosebud mouth, pink cheeks, and soft blue eyes is sent to you already delicately painted by hand on the fabric. The wee dresses and underthings are made in simple fashion of quaint and dainty materials, and even the bonnet and shoes are as easy to make as can be. For there is a complete instruction sheet for making the dolly and her clothes, and the cutting lines are all stamped on the fabric, with careful markings to help in every step of the construction — even to the dimple in her chin!

'Tis true Penelope's curls are made of dark brown wool — but she has the most adorable coiffure you ever saw.

Penelope at the party—Oh, where is the mistletoe?

To prosaically buy a Penelope doll person "ready made" in the exclusive commercial circles where her sisters sometimes appear, you must have twenty-five dollars in your reticule to tempt her out of the shop! But if you make her, she costs only $2.50!

Penelope wears a petticoat — Oh, my, yes — and very full and frilly it is, too.

Penelope in her pantalettes and quaint chemise is quite as winsome as in her pretty frocks. Oh, lady, lady, if you want to be the best loved Santa Claus that ever was — just make Penelope!

Penelope retires in her modest "night rail."

Pretty Miss Penelope

One thing leads to another. In another *Modern Priscilla* magazine, the date of which I neglected to note, further evidence of Dorothy Heizer's work came to my attention.

Pretty Miss Penelope, a Christmas doll in kit form, was offered to the magazine's readers. This time the doll's body was stamped on flesh-colored fabric, ready to cut out, sew, and stuff. The face, with pink rosebud mouth, pink cheeks, and soft blue eyes, was already delicately hand painted on the fabric and ready to be attached to the completed doll. The cutting lines for the clothes were stamped on the fabric and a complete instruction sheet made everything easy to finish.

Needle-sculpturing was apparently included in the instructions, since the writeup about the dolls tells us the instructions include "every step of construction — even to the dimple in her chin!" The writer of the article goes on to say:

> To prosaically buy a Penelope doll person "ready made" in the exclusive commercial circles where her sisters sometimes appear, you must have twenty-five dollars in your reticule to tempt her out of the shop! But if you make her, she costs only $2.50!

It will be most interesting to see how many other doll kits by Dorothy Heizer come to light in the future, for apparently Mrs. Heizer worked with *Modern Priscilla* magazine on more than one occasion. It might have been a series of offerings. Perhaps she designed one kit per year for the periodical. Other readers may be able to help in the quest for more Dorothy Heizer doll kits.

Other Periodicals

Many other magazines have included patterns in their pages or offered kits and patterns for cloth dolls by mail. Time and space do not permit comprehensive listings of all such offers. However, here are a few additional samples from the pages of a variety of publications, in no particular order.

12-7

12-7   Matilda Anne and the Snuggles Bunny. A magazine tie-in with a local department store, Best and Company. Shown in the May 1931 issue of *Needlecraft Magazine,* Matilda Anne measured a full 27″. (Rothert collection)

12-8

*She's only a rag dolly —
but wouldn't you love her if
you were just about two?*

DESIGNED
BY
KATHLEEN
EAMES
LITTLE

No. 36-12-36. This stuftie doll is a little over a foot high — a nice size. Her playsuit is blue percale — white piqué with blue trim for the cap. For "best" she wears a white lawn dress and a crocheted jacket, bonnet and bootees of light blue wool — all of which makes an excellent start for a doll's wardrobe

12-9

12-8   **Belinda and Lucinda.** From the November 1934 issue of *Woman's Home Companion* comes this illustration of two charming little old-fashioned dolls designed by Edith Flack Ackley, a name well known to most doll collectors. The doll bodies were stamped on unbleached muslin. The kit included all instructions, plus patterns for clothing, for a mere fifty cents. (Author's collection)

12-9   **Patty Pinkcheeks, 12½".** (Or Betty Blue-eyes, Getta Yellowhair, Bertina Bow-legs). Frog-leg baby in a style similar to the Bye-lo bodies. Designed by Kathleen Eames Little. Directions were given in the issue for crocheting sweater, cap, and booties. The kits furnished all remaining materials for doll, dress, rompers, and bonnet. From the December 1936 issue of *Home Arts — Needlecraft.*

12-10   **International Doll, 12″.** This hot-iron transfer pattern included six costumes and could be ordered for twenty-five cents. Shown in the December 1938 issue of *Home Arts — Needlecraft.* (Author's collection)

12-11   **Brother and Sister Dolls, 22″.** By Mario Marques. From the Spring-Summer 1974 issue of *McCall's Needlework and Crafts.* Graph patterns for felt dolls of three nations, wearing bikinis, with fabric hearts sewn to their chests. In the same issue were instructions for a 17″ patchwork country girl and boy, made of scraps of handwoven fabric (left over from other weaving projects!).

12-12   **Homebody Dolls, 24″.** Designed by Mimi Shimmin. From the September 1978 issue of *Better Homes and Gardens.* Pattern was given for boy and girl dolls, plus complete outfits. Dolls are cut from simplified pattern. Finishing adds character. (Author's collection)

12-10

12-11

12-12

The Grocery Store Magazines

Who has not stood in a checkout line at a grocery store and leafed through yet another issue of *Woman's Day* or *Family Circle,* trying to decide if there is enough cash in the billfold to cover the expenditure, or in the case of writing a check in payment, whether or not something of vital interest is included in the issue? This author must admit that the magazine usually goes into the shopping cart. Who can resist, especially when there are instructions for something to make in the issue?

Over the years, my pile of magazines has become a collection and most recently a remarkable source of information about cloth dolls. Both magazines have long furnished graph patterns as well as offered full-size patterns or kits by mail for a large number of cloth doll designs created by freelance designers or on-staff artists.

We know the names of some of these designers: Joan Russell, Jo Smith, Robin Tarnoff, Rainie Crawford, Frances Gutman, Marcia Shenton, Gail Selfridge, Joan McElroy, and even Madame Alexander.

Other designers, whose creations have been offered in kit or pattern form in major magazines, have not been as fortunate. They received no credit for their designs. It is possible, of course, that at least a few of the patterns were created by on-staff artists or as group projects within a department. The majority, however, were done by freelance designers, many of whom live in a wide circle around the great publishing center of New York City. Unless the artists in question come forward, there is little possibility we will ever know who really designed these dolls.

Both *Woman's Day* and *Family Circle* have offered a wide variety of graph patterns, full-size patterns by mail, and kits over the past twenty-five years. Both magazines focus most of their attention on the gift-giving season at the end of the year. Thus the November issues in the earlier years carried gift-making patterns and instructions.

At one point in my pattern-collecting, I became frustrated with this timing and wrote to both magazines, chastising them for not giving needleworkers more gift-making time. "Please give us the Christmas gift-making ideas and instructions in October, or even September!" I wrote. No reply was forthcoming. However, about two years later, the schedules had been altered and October became the month for such features. I like to think my letters may have had some influence in the matter, especially since it would require about that length of time to adjust magazine publishing schedules.

Family Circle features its gift ideas under headings such as "Christmas Gifts to Make," "Early-bird Christmas Gifts to Make," and "Catalog of 105 Exciting Gifts to Make From 10¢ to $10." In addition, they have done a "Christmas in July," as well as offered last-minute suggestions in the December issues. In both magazines, kits and patterns are also offered by regular advertisers.

Woman's Day has showcased gift-making suggestions for years as "100 Christmas Gifts, with complete instructions for making." The 1958 issue, however, had "Complete Instructions for 63 Christmas Gifts." In 1960, the number of designs had risen to seventy-five. Since 1961 the magic number has been one hundred, although 1966 seems to have been a special year. The title *that* issue was "100 Great Christmas Gifts to Make." (This issue featured Joan Russell's Kate Greenaway boy and girl on the cover.)

Sometimes, even when a graph pattern for a doll is given in the issue, a kit or full-size pattern is also offered. An example is Rainie Crawford's Lucy, which appeared on the cover of *Family Circle*'s February 20, 1979, issue. A graph pattern for Lucy, her wardrobe, and her teddy bear was given in the magazine. A kit was available by mail. (Crawford also sells her designs as "patterns*plus" through her own mail-order business.)

Also noteworthy is the fact that occasionally the magazines have offered more than one set of dolls or graph patterns or kits in the same issue. A case in point is the November 1961 issue of *Woman's Day* in which patterns for Santa, an elf (featured on the cover), and a set of Bedtime Story Dolls, all designed by Joan Russell, were offered. Similarly, in 1966, they featured Russell's Greenaway Boy and Girl, her Indian Dolls to Make, and the Madame Alexander Cuddly Dolls.

In years to come, collectors will be combing the flea markets and garage sales, hoping to find one of these patterns or a finished doll.

Family Circle Patterns and Kits

Even though *Family Circle* has been less generous in their offerings of cloth doll patterns and kits than *Woman's Day,* there were a few notable designs published over the years that are listed here. A very recent addition to our list of designers is Deborah Harding, who created the Delightful Brother and Sister Dolls to Sew. These dolls appeared in the November 24, 1981 issue of *Family Circle.*

I admit to less enthusiasm in collecting the *Family Circle* magazine. There will, therefore, be many more gaps in the listing of dolls from this publication.

It is important to note that patterns and kits listed **are no longer available** from *Family Circle.*

December 1964

Santa, cover doll, 30", by Nancy Becker. Graph pattern only.

August 1973

Big Dolls Teach Children to Zip, Button, Tie, 24". Three dolls by Frances Gutman. Pattern to order.

October 1975

Country Cousin, 21", no design credit. Kit to order only.

November 1975

Doll of My Heart, no design credit. Pillow doll with heart designs all over dress for coloring with permanent markers. Graph pattern only.

October 1976

Tennis Doll, 20", no design credit. Kit by mail only.

July 26, 1977

Mary with Her Little Lamb, 18", no design credit. Kit to be ordered only.

Floppy Corrine, 24", no design credit. Kit to be ordered only. Both Floppy Corrine and Mary with Her Little Lamb were part of *Family Circle*'s "Christmas Gifts in July" feature.

October 18, 1977

Farm Girl and Farm Boy, 18", no design credit. Kit to be ordered only.

November 15, 1977

Jolly Santa, 13", no design credit. Graph pattern only. This Santa is featured on the cover of the special "Catalog of 105 Exciting Gifts to Make from 10¢ to $10."

Country Girl and Boy Rag Dolls, 23", no design credit. Graph pattern only.

October 23, 1978

Pinocchio, 24", no design credit. Kit by mail only.

Darling Lilly Dolly, no size, no design credit. Kit by mail only.

February 20, 1979

Lucy and Her Bear, 15½" and 6", by Rainie Crawford. Graph pattern inside the magazine. Kit by mail order.

June 26, 1979

Beach Baby, 22", no design credit. Graph pattern only. This is a real novelty. An open-top, canvas doll to be filled with sand, dumped, and refilled. A beach toy, but a complete cloth doll with separate limbs that could be stuffed with polyfill or other material if desired.

February 1, 1980

Farm Girl and Farm Boy, 21", no design credit. Kits by mail order only.

February 19, 1980

Mother and Daughter Dolls, no sizes given, no design credit. Instructions available by mail. Daughter doll has her own toy clown. Part of the "Americana Crafts" feature.

October 7, 1980

Heidi, no size given, no design credit. Kit by mail order only.

December 16, 1980

Gingerbread Man and Woman, 19½", by Deborah Harding. Graph pattern only. These are pillow dolls cut from cotton print and calico scraps, designed to resemble giant gingerbread cookies.

November 24, 1981

Delightful Brother and Sister Dolls to Sew, 20", by Deborah Harding. Graph pattern only.

12FC-1

12FC-2

12FC-3

12FC-4

Little boys and girls are naturally inquisitive and they welcome the chance to try something new and different. Our dolls can be made by you to satisfy your child's urge to investigate. They are 24" high, and each makes for a lovable armful. Their clothing is easy to make. It not only comes on and off, but has challenging buttons, snap fasteners, zippers, buckles and laces, large enough to provide small fingers with valuable practice—and gives you a chance to demonstrate clearly how these difficult things work. The doll bodies (totally washable) can be tossed into the washer. You'll probably have to buy the fabric for making them, but odds and ends take care of the clothes. For stuffing, which must be washable, too, we used 100% polyester fiberfill (or even discarded nylon hose). To order your free instructions by mail, see box on page 98   By FRANCES GUTMAN

BIG DOLLS TEACH CHILDREN TO ZIP, BUTTON, TIE

12FC-1 **Country Cousin, 21".** Kit offered by *Family Circle* magazine in its "Early Bird Christmas Gifts to Make." October 1975. No designer named.

12FC-2 **Heidi.** Kit offered in October 7, 1980 issue of *Family Circle.* No size or designer given.

12FC-3 **Tennis Doll, 20".** Kit for doll stamped on cotton and felt. All materials included, except stuffing. From *Family Circle,* October 1976.

12FC-4 **Big Dolls Teach Children to Zip, Button, Tie, 24".** By Frances Gutman. A free set of instructions could be ordered from *Family Circle,* August 1973.

Woman's Day
Patterns and Kits

Joan Russell's designs, showcased in *Woman's Day* magazine for more than ten years, are well-known to many dollmakers. Other designers who have supplied *Woman's Day* with patterns and kits are Jo Smith, Robin Tarnoff, Joan McElroy, Marcia Shenton, Gail Selfridge, and Madame Alexander. There may be others.

Following is a partial listing of doll designs offered in *Woman's Day* since 1958, the year I began collecting their magazine. There may have been earlier examples. However, these are not available to me at this writing. Please note that stuffed animal toys are not mentioned, except in such instances as they directly relate to the character of the doll (for example, Mary and Her Lamb).

The patterns and kits itemized here **are no longer available** from *Woman's Day*.

November 1958
Atomic Annie, a 38″ novelty doll with very straight limbs, no designer given.

Gingham Girl, another novelty of red and white checked gingham, 17½″, no design credit.

Featured on the cover were hand puppets, no design credit, graph pattern.

November 1960
Baby Doll, 14″, five outfits, no design credit, but probably Joan Russell.

November 1961
Christmas Toys, including Santa Claus and an elf featured on the cover. No sizes given, no designer credits. Graph patterns in magazine for both dolls plus seven animals. Full-size patterns available by mail.

Bedtime Story Dolls by Joan Russell, available only as full-size patterns by mail order, including a 16″ Alice in Wonderland, a 16″ Little Lord Fauntleroy, a 12½″ Hansel and Gretel, a 14″ Mary (with her lamb), and a 13½″ Goldilocks (with her three bears). Included with this portfolio of patterns was a 17″ fake-fur Puss-in-Boots.

November 1962
Duck and Four Dolls, cover dolls. Featured Eino of Lapland, Maria of Bolivia, Katrina of the Netherlands, and Margaret of Scotland. No sizes given, but probably 16″. No design credit, although certainly Joan Russell, as these dolls are companions to those offered in the bonus feature. Graph patterns. Full-size patterns by mail. (The duck was a large, sit-on stuffed toy.)

Dolls From Many Lands (the bonus feature) by Joan Russell. Nnkea from Nigeria, Apolonia from Czechoslovakia, Angeline from Italy, Gisela from Germany, Brigid from Ireland, and Hanako from Japan. Available only as full-size patterns by mail.

November 1963
Ballerina, 11″, no design credit. Graph pattern only.

Little Women by Joan Russell. Four dolls: Meg, Jo, Beth, and Amy. Each shows the designer's attention to detail. Russell made a pilgrimage to Concord, Massachusetts, to visit Orchard House, the home of Louisa May Alcott, for background and inspiration in designing these dolls. I believe these to be her best work. Full-size patterns by mail only. Set included wardrobes and trunk patterns.

November 1964
Five Babies by Joan Russell. These 17″ cover babies include Sleepy Head, Angel, Cherub, Red Head, and Cry Baby. Graph patterns. Full-size patterns by mail.

November 1965
The Mad Tea Party by Joan Russell. No finished sizes given for Alice, the Mad Hatter, the March Hare, or the Dormouse, all featured on the cover. *Alice's Adventures in Wonderland* had been published exactly one hundred years before *Woman's Day* presented this set, another excellent example of Russell's work. Graph patterns given in the magazine. Full-size patterns available by mail.

Annie and Arabella, 17″ and 8¾″, by Joan Russell. Graph patterns included complete wardrobes for both dolls and were a part of *Woman's Day*'s "100 Christmas Gifts" section, along with White Rabbit from the Mad Tea Party. Full-size patterns available by mail.

Gingham Twins, 11″, no design credit. Graph patterns only.

Sleepyhead Doll, 17″, no design credit. Graph pattern only.

November 1966
Kate Greenaway Boy and Girl, cover dolls, by Joan Russell. No size given. Graph patterns. Full-size patterns by mail.

Indian Dolls to Make by Joan Russell. Included Indian maidens of the Cherokee, Pueblo, Navajo, Iroquois, Seminole, and Sioux, plus a Navajo papoose. All costumes are done with the typical Russell eye for detail and authenticity. Full-size patterns by mail only.

Cuddly Dolls by Madame Alexander, 14½″. One basic doll

with five different outfits. Featured in the "100 Christmas Gifts" section. Graph pattern only.

November 1968

Ten O'Clock Scholar and Miss Muffet, cover dolls by Joan Russell. No size given. Graph patterns.

Mother Goose Dolls to Sew by Joan Russell. Finished sizes not given. There are five character dolls (including the two on the cover): Miss Muffet (and her spider), Ten O'Clock Scholar, Wee Willie Winkie, A Fine Lady (and her white horse), and Mistress Mary. Full-size patterns available by mail only.

November 1969

Circus Stars to Sew by Joan Russell. Featured Lady Reinlightly, the Bareback Rider, and Sparky, the Firefighting Clown, plus six circus animals. (Roarmore the Lion was featured on the cover and a graph pattern was given for him inside the magazine). Patterns for the full set available by mail only.

December 1970

A Dozen Dolls From One Easy Pattern, 13", by Gail Selfridge. Simple graph pattern given. Variations achieved in fabric selection.

December 1972

This is Amy — She's a Doll, 14", by Joan Russell. Amy is a small edition of Russell's youngest daughter and has her own Amy doll, just 7", with two outfits. Full-size mail-order patterns only.

November 1973

One-World Costume Dolls by Joan Russell. Six dolls, 16", include: Caitlin of Wales, Howja of Alaska, Ari of Greece, Manuelo of Mexico, Esi of Ghana, and Soo-Ni of Korea. Available as full-size, mail-order patterns only.

April 1975

Pocket-Size Dollmates, 8½", by Jo Smith. Four dolls, graph pattern.

November 1975

Darling Dolls for Yankee Doodle Children by Joan Russell, no sizes given. Six dolls: Priscilla, her doll Prudence, Hannah, Oliver, Abigail, and Harmony (a baby). Also included were instructions for making Harmony's cradle. Full-size patterns were available by mail only.

April 24, 1978

Dear Rosamond, 18", by Joan McElroy. With changes in hairstyle and costume, Rosamond becomes a flower girl, shepherdess, homesteader, or president's lady. Graph pattern in magazine only.

November 20, 1978

Happiness Is a Family of Elves by Joan Russell. Instructions for Daddy Elf, Mommy Elf, and three Kiddy Elves, as well as mushroom tables and chairs. Mail-order pattern only. Sizes were 4½" to 9".

November 22, 1979

Polly and Her Dolly, kit only, no finished sizes or design credit given. Embroidered features and details. Dressed in old-fashioned outfits.

February 12, 1980

Heartthrobs, 17" pillow dolls, boy and girl with heart-shaped bodies. No design credit given. Graph pattern in magazine only.

September 2, 1980

Darling Dolls, 16", by Robin Tarnoff. Children include: Jeremy, Amy, David, and Ashley (a girl). Heat transfers for facial features included in the magazine. Graph patterns only.

November 4, 1980

Dauntless Duo, 18". Kids ready for the cold in snowsuits of quilted fabrics that are an integral part of the bodies. No design credit. Graph patterns only.

November 24, 1981

Lovable Lucy — A Doll to Cherish, about 7", by Robin Tarnoff. Heat-transfer patterns bound into the magazine.

October 13, 1981

The Overalls Gang, 20", by Robin Tarnoff. Children include: Jeff, Sarah, Barry, and Cindy. Kits only by mail order.

December 22, 1981

Itty Bitty Dolls, 5". Flat dolls by Robin Tarnoff. Heat-transfer patterns bound into the magazine.

Twinkly and Cupid, no dates or descriptions available.

Attempts to obtain biographical material on Joan Russell having failed, I was delighted to find a reference to the designer in the regular feature, "It's All In A Woman's Day," in the November 1973 issue. In part, the item reads:

> Toy designer Joan Russell got off to an early start making doll clothes with her mother and grandmother and marionettes with her Girl Scout troop as a youngster in Howard Beach, New York. Today, a wife and the mother of three in Closter, New Jersey, she still creates with her needle — clothes for her family and stuffed dolls exclusively for us. "One-World Costume Dolls" . . . is the latest addition to our annual, and beloved, Joan Russell collections. The correct costumes for our adorable ambassador dolls were carefully researched by Mrs. Russell. And Writer-Editor Barbara Bernal made sure their names were authentic, too, by calling on such sources as the Ghanian Consulate and a Korean antique store.

12WD-1 **Cuddly Dolls, 14½".** Created especially for *Woman's Day* readers by Madame Alexander. A graph pattern was given. There were five variations of the basic doll. Soft wool jersey, yarn hair, and felt features were suggested. From the November 1966 issue of *Woman's Day*.

12WD-2 **Pocket-Size Dollmates, 8½".** Designed for *Woman's Day* by Jo Smith. By varying the body fabric, it was suggested, an entire one-world grouping of small dolls could be made. From the April 1975 issue of *Woman's Day*.

12WD-3 **Dear Rosamond, 18".** By Joan McElroy. With changes in hairstyle and costume, Rosamond becomes a flower girl, shepherdess, homesteader, or president's lady. Graph pattern was given in the April 24, 1978 issue of *Woman's Day*.

12WD-1

12WD-3

12WD-2

12WD-4
12WD-5

12WD-4 **Kate Greenaway Boy and Girl.** Cover dolls by Joan Russell. No size given. Graph patterns in the issue plus full-size patterns by mail. From the November 1966 issue of *Woman's Day.*

12WD-5 **Darling Dolls, 16″.** By Robin Tarnoff. Heat-transfer designs for a dozen different faces were bound into the September 2, 1980 issue of *Woman's Day.* Graph patterns only.

EXCLUSIVE DESIGN!

The dolls are identical—sixteen inches of stuffed muslin with arms and legs that move this way and that. But the faces? All different. All adorable. All done with the special iron-on transfers you see at right. Directions and diagrams for easy-to-make dolls and clothes, page 148. Designed by Robin Tarnoff.

DARLING DOLLS

Give each enchanting doll a different iron-on face.

Jeremy   Ashley   Amy

National Doll World Patterns

A relatively new magazine, *National Doll World,* is a dollmaker's dream. In nearly every issue, full-size patterns for at least one, often several, cloth dolls are given. Here is a list of those patterns, beginning with Volume 1, No. 1, the April 1977 issue, along with the designers' names in most cases. Many back issues of this magazine are still available from the publisher. Issues that do not contain patterns are not listed.

April 1977
Alicia, a Teri Doll Original by G. P. Jones
Victoria, a Jen Kost original
Happy Day Clown by Dorothy Fitzgerald

June 1977
Tommy, a Teri Doll Original by G. P. Jones
Lovely Melanie, a Karen original

October 1977
Peanut Farmer by Jen Kost
Jody, a Teri Doll Original by G. P. Jones

February 1978
   Auntie Annie Pillow Doll by Jaye Wallace
   Baby of the Month by Dorothy Huber (Note: Each Baby of
      the Month pattern featured two babies, as the magazine
      was issued bimonthly.)
   Alison Lea by Cornelia M. Barr

April 1978
   Baby of the Month by Dorothy Huber
   Dollhouse Dolls You Can Make by Mrs. J. D. Mackey

June 1978
   Turn-of-the-Century Bride, a Teri Doll original by G. P. Jones
   Baby of the Month by Dorothy Huber

August 1978
   Hap-E Bay-B P.J. by Jen Kost
   Baby of the Month by Dorothy Huber

October 1978
   Twenties Sweetheart, a Teri Doll Original by G. P. Jones
   Baby of the Month by Dorothy Huber

December 1978
   Night Before Christmas Dolls by Sue Ann Teichman
   Baby of the Month by Dorothy Huber

February 1979
   Miss Ida of 1893 by Jen Kost

April 1979
   Hippie Doll, 13″, by Lola M. Fascetti

June 1979
   Polly and Peter by Carrie Linabury

October 1979
   Ms. Halloween by Patti Eaglo
   Sammie Kaye by Jen Kost

December 1979
   Dolls of the Seasons, Winter, by Patti Eaglo
   Malina, the Ballerina, by L. M. Coons

February 1980
   Beautiful Baby Bright Eyes by Leota J. Williams
   Matryashka Doll by Lola M. Fascetti
   Needle-Shaped Faces by Jen Kost
   Valentine Pillow-Doll by Betty Nordwall

April 1980
   Additional Costumes for Ms. Halloween by Patti Eaglo

June 1980
   Pinocchio by Sue Ann Treichman

August 1980
   Shirley Temple by Naomi Carwile
   Sally and Sam by Maxine Clasen

October 1980
   The Pin-Up Girls by Dian Girard
   Voodoo Doll by Betty Jean Aitken

December 1980
   Noel Angel by Patti Eaglo
   Mr. and Mrs. Santa by Maxine Clasen
   Elves by Maggie Duran
   Fantasy Mermaid by Marjorie Colbruno

February 1981
   Baby's Baby by Shirlee Hill

April 1981
   Joey by Maxine Clasen
   Rag Doll Faces by Chris Reed

June 1981
   Amelia Ann by Nancy Porras

August 1981
   Home Gnomes by Lisa A. Lael

October 1981
   Kanah, the Kitchen Witch, by Jen Kost
   Jack and Jill, Quick and Easy Dolls, by Sue Ann Teichman

December 1981
   Night Before Christmas Dolls by Patti Eaglo
   Betsy, An Historical Cloth Doll, by Ann Larberg

February 1982
   Two New Costumes for Amelia Ann by Nancy Porras
   Amelia Ann by Nancy Porras

April 1982
   Sarah Robinson's Articulated Doll by Elizabeth Andrews
      Fisher
   A Pair of Party Dolls by Kathleen Taylor
   Rag Doll Cards by Mary Ellen Smith
   Construction Tips for Professional-Looking Fabric Dolls,
      With Patterns, by Teresa L. Rudes.

June 1982
   Pocket Pals by Kathleen Taylor
   Marjie by Catherine Zweisler
   Happy Clown by Dorothy Fitzgerald

Space limitations do not permit additional listings of the patterns that were available in dozens of other publications. There are, however, several possibilities for the dollmaker who wishes to locate back issues of these periodicals. Flea markets abound with dealers who specialize in old magazines. Garage sales often include piles of back issues. (It's a shame to throw these perfectly good magazines away. Maybe someone will buy them.) Local used-book dealers often include magazines in their wares.

For the serious dollmaker or pattern collector, there is one other course to ensure complete sets of patterns in the future: Subscription. Usually subscription rates have a built-in savings when compared with newsstand costs, and there is also the time savings in not having to go out to find the latest issue.

Finally, look on the newsstands to familiarize yourself with what is available. There may be several publications never encountered before. Buy copies of new magazines or those you have never read, judge the value of each in terms of your own needs, then buy a subscription if you feel the publication has features you would like to read regularly.

I cannot resist one final example. In the Winter 1977 issue of *Ladies' Circle NEEDLEWORK*, are patterns and instructions for no less than seventeen cloth dolls. Dolls to Make and Love, by Elma McCarthy, shows six dolls. Dolls to Cuddle, no design credit, has five dolls. Fun with Felt: Tyrolean Family, by Sharon Valiant, gives patterns for four dolls. And in Merry Christmas: Two Little People, by Jane Slovachek, there are, of course, two dolls.

Cover price of the magazine was just $1.50, a bargain, indeed, for seventeen doll patterns plus the other interesting material included. Which serves to point out a final thought: Each issue of these periodicals explores other doll subjects and gives patterns and instructions for a variety of different types of dolls, in addition to the cloth doll patterns.

Patterns from the Newspapers

The newspaper patterns are carried widely across the country in local newspapers as well as some national publications under several different names. In many areas, they are the Laura Wheeler patterns. Elsewhere they are the Grit patterns, the Parade patterns, or some other name. These latter seem to take their names from the publications in which they appear. They are all mailed to the home needleworker from post office box numbers at Old Chelsea Station in New York City.

Several factors tie all the offerings together. In my hometown newspaper, *The Kansas City Star*, the Sweet Pea doll #905, from the Popeye comics, was offered as a Laura Wheeler pattern. My sister in Florida ordered the same pattern as part of a set of the Popeye Family from Parade Pattern Service, also at Old Chelsea Station, but with a different box number. The same holds true for the Dolls of All Nations series. They are available as Laura Wheeler patterns and as Grit patterns.

I was unable to learn anything about the artist or artists who created these patterns or about the company that markets them. The first of a series of inquiries was answered with a routine offer of a catalog that could be ordered for $2. Further inquiries brought no reply. Granted, a catalog would no doubt be interesting and helpful, in that it would list the full complement of patterns available. However, background on the artists involved and on the company was the object of the inquiries. Perhaps at some later date, and even through the influence of

this book, more information will be forthcoming. For now, however, we must be content with mere illustration of some of the subjects of these patterns.

The designs run the gamut from play dolls to foreign costume dolls to dolls based on comic strip characters. There is a cowboy pillow doll and a 44″ clown. There are several crocheted dolls, a little ballerina, and dozens of others. The illustrations show only a sampling of the patterns available.

12NP-1

12NP-1   **The Laura Wheeler Patterns.** Selections cut from pattern advertisements in local newspapers. Note that the Popeye Family dolls are the same as those offered in the Parade patterns, although Olive Oyl's costume is different. The pose of the Sweet Pea doll is identical in both cases. The artwork is uniform in all ads, indicating a common source. Comic Characters are copyrighted by King Features Syndicate. All copyrights apply. (Author's collection)

12NP-2 **Popeye Family Dolls.** From pattern envelope of Parade Pattern Service. This envelope carries the same street address as that given in the Laura Wheeler ads. All copyrights apply. (Glassmire collection)

12NP-3 **Selection of Grit Patterns.** Note the same style of drawing is used in all of these ads, indicating a common source. Cartoon characters are copyrighted by King Features Syndicate. All copyrights apply. (Author's collection)

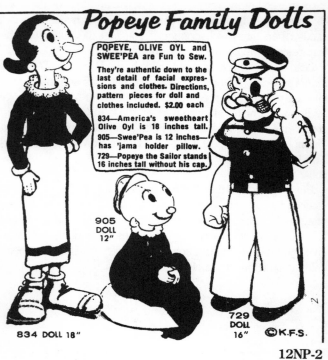

Popeye Family Dolls

POPEYE, OLIVE OYL and SWEE'PEA are Fun to Sew.

They're authentic down to the last detail of facial expressions and clothes. Directions, pattern pieces for doll and clothes included. $2.00 each

834—America's sweetheart Olive Oyl is 18 inches tall.
905—Swee'Pea is 12 inches—has 'jama holder pillow.
729—Popeye the Sailor stands 16 inches tall without his cap.

905 DOLL 12"

834 DOLL 18"

729 DOLL 16"

©K.F.S.

12NP-2

Felix The Cat
20" TALL
456

456 — Felix the Cat is about 20." The feisty little black cat has won the hearts of children everywhere. Directions, pattern pieces for cat and removable clothes. Send $1.75.

Inky & Dinky Cats
12" TALL

7358 — These famous cartoon cats — Inky & Dinky are soft toys every child will want. They're about 12" tall. Directions, pattern pieces for cats and clothes included. Send $1.75 for this pattern.

7358

©K.F.S.

12NP-3

Dolls of All Nations Patterns

976 18" DOLL

983 16" DOLL

Each doll sparkles with the appeal of its own individual personality and is dressed in character. You get easy-to-follow directions, diagrams and details plus tissue pattern for each doll and its removable clothes.

976 — Miss Italy is wearing a lace shawl and embroidered apron. She's about 18" Send $1.75.
983 — Miss France is about 16" tall and is wearing a lace-trimmed headpiece. Send $1.75.
7325 — Miss Holland wears a Dutch cap and wooden shoes. She's about 18" tall. Send $1.75.

7325 18" DOLL

STAR PATTERN SERVICE

Dagwood and Blondie

736
DOLL
25"
TALL

©K.F.S

7207
DOLL
25"
TALL

515

736 — Here's Dagwood Bumstead, a movie and cartoon star, now a soft toy. Tissue pattern pieces for doll about 25" tall and clothes included ... $2.25

7207 — Here's Blondie, right out of the cartoon strip, now she's a soft toy. Tissue pattern pieces for doll about 25" tall and outfit included ... $2.25

515 — Paint 'n' embroider the Bumsteads in action on 12" blocks for a 60½ x 89½ quilt everyone will love. Twenty-four motifs, charts, yardages incl ... $2.25

12NP-4

12NP-4 Dagwood and Blondie. A recent offering from the Star Pattern Service. Includes character dolls as well as related quilt pattern. All copyrights apply. (Author's collection)

Commercial Pattern Publishers

The yard goods department of nearly every discount or department store also features the patterns of several major pattern companies — Vogue, McCall's, Butterick, and Simplicity, the Big Four. Each of these publishers has a selection of stuffed toys and dolls in its retail catalog. Many collectors seek out such patterns at garage sales, flea markets, estate sales, and the like. Pattern exchanges exist for the purposes of finding specially desired patterns or for locating missing pieces that might render a particular pattern usable again.

Patterns for Raggedy Ann and Raggedy Andy have been among the most popular sold through the pattern departments and the most consistently offered. The Raggedies have had what is called in the theater a long run. Many a Christmas stocking has been filled with income from a small seasonal business of producing Raggedies made from these commercial patterns and selling them to friends and acquaintances. The more industrious home sewers have even supplied shops with sufficient quantities to last through the gift-buying season.

The variety of designs makes the commercial patterns a valid category for the pattern collector. Additionally, commercial patterns are subject to the same supply and demand as other items created for the purpose of earning a profit. Many designs have come and gone, a fact that adds spice to the hunt for any collector.

Make These Stuffed Dolls

No. 250. Printed Pattern for Stuffed Twin Dolls and Doll Clothes with Transfer for Faces. Blue. Price, 35 cents. These boy and girl twins are going to be great pets when you include them in your family. Their bodies can be made of peach gingham, percale or unbleached muslin. The faces are to be embroidered, the hair made of yarn. Pattern for complete clothes outfit—underwear, dress or suit, coats and hats for each doll. Full directions. Dolls can sit down. Size 25 inches tall.

No. 346. Printed Pattern for Stuffed Kewpie Doll with Clothes and Transfer. Yellow. Price, 25 cents. A simplified doll pattern, in two pieces only—back and front—and a Kewpie at that, the idol of children. Stamp the doll on flesh-colored chambray, percale, gingham or Crêpe de Chine, and buttonhole the edges together. The brief costumes can be made of cotton prints or gingham, and the sleeping suit of flannelette or eiderdown. Finished doll about 14½ ins. high.

No. 426. Printed Pattern for Twin Dolls with Transfer. Blue. Price, 35 cents. "The Twins"—flaxen-haired and gaily garbed—are undoubtedly of Tyrolean origin. Their bodies are to be made of flesh color gingham, features embroidered, and hair of Germantown wool. Their costumes, of light weight flannel or wool broadcloth, are most attractive trimmed with pinked strips of material or with rick rack. They are 23 inches tall. Full directions for making and stuffing. Materials required stated in pattern. Dolls are flexible and can sit down.

Copyright Rose O'Neill

A page taken from a 1938 McCall's Pattern Company pattern book is indicative of the variety of pattern types offered by pattern publishers. There's everything from twin children, a boy and a girl, to a pair of Tyroleans, to the favorite Rose O'Neill Kewpies. (See 12-3.)

12CP-3

12CP-1

12CP-2

12CP-1 **Button-Nose Rag Doll, 31″.** Good Housekeeping Pattern Service, copyright ©1940. There are twenty-nine pieces in this unmarked tissue pattern. Suggested is yarn hair, embroidered features. (Author's collection. A gift from the late Donna Stanley, founding editor of *Collectors United*)

12CP-2 **Raggedy Ann and Raggedy Andy, 36″.** McCall's Pattern No. 4268, copyright ©1974, The Bobbs-Merrill Company, Inc. Pattern includes two-color heat transfer for faces and hearts. (Barber collection)

The Raggedies were subjects of many different patterns over the years. Another such pattern is McCall's No. 5713, for 10″, 15″, 20″, and 25″ dolls, with one costume each. A McCall's Carefree Pattern™, it is copyrighted ©1977 by The Bobbs-Merrill Company, Inc. and carries a use notice: "Sold for individual home use only and not to be used for commercial or manufacturing purposes."

12CP-3 **Little Orphan Annie and Sandy, 38½″ and 24½″.** McCall's Pattern No. 5898, copyright ©Chicago Tribune-N.Y. News Syndicate, Inc., copyright The McCall Pattern Company ©1977. A trademark of Thomas Meehan, Charles Strous, Martin Charmin. This pattern envelope carries same use restriction notice as No. 5713 in 12CP-2. A large, shaggy Sandy accompanies this version of the popular comic strip character-turned Broadway stage and Hollywood film star. Andrea McCardle played Annie and Reid Shelton was Daddy Warbucks in the stage hit. The stage and movie versions of "Annie" have increased the popularity of toys and dolls relating to the characters, while at the same time possibly increasing the number of interested collectors. Those who have valued the old composition Annie dolls may now add rag dolls by Knickerbocker as well as homesewn versions to their collections. Modern materials make this pair particularly effective. Annie has yarn curls, and Sandy's lush, full, shaggy coat is achieved by use of synthetic "fur" fabric. (Barber collection)

12CP-4 **Awake or Sleeping Baby Doll, 16".** McCall's Pattern No. 5796, copyright ©1977, The McCall Pattern Company. Also includes wardrobe and quilt patterns. (Charlson collection)

12CP-5 **Boy and Girl with Old-Fashioned Wardrobe, 32".** Little Vogue Pattern No. 1336, copyright ©Vogue Pattern Service, no date. (Barber collection)

12CP-6 **Set of Dolls and Sleeping Bags.** One size, copyright©1977, The McCall Pattern Company. Dolls may be made up to represent children of many lands. Clothes are given for Indian, Eskimo, Oriental, etc. (Barber collection)

12CP-4

12CP-6

12CP-5

12CP-8

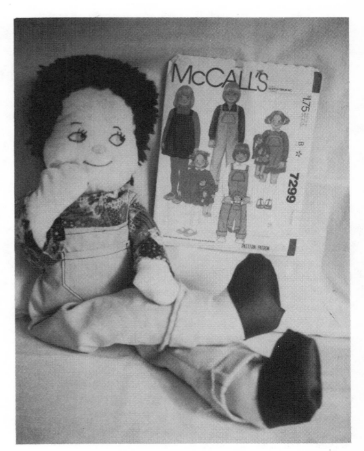

12CP-7

12CP-7   **Rag Doll with Matching Children's Clothes, 21″**. McCall's Pattern No. 7222 makes the doll and clothes. Pattern No. 7299 is for the matching children's clothing. Copyright ©1980 The McCall Pattern Company. Doll and a matching outfit were sewn for Jon Scheuler by his grandmother.

12CP-8   **Little Lulu, 17″**. McCall's Pattern No. 1447. From the Summer 1949 issue of *McCall Needlework*, a magazine featuring McCall's patterns exclusively. Recommended fabric is muslin with corkscrew curls of yarn "set" on a pencil. Included was blue transfer for embroidering features. Copyright ©1948 M. H. Buell (Author's collection)

13   On Building a Collection

How do you decide what type of doll to collect? Should you keep to a narrow field or buy anything that comes along? Should value and possible appreciation be considered? Or should doll collecting remain a matter of the heart, not to be considered a financial investment? How can you learn about dolls in order to avoid mistakes? Or does it really matter? Should you simply use the mistakes to your advantage?

All these and many more questions are apt to be asked as the doll collecting urge becomes a habit and then a way of life. I can only answer from my own experience, which may or may not be the answer for you.

Deciding on the type of doll to collect is often not a matter of concern. Spontaneity, excitement, recognizing the duplicate of a childhood doll, or being caught up by auction fever — all have served to create new doll collectors who simply gathered in, without thought of the future or storage space available, what lay before them. The appeal of the moment has ignited in an otherwise sane individual the longing to possess a fragment of their own or someone else's forgotten childhood.

Keeping to a narrow field, given the circumstances and disposition of many new collectors, is virtually impossible. Few new collectors have the determination of spirit necessary to refrain from straying from their chosen categories. A doll in question may be a bargain or one that could be sold or traded for something more desirable or more suitable to a growing collection. And so it goes. Dolls are often added in a helter-skelter fashion based merely on a whim of the moment or the immediate appeal of the subject. It is a phase through which most of us pass.

On the other hand, there are collectors who see this method not as a phase to be worked through, but as a standard way of doing business. They take pleasure in the great diversity of their collections, seeking always for new categories, novelties, one-of-a-kinds, and whatever presents itself.

Cloth doll collectors are nearly always collectors of bisque dolls, china dolls, rubber dolls, composition dolls, and any other type available. As yet, I have encountered no purists who collect cloth dolls only. Perhaps there are a few. Many of the finest cloth doll collections known to me began as adjuncts to collections of the "better" dolls — the bisques and chinas. In the minds of such collectors, the rag babies ranked in value somewhere below the compositions and celluloids. Then something seems to have happened to these collectors.

Somewhere in their experience such collectors have begun to appreciate the basic appeal of cloth dolls. The variety, quality, availability, and relatively low cost of cloth dolls captures the attention of many collectors looking for broader horizons. Just as the number of collectors of quality foreign costumed dolls has grown, so have the ranks of the cloth doll collectors increased in recent years.

What turning point takes a person in a certain direction? Often there is no easily definable time when a collector decides to become a cloth doll collector. Perhaps so simple a thing as finding a neglected rag baby at the bottom of a box purchased at a farm auction provides the impetus to seek out other cloth dolls. The reasons for a particular collecting interest can be as varied as the number of collectors questioned — a childhood interest, a dream realized, a memory recognized. Similar threads are woven through all the stories.

"My mother wouldn't buy a Shirley Temple doll for me," said one collector. "After my daughter was born, I began buying 1930s compositions for her, even though she wanted Barbies. Soon I realized I was buying the compos for myself."

Later, the daughter's Barbies were sold to buy designer jeans, while the mother's compositions helped support a growing hobby that has evolved into a comprehensive collection including many fine bisques and chinas as well as composition and cloth dolls.

Another collector admitted to a longstanding liking for dolls, but was afraid people would think she was silly. She liked Ginny dolls and bought a few. One thing led to another, she says, adding that she had intended to buy only the smaller dolls. Her resolution was destroyed when an acquaintance who had boxed up a large number of composition characters to take to the dump, gave them to the collector instead. Later she rescued a P. D. Smith doll from a trash consignment. Still later she began making dolls and is now what she calls a semi-dealer.

Branching out into cloth dolls has often taken the same sort of undirected, accidental course for many collectors. There are, however, some who very wisely and consciously chose their course. They recognized early in their collecting careers the intrinsic as well as aesthetic value of the cloth dolls they were finding. Others felt something of a sentimental pull toward the often handmade rag babies they were finding in old trunks and toy boxes, for it seems more than a little likely that the rag dolls and toys were the recipients of the most exuberant loving and playing since they were soft, satisfying objects.

For whatever reason, the cloth dolls of the nineteenth century and the early twentieth century, as well as those of more recent years, have grown in value in the eyes of collectors. They are now being preserved in both private and museum collections. Cloth dolls created by modern artists are also worthy of consideration by collectors. These are the hard-to-find, limited production dolls of the future. We can appreciate this fact even more when we consider the present value of a Dorothy Heizer doll, for example.

Additionally, the commercially produced dolls of today will take their places in the collections of the future as have the Philadelphia Babies and the Martha Chase rag dolls. The modern commercial dolls purchased and preserved in their original form will be the gems of future collections. Today's collector can, in the meantime, enjoy them and enrich his or her own collection by choosing carefully from the manufacturer's offerings each year. The short-lived Hallmark series is a case in point.

What shall we collect, you and I? Shall we carefully buy only what may appreciate in value, scorning something we would enjoy in favor of financial gain alone? I think not, for where is the fun in that? Collecting can be a profitable hobby. We have all watched as our collections doubled, tripled, even quadrupled in value over the past twenty years. This aspect of the hobby cannot be overlooked. Dolls, toys, stamps, coins — all such collectibles are valuable possessions.

But if we cannot see beyond the dollar value of a collection, then we lose much of the intrinsic value. If we do not share what we can with others, another portion of the value is lost. If we cannot see ourselves as present stewards of a bit of heritage to be passed on intact and even enhanced, we have lost the final portion.

The dolls shown in this chapter are examples of the quality and variety to be found in cloth doll collections. The majority of what may be considered the most important cloth dolls are found here. For the most part, these dolls are in excellent condition. The collection provides an overview of cloth doll history and represents dolls any collector could cherish.

13-1

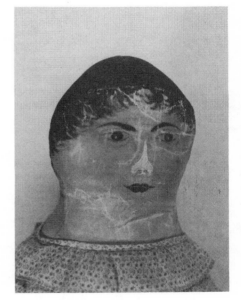

13-1 **Hester, 29″.** This very old doll is marked: **Hester 1860.** From an old family collection in Pennsylvania. Sewn with a chain-stitch machine, the doll has painted dark brown hair, blue painted eyes, mitten hands, probably original dress. Features are painted in artist's oils. (Rasberry collection)

13-2   **Sheppard Dolls, 20″ and 21″.** Painted wigs and features display evidence of much handling. Note unusually deep molding of eyes of doll on the right. Also called Philadelphia Babies, these dolls were made by the J. B. Sheppard Company of that city from 1860. Dolls were 18″ to 22″. (Rasberry collection)

13-3   **Mid-Nineteenth Century Lady, 22½″.** Possibly molded from a china or papier-mâché head. Cloth with black painted hair and solid black painted eyes. This prim-faced lady is an excellent example of a very rare type. Her features are hand painted in oils, her shoulder head is a deep one, and her dress is quite old. Her chin is well defined, her thumbs are gusseted, and her fingers are stitched. She won a first place ribbon at the United Federation of Doll Clubs convention in San Diego, California, in 1977. (Rasberry collection)

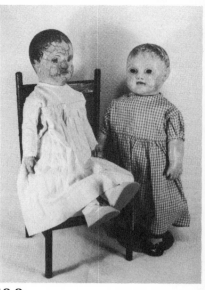

13-2

13-2

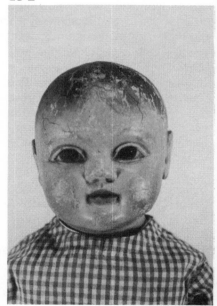

13-3

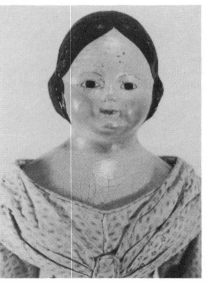

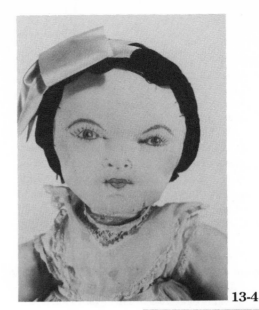

13-4

13-5

13-4   **Handmade Girl, 23″.** Reportedly sold at Marshall Fields in Chicago in 1893. The style of body design dates this as an early doll, although the clothes are probably of later date. Hair is of brown yarn, features are hand painted, almost in portrait style. Probably created by a seamstress/dollmaker who supplied the store in relatively small quantities. (Rasberry collection)

13-5   **Lithographed Man, 15″.** Wears high boots, red hat, red and black striped pants, European-styled tunic. He is very soiled and has no marks. Even so, he took Honorable Mention at the United Federation of Doll Clubs convention in Denver in 1978. (Rasberry collection)

13-6 **Handmade Farmer, 18″.** Sewn-down yarn hair, drawn and painted features on a flat face, a cotton broadcloth body, and excellent hands with stitched fingers. His shoes are of shiny oilcloth and his blue pants and red plaid shirt are cotton. His appearance indicates he is an early doll, unmarked. (Rasberry collection)

13-7 **Early Cloth Girl, 25″.** Stuffed cotton body, excellent large hands with separate thumbs and stitched fingers. Wears white windowpane check bonnet and apron, red dress, black hightop shoes, all very old, possibly original. Hair and features are artistically hand painted with artist's oils. (Rasberry collection)

13-8 **Early Cloth Woman, 20″.** Wears old, possibly original, print dress of pink, brown, and gray on white, with pink dotted Swiss hat trimmed in blue, black lace stockings, black shoes with buckles. Features are hand painted as is the hair. Arms are of brown cloth. (Rasberry collection)

13-6

13-8

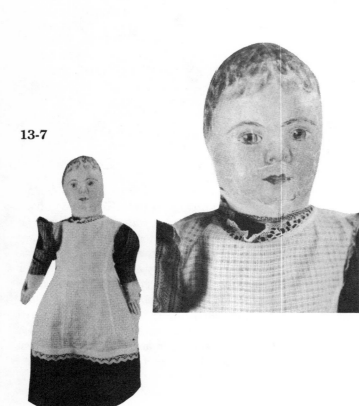

13-7

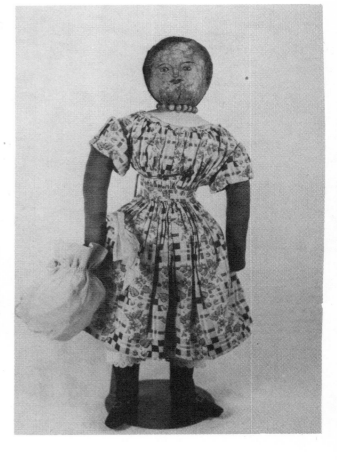

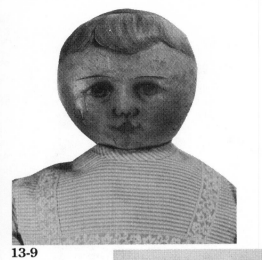

13-9

13-10-12

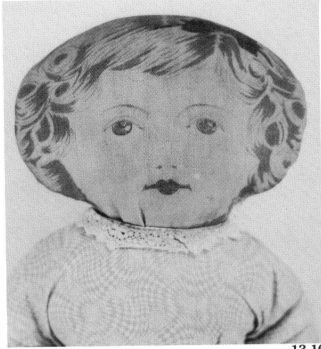

13-10

13-9   **Columbian Doll, 26½".** Light brown painted hair, hand-painted features, blue eyes. These dolls were made by Emma Adams and her sister Marietta. Features and hair of this doll are excellent. Note the shadow effect under the front hair. Probably painted by Emma Adams herself, or if a later doll, then by a highly skilled artist employed by her sister who continued the business after Emma's death. Clothing is of later date. (Rasberry collection)

13-10   **Art Fabric Mills Girl, 22".** Wears very old dress, printed-on boots, wine-colored ribbon at waist and wine-colored stockings, is cotton-stuffed. On right foot is **ART FABRIC MILLS/PATENTED FEB 13, 1888.** Doll has very well-defined fingernails. Hands are closed in fists. (Rasberry collection)

13-11   **Lithographed Girl, 24".** Also has closed hands, hand-stitched fingers, wears bright red stockings, blue ribbons, black high-buttoned shoes. (Rasberry collection)

13-12   **Lithographed Girl, 25".** Red ribbon printed in her printed hair, wears red printed-on socks, black printed-on high-button shoes. This doll and 13-10 and 13-11 are in unusually fine condition, even down to their feet, which are usually found quite worn. (Rasberry collection)

13-13 **London Rag Baby, 17″.** A beautiful example of the type. This doll has painted blue eyes, molded face, is dressed all-original in red with ecru trim. The body is of red sateen and white muslin, unmarked. Fingers are stitched. Earliest of these dolls date from 1865. They are unique in that the muslin face covers a support of wax, thus rendering them somewhat more fragile than other cloth dolls. (Rasberry collection)

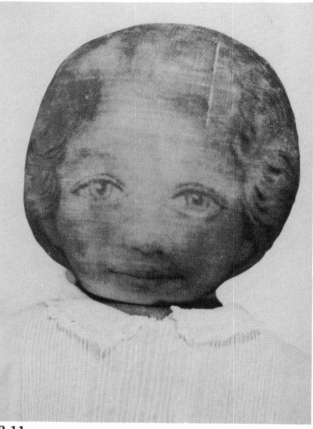

13-11

13-12

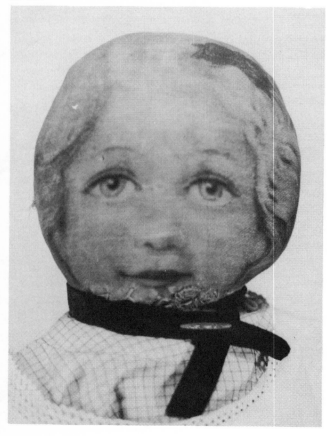

13-13

13-14

13-15

13-16

13-14 **Handmade Old Woman, 19½″.** Velvet face with blue glass eyes inserted, applied nose, crudely painted mouth. The muslin body is excelsior-stuffed. Lower legs are of red cotton to represent stockings, black cotton boots are sewn on. She wears a flannel petticoat, brown velvet bonnet, brown checked gingham dress, all probably original to the doll, which dates in the late 1800s to early 1900s. (Rasberry collection)

13-15 **All-Cloth Woman, 19″.** Light brown floss hair, painted brown eyes, applied nose and well-defined bosom, dressed all original in brown velvet vest, brown print skirt, cameo on vest. Note the large, well-defined hands with machine-stitched fingers. (Rasberry collection)

13-16 **Dean's Rag Book Lithographed Doll, 14″.** Brown hair and eyes with green eye shadow, brown shoes, pink underwear. Marked on the right foot: **DEAN'S RAG KNOCK-ABOUT TOY SHEETS/WASHABLE AND HYGIENIC/ TRADEMARK/REGISTERED IN ALL COUNTRIES.** On the left foot: **Circle/Must Be/ Covered by/Numbered/Certificates as/Guarantee of/Hygienic Stuffing/Registered.** (Rasberry collection)

347

13-17 **Handmade Black Woman, 15½″.** Black sateen with black embroidery floss hair, white shoebutton eyes with painted pupils, wearing original striped cotton skirt, white blouse and apron trimmed with embroidery, mobcap with lace, and kid leather shoes. (Rasberry collection)

13-18 **Kathe Kruse Baby, 13½″.** Brushstroke painted hair, blue painted eyes, hardened fabric head with molded ears. Marks: **Kathe Kruse/31192** (undecipherable third line). Excellent example of the earlier Kathe Kruse children with solemn little faces and appealing natural look. (Rasberry collection)

13-19 **Kathe Kruse Child, 18″.** Dressed all original in red and green ensemble, cotton dress with knitted sweater and hat, white felt underpants, original tag. Note the beautifully painted hair. (Rasberry collection)

13-17

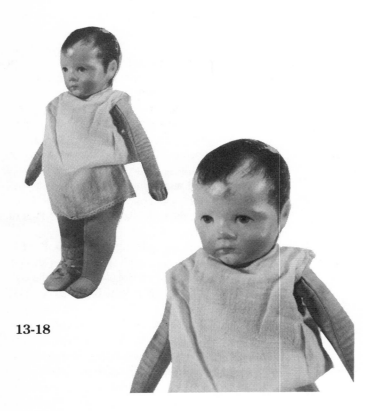

13-18

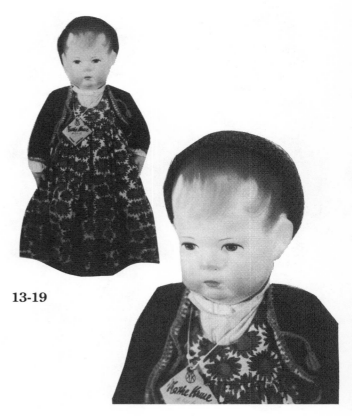

13-19

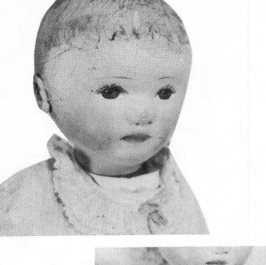

13-20

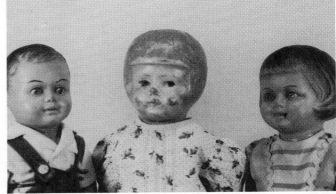

13-22

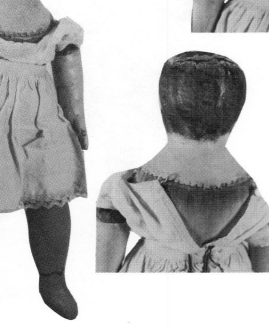

13-21

13-20	**Chase Baby, 23½″.** Light brown painted hair, brown painted eyes, applied ears, nicely formed cheeks and nose. Hands are beautifully realistic with gusseted, separated fingers. A beautiful example, unmarked. (Rasberry collection)
13-21	**Chase Girl, 18″.** Painted blue legs to simulate stockings and shoes, well-shaped head with painted hair in slight waves, deep shoulderplate, mitten hands with stitched fingers, separate thumb. Original dress (not shown) is yellow dotted Swiss. Original slip and two-piece underwear. (Rasberry collection)
13-22	**Trio of Chase Children, 16″.** Boy and girl on either side are modern productions. Girl in the center is an older, stiffened cloth doll. Modern dolls are treated with vinyl paint. Older models were painted with oils. None of the dolls is marked. Modern dolls wear original clothing. (Rasberry collection)

13-23 **Kamkins Child, 19″.** Mohair wig, painted blue eyes. The mask face is cloth embedded in a rubber base. Body is cotton-stuffed cloth. Clothing is all original. Created by Louise R. Kampes, c. 1920s. (Rasberry collection)

13-24 **Petzold Boy and Girl, 14″.** Dressed all original in felt and fabric costumes. These dolls were created by Dora Petzold in Germany. Boy wears brown velvet suit. Girl wears red felt skirt and jacket. Girl's wig is light brown mohair. Boy's is blond mohair. Note beautifully molded faces. (Rasberry collection)

13-25 **Lenci Boy, 20″.** Mohair wig, molded felt face, painted features, brown eyes, all-original outfit, gray woven check cap, tan felt trousers, black knit sweater. This young fellow won a blue ribbon at the 1982 UFDC convention in Kansas City, Missouri. (Rasberry collection)

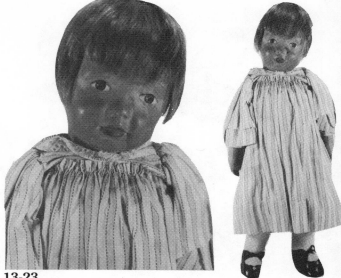

13-23

13-24

13-25

13-26

13-28

13-27

13-26	**Lenci Girl, 22″.** Tightly curled mohair wig, brown painted eyes, pink felt dress, white undergarments, green coat and shoes, all original. (Rasberry collection)
13-27	**Lenci Boy, 16½″.** Curly blond mohair wig, all-original felt clothing. This young boy, as well as 13-25 and 13-26, represent some of the finest of the Lenci children. (Rasberry collection)
13-28	**Lenci Smoking Doll, 26″.** Blond mohair wig, drooping lids, brown painted eyes, all-original outfit of turquoise felt trimmed with black. An unusual Lenci, highly desirable as a collector's item. Marks: **Lenci** on metal button attached to hem of jacket and **Lenci/MADE IN ITALY/162.** (Rasberry collection)

13-29 **Lenci Amore Girl, 11″.** All-original felt costume, brown eyes, mohair wig. Mark on cloth tag sewn to dress: **Lenci Torino.** On box: **Amore/Series P.F. No. 2.** (Rasberry collection)

13-30 **Lenci Exotic Dancer, 20″.** All-original felt costume. A most unusual doll. (Rasberry collection)

13-31 **Lenci Girl, 19″.** Blond mohair wig, beautifully painted face with blue eyes, wears red-trimmed black and white checked cotton dress, red felt shoes. Two tags on dress hem read: **Bambola Italia/Lenci/Torino/Made in Italy** and **ARS Lenci/Made in Italy Torino/New York, Paris, London, Manchester.** (Rasberry collection)

13-29

13-30

13-31

13-32

13-34

13-33

13-32	**Foxy Grandpa and His Two Grandsons, 11″ and 8″.** Yarn wigs, painted features, felt clothing, straw hats. Characters were adaptations from the Carl Schultze cartoons that ran in the Sunday newspaper supplements during the first decade of this century. (Rasberry collection)
13-33	**Palmer Cox Brownies, 7″.** All lithographed flat and lightly stuffed. The Arnold Print Works produced these dolls by the yard. Twelve brownies to the yard included: Dude, Highlander, Indian, Chinaman, Sailor, John Bull, Soldier, Uncle Sam, Policeman, Canadian, Irishman, and German. Marks: **Copyright 1892 by Palmer Cox** on back of the foot. (Rasberry collection)
13-34	**Dy-O-La Advertising Girl, 10″.** Lithographed cloth, stuffed with cotton and excelsior. Marked on back: **MOTHER/USES/DY-O-LA.** On front: **MY NAME IS/SCARLET.** (Rasberry collection)

13-35   **Snap, Crackle, and Pop, 10½″ to 11″.** Lithographed cloth, sewn with outside seams. Advertising pieces for Kellogg's Rice Krispies in the 1930s. The name of each character appears on his hat. (Rasberry collection)

13-36   **Bye Bye Kiddie, 21″.** Blond mohair wig, painted, molded features with blue eyes, well-defined hands. Doll is dressed all original in blue-gray taffeta dress with embroidery trim, pink collar and ribbon, long white stockings, black shoes, blue hat. Marks: **Bye Bye Kiddie/Pat./Alta &** (second name undecipherable) **©Doll Co.** (Rasberry collection)

13-37   **Russian Tea Cozy Doll, 15″.** All cloth with molded, painted face, quilted flannel petticoat (to keep the teapot warm), plaid apron. Cloth tag printed in Russian sewn to apron. Handmade. (Rasberry collection)

13-35

13-36

13-37

13-38

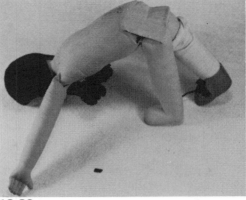

13-39

13-39

13-41

13-40

13-38	**Abraham Lincoln, 13″.** Handmade portrait doll is all original with stiffened fabric hands and face, applied ears, yarn hair with part stitched in white thread. Artist unknown. (Rasberry collection)
13-39	**WPA Girl, 22½″.** Body is hard-stuffed peach muslin, shoulderhead is painted stockinette, fingers are machine-stitched, feet have heavy cardboard or thin wood inserts to keep them flat, clothes are a combination of cotton and felt. Doll is in all-original condition and body has unusual seat design. Hair is black embroidery floss. Features are hand painted in oils. One of many designs created by artists commissioned by the Works Progress Administration during the Great Depression of the 1930s. (Rasberry collection)
13-40	**SFBJ Lady, 18½″.** Golden floss hair, felt face, light peach-colored cotton body, dressed all original. Marks: **SFBJ** on metal disks on shoulder joints. Relatively rare. (Rasberry collection)
13-41	**Golliwog.** Lithographed features, synthetic fur wig, button eyes. Red pants are part of body as is yellow vest, black shoes, and spats. Wears removable felt jacket and tie. Marked on heart-shaped tag: **Safety for your child Peace of mind for you/A Dean's Childsplay Toy/Hi! I've set my heart on you.** Reverse: **Dean's Childsplay Toys Ltd. #802/Reg. Sussex England/ Makers of Soft Toys for Over 70 Years.** (Rasberry collection)

13-42   **Alexander Little Shaver, 9½″.** Blond yarn hair, molded, painted face with blue eyes, pink cotton body, all-original outfit of pink, brown, and black dress, black velvet shoes, flower hat and veil. Alexander cloth tag sewn into clothing. (Rasberry collection)

13-43   **Betty Boop.** Lithographed doll from the 1970s based on the 1930s comic strip character. Marks: **The Original/Betty Boop/Rag Doll/Reg. No. PA.377/Copyright ©King Features Syndicate Inc./All New Materials/Cotton and Synic Fibers. Designed by Patti/COLORFORMS/Colorforms, Inc./Norwood NJ-07648 U.S.A./MADE IN TAIWAN REPUBLIC OF CHINA.** (Rasberry collection)

13-42

13-43

14 Unidentified Rag Dolls

Unmarked dolls, in addition to those shown in this chapter, may be found throughout this book. The others, however, may claim family ties to certain categories and are therefore only half-orphans.

One very important point that needs to be made early on is this: Perhaps these dolls are unknown, and therefore unidentified, only to me. Perhaps there are readers who know these dolls. I can only hope such readers will share their knowledge so the unidentified dolls may be removed from the rolls of the unknowns and properly acknowledged.

Much research, comparing, and questioning has gone on during the making of this book in an effort to reduce the size of this chapter. Many earlier unknowns, as a result of such inquiry, have been identified and are now listed in their appropriate sections. But some defy identification and may never be known. We must content ourselves, at least for now, with what we have and hope to solve the other mysteries in the future.

Occasionally an unmarked doll appears, only to be quickly matched with a tagged specimen or one still in the wrapper or box. Some of the flats printed out and distributed by the yard when sewn have no means of identification. It is great good fortune if one is able to find an uncut example with all the copyright information, manufacturer's and advertiser's names, instructions for completing the dolls, and even the date. Such uncut or still-in-the-wrapper items are treasures, for very often this is the only means of identifying a piece.

There is also the possibility of finding, in some old periodicals, the original offer for a particular doll as premium. Even so, such finds do not always answer all questions. Since photography was not a common means of illustrating early ads, an artist's rendition of a doll may not come close to the actual appearance of the doll as distributed. Or a design may have been changed between the time the advance advertising was issued and the date the doll was released. These things did not happen often, but collectors should remember that such things did occur.

Many of the dolls shown in this chapter wear familiar faces. A collector may feel that he or she recognizes the doll, but will be unable to recall its name or origin. Others, I expect, will be immediately recognizable to some reader who will hopefully write to clear up the matter.

Other dolls in this chapter may never be identified and will remain among the challenging mysteries that collectors love. This accounts for the fascinating charm of these "nobodies." They present a challenge, a mystery to solve, and that is a great part of the joy of collecting.

14-1

14-1   **Three Little Girls.** Lithographed and formed face, jointed hips and shoulders. Used to illustrate editorial material in the November 1913 *Playthings*. No further description given. (Courtesy the magazine)

14-2   **Leprechaun, 17″.** Painted features, stuffed felt, flannel ruff, felt hat, applied design, unmarked. (Rothert collection)

14-3   **Sailor, 7½″.** Hat, all cloth, World War II vintage, red-brown floss wig, mask face of tricot with painted features. Body of stuffed, pale peach tricot on wire armature, blue felt suit, neckerchief missing. (Author's collection)

14-4   **Dutch Girl, 11″.** All cloth, painted mask face, simple flat-constructed body of peach cotton, mitten hands. Wears rayon socks, blue cotton dress, white organdy hat and apron; carries red, white, and blue flag. Owner has a matching boy doll. (Brockington collection)

14-5   **Girl Doll, 15″.** Blond yarn wig, blue eyes, painted features on oilcloth mask face, cloth body, well-made, all-original organdy outfit. Owner has wondered if this could be an early Alexander since the clothing is so well made. (Rickleffs collection)

14-2

14-3

14-4

14-5

14-6

14-8

14-7

14-6   **Palmer Cox-type Brownie, 8″.** Painted hair and features on stockinette over a wire armature. Definitely a Cox-type, but unmarked. (Ortwein collection. Photograph by Jackie Meekins)

14-7   **Soldier, 15″.** Khaki-colored body is uniform; hair on back of head and circular ends of limbs are of rust-colored wool. Mask face with painted features. Owner was told this doll was given as an incentive to buy war bonds. (Meekins collection. Photograph courtesy the collector)

14-8   **Man Doll, 15″.** Of similar construction to 14-7. Body of olive-colored poplin with felt shirt and jacket. (Perry collection. Photograph by Jackie Meekins)

14-9 **Dutch Girl, 22″.** Muslin body, painted mask face, mohair wig, dressed all original in wooden shoes, brown linen apron and blouse, gold bead necklace; unmarked. (D'Andrade collection)

14-10 **Sailor Boy, 11″.** Molded felt construction, painted features, mohair wig, all original, unmarked.

14-11 **All-Cloth Girl, 17½″.** Molded mask face, stiffened cloth body, swivel neck, stitched joints, painted brown eyes with inserted lashes, golden brown mohair wig, dressed in original yellow dress (not shown) and hat. Original price tag still attached reads $1.95. (Hoy collection)

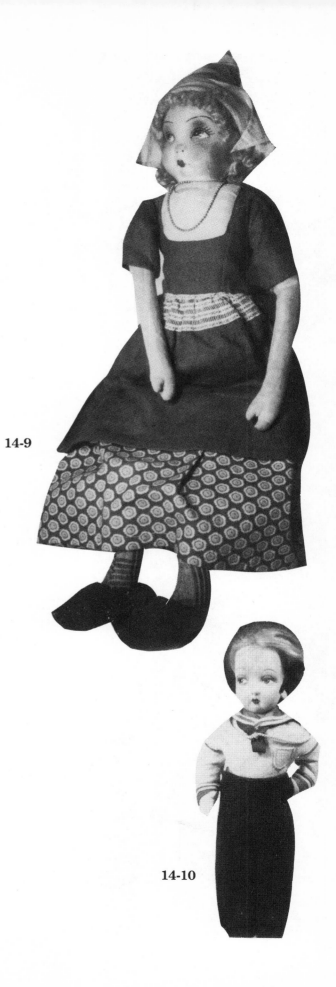

14-9

14-11

14-11

14-10

14-12

14-13

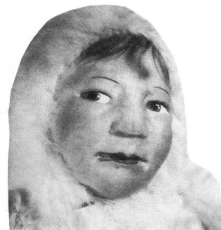

14-14

14-14

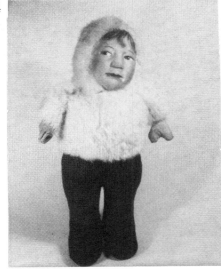

14-12   **Large Child, 24″.** All cloth with mask face, yellow yarn wig, painted blue eyes with lashes inserted in slit in cloth, body of unbleached muslin, limbs of peach-colored muslin, c. late 1930s, early 1940s. (Joplin collection)

14-13   **Chinese Man, 24″.** Lithographed features, ears sewn on, body stitch-jointed, stuffed with excelsior, limbs stuffed with cotton. All-original silk and cotton outfit. (Calia collection)

14-14   **Eskimo, 19½″.** Mask face with painted features and hair. Clothes and body are one. Right hand has hole to hold a harpoon, perhaps. (O'Rourke collection)

14-15   **Pirate, 19½".** Molded felt head, stuffed cotton body and limbs, painted features and hair. Original outfit, except shirt is missing. The strong portrait look of this doll and the size are similar to 14-14 and would seem to indicate they may have come from the same source. (O'Rourke collection)

14-16   **Infinity Boy Doll, 13¾".** Lithographed cloth, blond boy with blue eyes wearing brown shoes and red and white checked romper. Holds an identical doll that in turn holds an identical doll, etc. A visual art trick. Source unknown. (Author's collection)

14-17   **Cloth Baby, 11½".** Softly stuffed, stitch-jointed cotton body, painted or lithographed features. Clothing is all original. (O'Rourke collection)

14-18   **Cloth Baby, 20½".** A most unusual rag baby with excellent seaming and construction. Head is of four pieces with two darts under the chin. Body is cut in six pieces with separate fingers well defined. Features are painted on the faded pink sateen material. Hair is indicated by careful swirling of the paint brush to simulate curls. A real work of art, this baby is probably quite old. (Hafner collection)

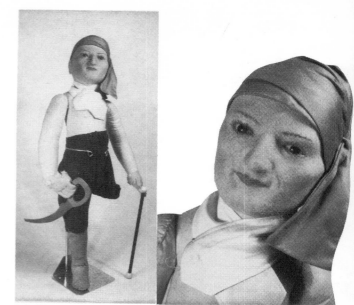

14-15

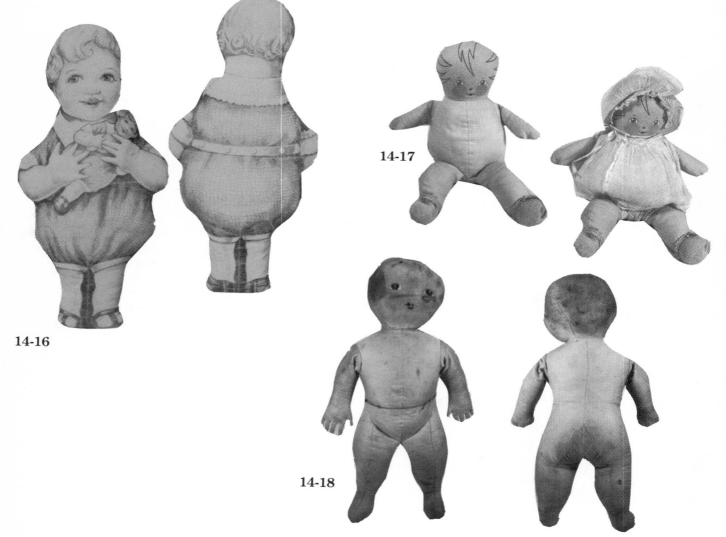

14-16

14-17

14-18

14-19 Little Miss Muffet, 10″. Lithographed oilcloth. Reverse of doll is Mary and Her Lamb, also with poem, probably one of a series featuring nursery rhyme characters, 1930s-1940s.

14-20 Dolly, 12″. Lithographed cloth, removable red and white dress. Quite possibly this doll and her dress were available as a flat to be completed at home.

14-21 Peasant Girl, 11″. Blond mohair wig, mask face covered with stockinette, stuffed cotton body, all-original outfit. Resembles some of the Mollye dolls, but is unmarked. (Adame collection)

14-22 Cloth Boy, 14″. Yellow floss wig, mask face, stuffed oilcloth body and limbs. All-original outfit consisting of red felt jacket, blue shorts, red and white checked shirt. (Hoy collection)

14-23 Scootles, 17½″. A rarity, at least in my experience. The question here is not *who* is this doll, but rather who *made* the doll? Scootles, created by Rose O'Neill and manufactured, among others, by Cameo, was done in various media. This beautifully formed doll has yellow yarn sewn-in loops for hair, painted blue side-glance eyes and painted lashes, a narrow orange painted line for a mouth, and wears its original romper of tiny red and white checked cotton with a white cotton collar. The body has a tucked seat similar to that of the frog-body Bye-lo, so it sits nicely. (Bigelow collection)

363

14-24   **Tear Drop Baby, 18″.** All cloth with painted mask face and percale clothing. Doll was shown in Sears, Roebuck Christmas catalog of 1964. No manufacturer given. (Author's photograph. Courtesy Sears, Roebuck and Company)

14-25   **Hawaiian Girl, 13″.** Black yarn wig, brown cotton body and head, mask face, painted features. Doll is machine-sewn with hand stitching up the back where it was stuffed. Given to the owner by an Air Force couple who had lived in Hawaii, c. 1959. (Rogers collection)

14-26   **Cloth Kewpie, 11½″ and 14″.** Painted mask faces, bodies of jersey cloth. Possibly made by Cameo, but not indicated. Advertised in the 1931-1932 Sears catalog for 98¢ and $1.49, respectively. (Author's photograph. Courtesy Sears, Roebuck and Company)

14-27   **Whoopy Clowny, 14″.** Another Rose O'Neill creation with froglike legs and a gimmick: "Toss the doll up in the air and he screams". From the Sears 1931-1932 Fall-Winter catalog. (Author's photograph. Courtesy Sears, Roebuck and Company)

14-28   **Nelly Kelly, 15″ and 19″.** Soft-stuffed dolls. Body and clothing together, removable apron, washable rubberized cloth faces, printed features. From the Butler Brothers Fall 1933 catalog.

14-25

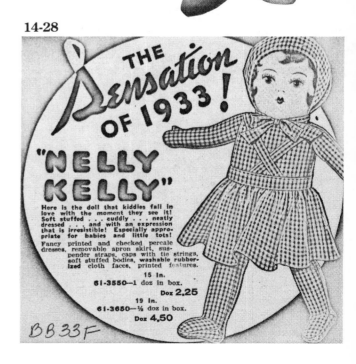

14-24

14-26

14-27

14-28

15 Some Gems Worth Hunting

Fig. 15-1

During research for my books, I constantly record information on file cards. I am, perhaps, a leading consumer in the 4 × 6 file card market. Whenever and wherever I discover clues to dolls I have never seen or photographed before, that information is entered on a card and filed away in my files.

As a result, there are always hundreds of mysteries to solve, hundreds of avenues down which my research may take me. In addition, there are always unsolved mysteries and incomplete cards when a book is finished. No book is ever truly finished, no subject completely closed.

Time and again when writing this book, I had to set items aside until there was a pile of cards labeled "next time," a pile that seemed to represent a challenge as well as a reminder of my own limitations. Time, money, energy, even the number of pages allocated for the book — all set limitations on what this book might become.

The dolls I have not seen haunt my thoughts. Collections not examined and photographed intrigue me. Who knows what dolls may be waiting for me? Riffling through a stack of incomplete reference cards, I find the names of many doll designers unknown to me as well as familiar ones, the latter connected with dolls I have "met" personally. A few examples will illustrate.

Mollye Goldman of Philadelphia designed a boy doll very much like Raggedy Andy. She registered her patent application on May 7, 1935 (Fig. 15-1). Camille C. Blair of Los Angeles filed her patent application for a doll on July 29, 1930 (Fig. 15-2). Lena Gould applied for her patent for a clown doll on August 21, 1914 (Fig. 15-3). These and others are known to me only through the sketches shown with the patent application information published by the United States Patent Office.

Other dolls have been carded for my files using information obtained from trade journals. Also opened to me were the catalog archives of two of the foremost mail-order houses in the country: Montgomery Ward and Sears, Roebuck and Company.

Fig. 15-2   Fig. 15-3

These archives are contained in locked vaults in both cases and are never opened to the public (and rarely to researchers).

Nevertheless, questions and uncertainties still persist because of the inherent nature of the material. First, as mentioned elsewhere, many of the old catalogs were artist-illustrated rather than illustrated with photographs. Hence the actual dolls shipped to customers often bore little or no resemblance to those illustrated. Sometimes there was no relationship to the advertised items. Both firms did a tremendous volume of business, especially at Christmas, the peak doll-buying season. Both firms have a policy regarding out-of-stock items. Whenever possible, in order not to disappoint a customer, an item of equal or greater value is substituted for a sold-out item.

What we are concerned with here, however, are the dolls offered in the catalogs and their manufacturers. In the Fall-Winter 1926 Sears, Roebuck and Company catalog, the firm's policy statement not only explains their substitution policy, but also names several suppliers:

> America's best known makers build dolls especially for us, for every doll must be of unusual value to gain a place in this catalog. Such makers as Horsman, Effanbee, Century, American Character (Petite), Ideal, Gem, and other well known factories put special value into "Sears Specials" during the quiet months. No one maker, it seems, can supply all of the vast amount we may need on a particular doll, therefore, in most instances we do not mention the maker's name, but you can depend on our sending you a good doll and a big value for your money.

Fig. 15-7

Fig. 15-4

Fig. 15-5

Fig. 15-6

What sorts of dolls from these two companies are listed on my cards? There is Lola Worrell's Floppy Flo made about 1922 to 1924. Flo had a bushy wig and long limbs. She was described as a rag doll, so we may assume that she was an all-cloth doll. There were, however, some catalog listings for rag dolls that actually had papier-mâché or composition heads.

On pages 206-207 of *Twentieth Century Dolls*, I sketched a Flapper Vamp based on an illustration found in a late 1920s Sears, Roebuck catalog (Fig. 15-8). This type of doll was especially popular in the last half of the 1920s and continued as a favorite into the 1940s, even appearing in vinyl form in the 1950s. The 1920s example (sketched here) was of rayon brocade with cotton stuffing and had a fluffy mohair wig. Its limbs could be tied in innumerable positions. Retail on the 24″ to 30″ item in 1926 was 97¢ to $1.79.

Was this doll one of Lola Worrell's dolls manufactured by her Flapper Novelty Company and merely renamed by Sears? Or did Flapper Vamp come from one of the dozens of other manufacturers, large and small, who had recognized a good seller and hopped on the bandwagon? We may never know.

Neither may we ever know the origin of the Buster Brown rag doll, "neatly dressed to represent the original, 25¢ each," as advertised in the 1909 Montgomery Ward catalog. I have handled a number of Buster Brown dolls, but am left to wonder if any have been the specific doll shown in the Ward's catalog sketch.

Then there is the question of Jennie L. Allen's rag doll, patented in 1918 in Long Beach, California. Did Jennie ever succeed in getting her doll manufactured? Perhaps her doll is one I have held in my hands and not recognized.

And what about the two-faced rag dolls created and patented by Lelia May Fellon in 1917, then assigned to Louis Amberg? There were eight separate design patents registered in her name. Have I ever seen one of these dolls and not known it?

Who made the American Lady distributed by Wards from 1901 through 1904? With her hair in bangs and a washable lithographed face and jointed limbs, she must have been quite a woman. The catalog description indicates she had removable shoes, stockings, underwear, bonnet, and dress.

In 1921 Eva M. Anderson of Waterloo, Iowa, had a patent for a doll made from two socks. Susie M. Atterhold of West Albany,

New York, used a stocking to make a doll with embroidered features in 1923. Marie K. Baker applied for a patent on a fabric doll in 1912. Frank Barnard's 1920 stockinette rag doll was dressed as a black minstrel.

Elizabeth Bell's 1908 stuffed doll on a wire frame (armature) was assigned to Belle Novelty Company of Delaware. Lenna Bergeson assigned her 1923 patent for a stockinette rag doll to Louis Amberg.

Glee Beug of Sturgis, South Dakota, took out a patent for a

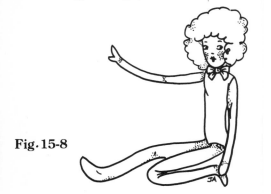

Fig. 15-8

rag doll in 1922. Then there was a long-legged man doll with hair parted in the middle and prominent ears, patented in 1921 by William Franklin Blaydes, Jr. The Otsy-Totsy-Dolls were a creation of Mayotta Brown, San Francisco, trademark registered in 1922. Some of Brown's dolls had yarn hair, but were these the Otsy-Totsy-Dolls? The record is not clear.

Two design patents were registered by Edson B. Card, White Plains, New York, for men dolls with elongated limbs. At the same time (1921-1922) Mr. Card copyrighted his Daddy Doll. Was this a male version of the Flapper types? It would seem so. The time period is right.

In Bishee, Arizona, Mary Caretto obtained a 1922 patent for her rag doll. No description available. Minnie E. Case was also working on rag dolls. In 1925 she patented a rag doll dressed as an Arabian. It was a time when the mystique of Lawrence had captured the imagination of the world. Josephine Merwin Cook, in 1920, patented a rag doll. Where are her dolls now? And has anyone seen Dolly Winkle? Dorothy M. Crosby, Duluth, Minnesota, patented her Dolly Winkle in 1918, but a recognizable example has not yet been found.

All across the land designers and dollmakers were trying to protect their ideas. From almost every state in the Union came applications for patents on cloth dolls. Maude Abbott Cummings (M. A. Cuming & Co.) of New York City patented her rag doll in 1920. What was so special about her design that Maude thought it should be protected by a patent?

Bertha E. Feist of New York City patented her two-faced rag doll in 1921, two or three years after Lelia Fellon had assigned hers to Amberg. They must have been different, these two dolls, or the Patent Office would not have allowed Bertha a patent. How were they different? What construction technique had Bertha used that Lelia had not?

In the mid-1920s Joseph G. Kaempfer and his wife were associated with the Simplex Stuffed Toy Manufacturing Company, making Eagle Brand dolls. Mrs. Kaempfer designed the clothing for the dolls. But were the dolls rag dolls in the true sense? Were the heads perhaps of composition or papier-mâché, with stuffed bodies and limbs? More research is needed here.

Grace Corry is a name known to most doll collectors, but where is her Figi Wigi rag doll of 1921? Is Figi Wigi the rag clown with the bobbing head, also listed in 1921, or are these two separate dolls? Century Doll Company's label should be on or attached to these dolls. As Grace Corry Rockwell, also in 1921, she designed Blue Eyes with a bobbing head for Century. All have escaped my notice.

Bully Boy Brewster, a soft doll by Gertrude Stacey, was designed for Giftoy Company in 1921. About the same time Penny Rose created an oilcloth doll named Esther, and Betty Bright patented a rag doll with yellow hair and red ribbon. What was remarkable about these dolls? Sufficiently remarkable, that is, to qualify them for patenting?

Then there is the small mystery of another Flo. In 1921 the Chessler Company made stuffed dolls by that name that walked and talked. But was Flo's head made of cloth or of some other material? About 1923 Cayuga Felt Products Company of Union Springs, New York, made what may be supposed, considering the name of the manufacturer, to have been dolls made of felt, at least in part. What *is* known is that the dolls were 13″ and had hand-tinted features. Have any survived in identifiable condition?

Finally, there is Julia E. Greene of Philadelphia. Julia registered her trademark in the United States for rag dolls in 1920, christening them the Beddy-Bye dolls, a particularly apt name for a soft, cuddly rag doll. To date I have seen none of these dolls. Perhaps I never will. Or perhaps it is only that I have not recognized them when we met.

The list could go on and on. Suffice it to say that my work on the subject is incomplete. The stack of cards still stands on a corner of my desk, waiting for the next time.

Bibliography

Anderton, Johana Gast. "Johana's Dolls." *Mid-America Reporter,* February, 1972.

_____. *Johana's Dolls, A Reprint of Her Columns and Articles.* North Kansas City, Missouri: Athena Publishing Company, 1975.

_____. *Twentieth Century Dolls, From Bisque to Vinyl,* 2nd Edition. Des Moines, Iowa: Wallace-Homestead Book Company, 1979.

_____. *More Twentieth Century Dolls, From Bisque to Vinyl,* 2nd Edition. Des Moines, Iowa: Wallace-Homestead Book Company, 1979.

Bailey, Albina. *Dressing Dolls in Nineteenth Century Fashions.* Des Moines, Iowa: Wallace-Homestead Book Company, 1975.

Boyd, Carol and Bill. "Anili, Madame Lenci's Daughter," *The Best of the Doll Reader.* Cumberland, Maryland: Hobby House Press, 1982.

Bullard, Helen. *The American Doll Artist.* Boston, Massachusetts: Charles T. Branford Company, 1965.

_____. *The American Doll Artist, Vol. II.* North Kansas City, Missouri: Athena Publishing Company, 1975.

Coleman, Dorothy S., E. A. and E. J. *The Collector's Encyclopedia of Dolls.* New York: Crown Publishers, Inc., 1968.

Gerken, Jo Elizabeth. *Wonderful Dolls of Papier-Mâché.* Lincoln, Nebraska: Doll Research Associates, 1970.

Johl, Janet Pagter. *The Fascinating Story of Dolls.* New York: H. L. Lindquist, 1941.

Kahler, Atha. *The Doll Dressmaker's Book.* Privately published, 1971.

King, Constance Eileen. *The Collector's History of Dolls.* New York: Bonanza Books, 1978.

McKee, Carol A. *Lenci Clothes.* Cumberland, Maryland: Hobby House Press, Inc., 1982.

Michel, Reverend Bernard E. "Dolls, Surplices, and Service," *The North American MORAVIAN,* July-August, 1972.

Quarry, Lucille. "Dolls That Are People." *Woman's Home Companion,* November, 1925.

Robison, Joleen, and Kay Sellers. *Advertising Dolls.* Paducah, Kentucky: Collector Books, 1980.

Russell, Joan. *The Woman's Day Book of Soft Toys and Dolls.* New York: Simon and Schuster, 1975.

Walker, Frances, and Margaret Whitton. *Playthings by the Yard.* Privately published, 1973.

Periodicals

Family Circle Magazine, North Mattoon, Illinois, New York Times Company.

Ladies Circle Needlework Magazine, New York, Lopez Publications, Inc.

Laura Wheeler Needlecraft, Old Chelsea Station, New York.

National Doll World Magazine, Seabrook, New Hampshire, House of White Birches, Inc.

Playthings Magazine, Madison Avenue, New York.

Woman's Day Magazine, Greenwich, Connecticut, CBS Publications.

Index

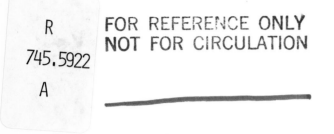